GRAND VISIONS

Marvels of Building & Engineering

Acknowledgements

Thanks to M for all her help. Thanks to New Holland's team of dedicated professionals who consistently and tirelessly turn the grand visions in my head into real books that you can hold in your hands. I'd especially like to thank my editors, Diane Jardine, Jenny Scepanovic and Rochelle Fernandez, designers Hayley Norman and Donnah Luttrell, publishing manager Lliane Clarke, publicist Warren Moore and lastly, but never leastly, Managing Director, Fiona Schultz.

First published in Australia in 2010 by
New Holland Publishers (Australia) Pty Ltd
Sydney • Auckland • London • Cape Town

1/66 Gibbes Street, Chatswood NSW 2067 Australia
www.newholland.com.au
218 Lake Road Northcote Auckland 0746 New Zealand
86 Edgware Road London W2 2EA United Kingdom
80 McKenzie Street Cape Town 8001 South Africa

Cataloguing-in-publication data:
Waterkeyn, Xavier.

Grand visions : marvels of building and engineering / Xavier Waterkeyn.
9781741107425 (hbk.)
Buildings.
Structural engineering.
690

Publisher: Fiona Schultz
Publishing Manager: Lliane Clarke
Project Editors: Diane Jardine, Rochelle Fernandez
Designers: Donnah Dee Luttrell, Hayley Norman
Printer: Toppan Leefung Printing Limited
10 9 8 7 6 5 4 3 2 1

Dedicated to

dreamers and visionaries

— grand and otherwise.

Where would we be without you?

GRAND VISIONS
Marvels of Building & Engineering

XAVIER WATERKEYN

NEW HOLLAND

contents

Introduction

Big thinking, big dreaming

Everything that ever manifests in the material world starts as a dream—an idea in somebody's head. Most of the time, ideas are usually humble. Most of us are content with low-key visions where our greatest achievements are having cozy lives with the people we love.

There's a lot to be said for humility of this sort. It's a major triumph to achieve contentment for ourselves, our friends, partners and children. Having a roof over our heads that doesn't leak, safety and security, warm clothes on our backs and warm food in our bellies on a regular basis might not seem like much, but even today only a minority of the world's population can take even these minimal things for granted. For most of recorded human history practically no-one could even count on that.

And yet, throughout all of human history there have been individuals and groups for whom even this hard-won minimal standard of living has not been enough.

There's abundant evidence that human beings thrive on a certain amount of discontent. From time to time you may even hear people who seem to have everything say things like, 'is this all there is?' and such comments usually come laced with a certain amount of guilt, as if we should be ashamed to find that having comfort alone isn't enough.

But there is a force underlying all of human activity that is just as powerful as the instinct to survive or the preference to live humbly. The Ancient Greeks called it *phusis*; loosely translated you could call this the 'dynamism of being'. Think of it as creative yearning, the desire for something bigger, better, grander than just a small, humble life. There are myriad ways that this yearning shows up in the lives of individuals and in the stories of human cultures—spiritual exploration, warfare, invention, artistic expression and most obviously and enduringly in large engineering projects.

Humans are creatures of the imagination, and some dreams succeed in capturing the imagination in such a compelling way that people will willingly dedicate their lives to fulfilling and realising those dreams. Throughout history some particularly powerful or persuasive people have recruited, persuaded, seduced, bullied or coerced thousands and sometimes millions of others to actualising their dreams.

The particular projects, buildings and monuments featured in this book were mostly chosen based on certain criteria. The project, for the most part, had to:

1) be conceived, designed and executed by one person or one group of people.

2) represent a significant investment and come at a high cost to the people involved.

3) demonstrate significant originality and invention. It had to break new ground.

Most measures, especially the ancient ones, are approximations. All costs are the original estimates, or modern estimates, based on scholarly analysis of the relevant economies. The equivalents in brackets are modern converted estimates, based largely on the value of the US dollar in the latter half of the first decade of the twentieth century. The reckoning is mostly based on the per capita share of GDP, which is a fancy way of saying 'This is how much it would cost to build today, given the current population of the country in question and their productive capacity'.

Grand Visions showcases how the spirit of yearning, *phusis*, has manifested in some of the most spectacular successes (and failures) in terms of engineering and construction in the annals of human endeavour. These projects and undertakings have often involved thousands of people, years, decades and sometimes centuries of time and significant investment of capital to come to fruition— grand visions into reality.

Part 01

Towers,

Pyramids &

Skyscrapers

Mountains have played a part in human spiritual experience since ancient times.

In virtually all human cultures people perceive God or 'the gods' as being 'up there'. Heaven is 'up' and in diverse societies the main deity either resides or manifests in the sky. The ancestor of the Japanese Emperors was Ameratasu—the goddess of the Sun. The Egyptian God Amon-Ra was the ancestor of the Pharaohs and also the god of the sun.

It stands to reason then that because humans don't have wings, the easiest way for people to get physically closer to their gods was to climb a mountain. Climbing also becomes a convenient metaphor for spiritual advancement, so mountains therefore can easily become sacred. They can also become the abode of the gods when the gods choose to get a little closer to people. The Greek gods lived on Mount Olympus and one of the Hebrew names for God in the Old Testament is El Shaddai—Lord of the Mountain. Mountains are a great place to meet the gods halfway—if you can survive the climb.

But what do you do when you live in a region where mountains are inconveniently located or even non-existent? The obvious answer is to build one. This isn't an easy task. In fact, it's horrendously difficult, but people with tools no more sophisticated than axes, chisels, hammers, sticks, rope and a lot of grunting have managed it with considerable panache on numerous occasions in the past.

Perhaps the most famous mountains are the Egyptian pyramids, but other cultures have built pyramids or pyramid-like structures in antiquity:

the Chinese

the Greeks and Romans

the Aztec, Inca and Maya

the Samoans

the Kushite Kingdoms of Nubia.

Of course, once having found a good idea, people generally want to see how far they can take it. For centuries after the pyramids, humans continued to want to build higher. Limitations of materials and construction techniques restrained them, and religions and visions of God changed, but the aim was still the same, so that the tallest buildings in the world became the towers of churches and cathedrals. Then in the late nineteenth century, breakthroughs in steel manufacture and the invention of the elevator allowed architects to design, and engineers to build new temples dedicated to a new god – commerce. These monuments to business now dominate our very idea of the word 'city'. We are still reaching for heaven, perhaps a heaven on earth, at least for some of us.

The Tower of Babel

The most famous legendary attempt to reach Heaven by physical means in the Western world is the Tower of Babel. The Torah, the first section of the Hebrew Bible, tells the story of the Migdal Bavel (Tower of Babel) in the Book of Genesis chapter 11: King Nimrod, the first man to found an empire after the flood, caused a tower to be built in Babylon out of baked brick and mortar in order to put his stamp on history; he thought 'let us make us a name'. God found this whole exercise rather arrogant, because the tower was to be built in honour of mankind and not Himself. He observed that the people were 'all of one language' in this great city and so, to put a dampener on human ambition, He gave each person a different language.

Confounded, the builders of the tower looked for people who spoke their own language, and because they had to spend all their time working out how to write dictionaries, they had no time to cooperate in the building of the tower. The project was abandoned, although other sources say that God later destroyed it with a high wind.

The Bible doesn't mention the tower's dimensions, but the ancient (and later suppressed) Book of Jubilee states that the tower had a rectangular footprint of 13 x 30 stades and a height of 5433 cubits and 2 palms. Based on a Royal Egyptian stade at 210 metres (689 feet), and a Sumerian cubit of 518.5mm (20.4 inches) this would have made the tower 2730 metres x 6300 metres and 2817 metres high (1.7 miles x 3.9 miles and 1.75 miles)—enormously wide and flat but still larger and taller than anything built or that could conceivably be built in the modern world. Based on these measurements the tower would have been a third of the height of Mount Everest.

Modern historians believe that the Migdal was inspired by Mesopotamian ziggurats (see page 22) that the ancient Hebrews saw during their Babylonian captivity, and this conjecture is borne out by modern estimates of the proportions of the building, based on what little survives of the ziggurats.

According to the Bible, King Nimrod's desire to say 'Hello' to God inspired in the deity a fit of linguistic inventiveness. To this day, people still have trouble co-operating on some large projects, even if they can all speak the same. In 1563 Pieter Bruegel painted *The Tower of Babel* which hangs in Vienna.

Probably the most famous of man-made mountains, Khufu's pyramid is the only survivor of Antipater of Sidon's list of seven wonders. The building is so solid it could possibly survive a direct hit from an atomic bomb and will almost certainly outlast any current civilisation.

The Pyramids

Pyramids of Giza

The very first Egyptian Pharaohs and aristocracy built tombs for themselves that we call mastabas, from an Arabic word meaning 'bench'. These were low, wide buildings built from either stone or, more commonly, mud-brick. Flat-roofed, rectangular prisms with sloping sides, the typical mastaba wasn't any larger than a small suburban house and served as the portion of a tomb above ground. The burial chambers themselves were located several metres underground.

Then the second pharaoh of Egypt's Third Dynasty, a man by the name of Horus Netjerikhet and better known to history as Djoser, decided early in his reign (2686–2667 BCE or 2630–2611 BCE—dates for these early kings are uncertain) that it might be a nice idea to have something more fitting for a god on earth to have as a tomb. So he engaged his multi-talented doctor, high priest, scribe and advisor, Imhotep—'the one that comes in peace'—to come up with something.

Imhotep's idea was to turn the mastaba into a square shape, then put a smaller square on top of that, then another, and so on. The end result was the Step Pyramid at Saqqara. Its original dimensions were 125.27 metres x 109.12 metres (411 feet x 358 feet)

at the base, reaching a height of 62 metres (203 feet). This pyramid, modest by later standards, contained 330,400 cubic metres (11,668,000 cubic feet) of clay and stone and was finished with a layer of polished white limestone. The Step Pyramid is only a part of a mortuary complex comprising around 15 hectares (37 acres) and surrounded by a wall of white Tura limestone (the best limestone in Egypt) 1,645 metres (5,397 feet) long and 265 metres (870 feet) wide.

Imhotep started a trend. Over the next 70 years more pyramids were built, including Khaba's 84 metres high step-pyramid at Zawyiet el-Aryan; Huni's attempt at Meidum (the famous 'collapsed' or 'false' pyramid); another faulty one, Sneferu's 101.1 metres (332 feet) Bent Pyramid at Dashur; and the Red Pyramid at Dashur, the world's first successful smooth-sided pyramid with a base measurement of 220 metres (722 feet) and a height of 104 metres (341 feet).

The Great Pyramid

Then along came Sneferu's successor, his son Khufu. The second pharaoh of the Fourth Dynasty, Khufu (whom the Greek historians

Towers, Pyramids & Skyscrapers

called Cheops), reigned from 2589 BCE to 2566 BCE. Unlike his father, who had a reputation for being not such a bad guy, tradition has it that Khufu was cruel and ruthless. His reputation as an egomaniac is reflected in the considerable resources that Khufu diverted to realise the construction of his tomb. Khufu engaged his vizier, Hemon, with the construction of what remains one of the most amazing artifacts ever built —Khufu's Horizon.

Over a 20-year period, starting around 2580 BCE and ending around 2560 BCE, labourers created a structure with the following dimensions:

base side: 440 royal cubits (at 0.524 metres per cubit) or 230.56 metres or 756.4 feet

base coverage: 5.3 hectares (13.13 acres)

original height: 280 royal cubits or 146.72 metres (481.4 feet). In fact, the Great Pyramid would remain the world's tallest building for around 3800 years until the completion of Lincoln Cathedral in the year 1300.

estimated mass: 5.9 million tonnes

volume: 2.5 million cubic metres (3.27 million cubic yards).

Most of the Great Pyramid is solid rock, as far as we know. There are three large chambers within, the names of which come from modern scholarship, since we have no idea what the Egyptians themselves called them and their true function remains a mystery.

The 'King's Chamber' is approximately in the centre of the pyramid. Its dimensions are 5.25 metres x 10.5 metres and it is 6 metres high (17.22' x 34.45' x 19.68').

The interior is quite bare, with a centrally placed 'sarcophagus' made from a single piece of Red Aswan Granite.

The sarcophagus would have been too large to fit through the narrow passages leading into the chamber and must have been placed there during construction and yet it's too short to accommodate even a medium-sized body without the body having to bend at the knees.

The 'Queen's Chamber', somewhat below but more centrally aligned than the 'King's Chamber', measures 5.74 metres x 5.23 metres and is 4.57 metres high (18.83' x 17.16' x 15'). It too is bare.

Twenty-seven metres (90 feet) below ground and below the structure of the pyramid itself is a third 'Unfinished Chamber', so called because its interior is rough-hewn and most Egyptologists believe it to represent a change of mind on behalf of the builders about the appropriate final resting place of the pharaoh. Like the other two chambers, it's bare and undecorated.

Building an ancient giant

It's been traditionally estimated that about 2.5 million blocks were used in the construction of the Great Pyramid, all ferried in barges from quarries across the Nile. The number 2.5 million is based on an assumption that the stones are of uniform size. However, although the lower level blocks routinely weigh 3 tonnes, most upper level blocks weigh around a tonne a piece. There are also some significant anomalies. While most of the blocks are limestone quarried from a site south east of the pyramids, there are pink granite rocks used in the Great Pyramid's 'King's Chamber' that weigh forty to sixty tonnes and there are estimates that the granite beams in the 'relieving chambers' above the 'King's Chamber' weigh from fifty to eighty tonnes a piece.

Lifting eighty tonnes in one piece is no mean feat. The modern world's most powerful moveable crane is a huge truck—the Liebherr LTM 11200-9.1. Its maximum capacity is 1200 tonnes but such lifting capacity has only been possible in the last few decades. Even today it would be hard to imagine putting a 20-metre (66 feet) long truck in position so that it could position a block of stone into place several storeys above ground height. Nevertheless, somebody did it.

The precision with which these rocks were placed is astounding. The pyramid as a whole is aligned to 4 degrees west of true north and the original proportions of height to base circumference (280 cubits/1760 cubits) conform to the ratio of 2 Pi with an error better than 0.05 per cent. This doesn't, however, imply that the majority of pyramids blocks are necessarily stacked as neatly as joined Lego bricks. For the most part the core blocks of the pyramids show noticeable irregularity. They couldn't have been too irregular though or the structures would have collapsed, but close examination reveals that there was considerable in-filling of spaces between blocks with rubble and mortar. So it's really impossible to guess how many blocks were actually used in the construction of the Great Pyramid, but it was enough material to pave a highway from New York City to Chicago, or Sydney to Adelaide, or to build 20 Empire State Buildings. Yet in spite of the interior irregularity, the pyramids look so geometrically perfect because the neatest stacking was reserved for the exterior layers of the pyramids, and the facing stones.

When it was completed the Great Pyramid must have been even more impressive than it is today. It would have been entirely encased in an estimated 120,000 polished white limestone facing stones and capped with a gold or gold-plated capstone. In the glare of full sun it would have shone with pain-inducing brilliance.

There's a popular misconception that Khufu and Hemon used slave labour to build the pyramids, but in 1990 archaeologists Zahi Hawass and Mark Lehner found tombs belonging to site workers. The modern consensus is that about 200,000 skilled and semi-skilled workers built the pyramid either for wages or as a form of taxation or both. Feeding and equipping this workforce would have taken up a considerable proportion of the Egyptian national budget at the time. Building could only have taken place during the spring—the idle time while the peasantry waited for crops to grow after the annual flood of the Nile. It's estimated that a working gang of eight could transport 10 stones across the Nile during their 3-month work stint. A team of four masons could dress one finishing stone per month and complete one core stone every three days.

There's considerable circumstantial evidence that Khufu paid a high price for his pyramid above and beyond the material resources. In a time when a person's reputation could be measured by the reverence that people placed on their statues, it's perhaps significant that there is only one positively identified likeness of Khufu known to exist—a 7.6 centimetre (3 inch) ivory statue found by Flinders Petrie in Abydos in 1903.

There's no evidence that the Great Pyramid was ever used as Khufu's tomb and no-one has ever found his mummy. The Egyptians believed that without the preservation of the body, the soul could not reach or remain in the afterworld, so if Khufu's body was destroyed, then at least according to beliefs that he himself might have held, his preparations for the afterworld were all for nothing. There's not even a trace of a back-up sacred statue of Khufu, a common practice at the time, in case the real body was destroyed.

Unfortunately the millennia have taken their toll. With the eventual demise of Egyptian civilisations, maintenance of the Pyramids would have been an ever-decreasing priority and in 1301 CE a major earthquake there loosened the facing limestone of the Great Pyramid. In 1356 Bahri Sultan An-Nasir Nasir-ad Din al-Hasan decided that all this wonderful prefabricated building material was too good to waste so he cannibalised it and used it to build fortresses and mosques in Cairo. With all the wear and tear the Great Pyramid eventually lost about eight metres from its original height.

Khafre's Pyramid

Khufu's son, Djedefra ('enduring like Ra') reigned for 8 years from perhaps 2528 BCE to 2520 BCE. He tried building a pyramid 8 kilometres north of Giza at Abu Rawash, but the project was a disaster. Nothing remains of his pyramid except a large pile of rubble.

Djedefra's successor, Khafre (or Khafra, 'appearing like Ra', 2520 BCE?–2494 BCE?), is credited with the building of the second largest pyramid at Giza as well as the Great Sphinx. Khafre's Pyramid is the only one that still retains a good share of its original facing stones and thus gives us a better idea of what the pyramids looked like when they were fresh.

Although it doesn't get as much attention as the Great Pyramid, Khafre's Pyramid is still impressive:

Base side: 214.5 metres or 704 feet
Base coverage: 4.6 hectares or 11.37 acres
Original height: 143.5 metres or 471 feet
Current height: 136.4 metres or 448 feet

So Khafre's Pyramid is not so much smaller than Khufu's, and it represents virtually the same investment of resources all over again. In fact, when you combine the total volume of the pyramids built by Sneferu, his son Khufu and his grandson Khafre, the combined total of all the other Pharaonic pyramids built during the 'pyramid age' represent only about 54 per cent of the mass of the pyramids of these three Fourth Dynasty pharaohs.

People remember Khafre a little more fondly than Khufu, but perhaps this is only because we know even less about him. We do have more images of him than we do of Khufu, because Khafre produced a lot of statues of himself, but the evidence of his presence in the pyramid that bears his name is also strangely lacking. Like his pyramid-building predecessors and his successor, evidence of his reign is largely confined to the mortuary temples associated with the pyramids, rather than the pyramids themselves.

Menkaure's Pyramid

Khafre was succeeded by Menkaure (or Menkaura, 'long lasting vital force of Ra'—2532 BCE?–2504 BCE? or 2490 BCE?–2472 BCE?) and was, like his two predecessors, probably a son of Khufu. Menkaure's Pyramid is the only large pyramid that showed any evidence of actually being a tomb. In 1838 archaeologist Richard Vyse found Menkaure's basalt sarcophagus as well as a wooden anthropoid sarcophagus within it. Unfortunately, on 13 October of that year the basalt sarcophagus sank along with the *Beatrice*, the ship that was carrying it to England. The wooden coffin made it in another ship and you can see it today at the British Museum.

Menkaure's Pyramid is a much more modest affair than its siblings. With an original height of just 65.5 metres (203 feet) it was barely taller than the original step pyramid. Although compared to Sneferu's Pyramid it had the virtue of having smooth sides and a square (103.4 metres or 339 feet) base, in every other respect it represented a step backwards from its immediate predecessors. Or did it? Could Menkaure's smaller size be a deliberate part of an even grander vision?

The fact that the big Pyramids of the Giza complex, unlike so many other religious buildings in Egypt, are virtually devoid of any inscriptions dedicated to their putative pharaohs (who weren't usually shy about self-promotion), or any other written or pictorial records for that matter, have made some people suspicious about the true origins of the buildings. This doesn't mean that the pyramids are devoid of markings though. There's ancient graffiti from quite a few work gangs hidden in various places. So we know at least that someone long ago wrote things like 'Drunks of Menkaure' and 'Friends of Khufu' on the walls.

The biggest mystery of the Pyramids

The biggest mystery of all remains: How were the pyramids built?

Many engineers are at a loss to explain how the Ancient Egyptians actually moved such huge stones of such great weight into place with such precision.

Modern attempts to recreate even a small part of the pyramids using speculative building techniques have failed miserably, although senior engineers at the Daniel, Mann, Johnson and Mendenhall construction firm have asserted that it would take a team of about 5000 men about 20 to 40 years to build the Great Pyramid using only the technology extant at the time.

This estimate gives you a hint of just how widely opinions differ as to the logistics of the construction of the pyramids, but we know, with a little more certainty, from examinations of skeletal remains, that the average age of the workmen at death was around 35. If the engineers and scientist are right, this makes the achievement all the more remarkable, because it means that people who began working on the project knew that they would most likely never live to see its completion.

Faith and religious fervour must have played no small part in the realisation of the pyramidal vision as they would for so many other grand projects in the millennia to come.

Whatever the reality of the techniques and motives behind the building of the Giza complex, the debates on construction continue. Some people believe that Khufu and his successors weren't responsible for anything more than a grand restoration project for buildings that had already existed for thousands of years before there even was an Egypt.

There are, in fact, traditions that state that the Giza Pyramid complex (including the Sphinx) is far older than Khufu. In this light some modern thinkers have cited complex arguments ranging from weathering patterns in stone to ancient star patterns to support the idea that the whole Giza complex is considerably more ancient than Egyptologists think it is and that it encodes deep mysteries in its ground plan.

The complex itself covers around 2.25 square kilometres (225 hectares or 556 acres). One intriguing theory posited by construction engineer Robert Bauval in 1994—the Orion Correlation Theory—claims that the placement for the three pyramids of Giza corresponds to the 'Belt' of stars in the constellation we know as Orion, but that the Egyptians knew as Osiris. Science writer Andrew Collins disputes this,

arguing that it's not a great fit for the modern arrangement of the stars.

Feel free to judge for yourself by comparing a star chart of Orion to the Giza complex ground plan. You can find an excellent computer model here: *http://oi.uchicago.edu/research* and search for 'Giza Plateau Mapping Project' under Research Projects of Egypt/Nubia.

Collins thinks that the pyramid ground plan 'correlation' is actually to the three crossbar stars of the Constellation of Cygnus.

However, author Scott Creighton lends support to the Orion idea by arguing that the arrangement of the three large pyramids at Giza and the six associated 'Queens' Pyramids' are actually a cleverly encoded warning about cyclic climatic catastrophes with a start date of 10 550 BCE and stretching as far into the future as the year 5614 CE. These antique origin theories imply that the buildings and monuments, or at the very least their site, are older than any civilisation that we currently know of.

Feel free to look at Creighton's flash animations for a detailed summary of his provocative theory on *www.thegizaoracle.co.uk*

Whichever way you look at it the Pyramid complex at Giza provides fertile raw material for active imaginations. Given that the Ancient Egyptians were obsessed with the sky and with 'secret mysteries' it may be that unorthodox theories might not be so far-fetched after all. It could be that the vision of the Ancient Egyptians, or perhaps their even more ancient predecessors, was far grander than we'd normally dare think.

The Ziggurats of Mesopotamia

The Pyramid Age in Egypt formally lasted until the reign of the first pharaoh of the Eighteenth Dynasty, Amhose I (1550 BCE?–1514 BCE?), but in reality few Egyptian kings built pyramids after about 1759 BCE—the end of the Twelfth Dynasty. Meanwhile, 1500 kilometres (932 miles) to the east the peoples living around what is today central and southern Iraq were building their own mountains for the gods.

The word 'Mesopotamia' comes from Greek historians and means, literally, 'the land between the rivers'. The rivers in question are the Euphrates (Greek-derived 'fertilising') and the Tigris (Greek-derived 'pointed').

The principal inhabitants of Mesopotamia at the time were the Sumerians and later the Akkadians. To the Sumerians, the rivers were the Buranun ('fruitful') and Idigna ('running water'). To the Akkadians the rivers were the Puratu ('fertilising') and Idiqlat ('swift').

The two rivers are very different in character. The Euphrates is slow and silt laden, whereas the Tigris is fast running and clear. The Euphrates carries so much silt that, over time, it's carried huge quantities from its delta into the Persian Gulf, to the extent that the ruins of the ancient city of Ur, which was once a coastal city, now lies over 200 kilometres (124 miles) inland.

Both Egypt and Mesopotamia depended on flooding rivers for their survival. But in contrast to the Nile, which before the building of the Aswan Dam flooded regularly every year, the flooding of the Euphrates was irregular and could fluctuate widely.

Another important difference was that while the course of the Nile changed very slowly over time, gradually moving east at a rate of two to three metres per year, the course of both the Tigris and the Euphrates changed quite radically over short periods, leading to profound changes in the location of settlements.

These geographical differences played a major part in the development of local religion.

To the Egyptians life was all about an unchanging eternity; to the Mesopotamians life could change suddenly and catastrophically. Scholars have long accepted that the biblical flood myths come from Mesopotamian sources.

Given the inherent instability of the Mesopotamian world view, there was good reason for them to do what they could to appease the gods and for this reason they built ziggurats (Akkadian ziqqurrat, 'built on a raised area').

The early development of ziggurats echoed the early development of Egyptian mastabas but here again there are significant differences. The early mastabas were tombs, but from the very beginning the ziggurats were intended as raised temple platforms to enable worshippers to be closer to the gods—and to avoid unpredictable rising floodwaters.

The later pyramids had interior chambers, whereas ziggurats eventually became solid, artificial mountains. Pyramids ended up with smooth sides, ziggurats never lost their stepped appearance and, as they grew in

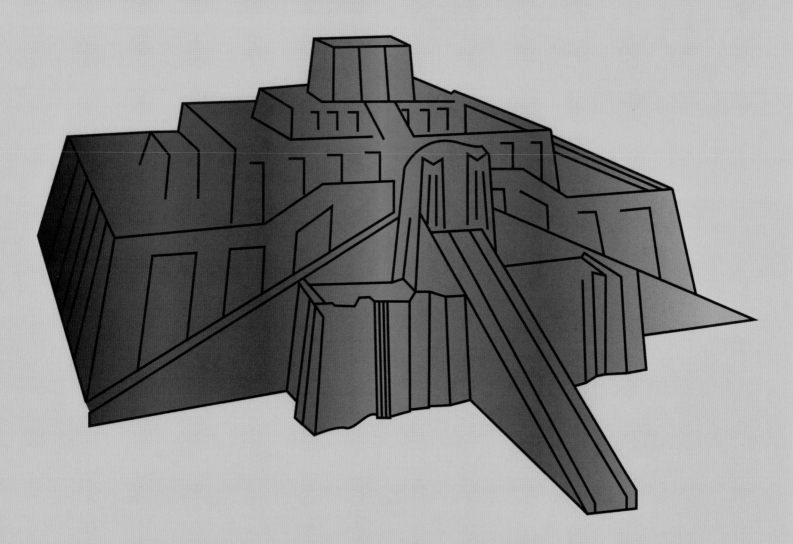

size, in some cases the steps became wide enough to plant gardens. In fact, the famous Hanging Gardens of Babylon were located on a ziggurat.

The area was once famous for its gardens and many scholars believe that the Biblical legends of the Garden of Eden were partly based on contemporary visions of Mesopotamia, especially Babylon.

So important were ziggurats to their religious, cultural and political lives that the Mesopotamians built settlements and whole cities around them.

The irony of Mesopotamia

While the ziggurats never achieved the size of the pyramids their realisation is all the more impressive because they were not

Ziggurats reached their peak with the building of the Etemenanki, the 'temple of the foundation of heaven and earth'. At its most splendid, the Etemenanki comprised seven large levels to a height of 91 metres (298 feet) with a square base of 91 metres (298 feet) to the side, but this was just the latest incarnation of various versions built on the same site over a period of over a thousand years. The first Etemenanki predates the ruler Hammurabi (1792 BCE–1750 BCE), the second last version was destroyed by Sennacherib when he sacked Babylon in 689 BCE, and was rebuilt by Nebuchadnezzar II. This final version of the ziggurat was destroyed by Alexander the Great when he captured Babylon in 331 BCE. Alexander fully intended to rebuild it, but his successors abandoned the idea after his premature death.

made out of stone but out of baked mud brick, the only viable building material in a region notably devoid of stone.

Of course, making this much mud brick not only for the construction of artificial mountains, but for the construction of whole cities, requires a lot of baking. This requires a lot of wood for burning and here is the central, tragic irony.

The Mesopotamian civilisations built out of baked mud because they didn't have stone and they needed buildings that would endure the irregular flooding of Euphrates.

But the more they built, the more wood they needed, and the more trees they cut down the greater their erosion problems—the greater the erosion, the worse the effects of the flooding.

This downward spiral, coupled with uncontrolled population growth, eventually led to such ecological collapse that the whole region experienced extensive desertification, and areas that once supported thriving civilisations were reduced to dustbowls. Whole cities had to be abandoned.

This explains why when you look at the region today it might surprise you that in ancient times it was called 'the fertile crescent' and that it was once the home of the Garden of Eden.

A notable preservation is the Great Ziggurat of Ur 64 x 46 x19.5 metres high (210 x 150 x 64 feet high). Built by King Shulgi around 2000 BCE, it survived precisely because Ur's fortunes declined as the result of war and the changing course of the Euphrates.

In fact, the Ziggurat is about all that's notably left of Ur. Being made of such a fragile material as low-temperature-baked mud brick, most ziggurats, and the cities that surrounded them, have returned to the dust from which they came.

024

Central American Pyramids

Half a world away a variety of closely related but nevertheless linguistically and culturally distinct Central American civilisations also tried the pyramid idea. Pyramid building started in this region from at least 3000 BCE to many hundreds of years after the heydays of Egypt and the Mesopotamian states.

For the most part the stepped Mesoamerican pyramids were more like the ziggurats of Mesopotamia in that they were artificial mountains with temples on top of them rather than the more geometric stone buildings of the Egyptians.

The Maya of the region now known as Southern Mexico, Guatemala, Belize, Western Honduras and El Salvador, were enthusiastic pyramid builders and their structures show considerable variation in building materials, form and style.

One notable location is El Mirador, in what is now the Department of El Peten, Guatemala. El Mirador was at its peak between about 250 BCE and 100 CE. It was then abandoned and later resettled before being finally abandoned in the ninth century, its location lost to history until it was rediscovered in 1926. Now a jungle-infested ruin, it still boasts three large pyramids including the largest Mayan temple ever built, La Danta—79 metres (259 feet) high and comprising a volume of 2.8 million cubic metres, larger than the Great Pyramid of Giza.

Not a bad effort for a city that is estimated to have had a population no greater than 80 000 at any one time.

Uxmal (archaic Maya 'thrice built') in the Yucatan in Mexico has an impressive display of beautifully preserved buildings mostly constructed between the years 700 and 1100. The 'Pyramid of the Magician' in particular looks much like it did when it was actually in use.

But the pièce de résistance is the Great Pyramid of Cholula—Tlachihualtepetl (Nahuatl 'artificial mountain')—built by the Aztecs in what is now Puebla, Mexico. Dedicated to the god Quetzalcoatl, it represents an even larger investment in time and resources than the Great Pyramid.

Scholars believe that the Tlachihualtepetl pyramid and temple complex was the result of over 1600 years of construction, beginning in the second century BCE and continuing into the early 1500s. Although it's only 66 metres (217 feet) high its base is a square of sides 450 metres (1476 feet), nearly double that of the Great Pyramid.

Now surmounted by a Spanish church built in 1594, it's a major site of pilgrimage. Beneath the church the pyramid comprises around 4.45 million cubic metres (5.89 million cubic yards), making it one-third larger than the Great Pyramid of Giza and also the largest single monument ever built. Archaeologists estimate that within the structure are about 8 kilometres (5 miles) of tunnels awaiting excavation and exploration.

The skyline of Manhattan has become so famous that it's almost instantly recognisable from almost any angle—all those skyscrapers jostling for space on an island that once didn't have anything on it but a lot of wildlife and a few fishing villages.

Manhattan's
Monuments

The Empire State Building demonstrates that even in the most capitalist capital of the most capitalist country on earth, money isn't the only consideration when attempting to realise a grand vision.

When Herbert Hoover was elected to the Presidency in 1928 the USA was riding high on one of the biggest economic bubbles in history. Then, on Thursday 24 October 1929, after the Federal Reserve decided to pull the plug on the money supply, the New York Stock Exchange traded 12.9 million shares in ever-decreasing value. On Black Tuesday 29 October, a further 16.9 million shares traded hands. By 31 October the market had crashed completely having lost 30 billion (4 trillion in modern terms). The 'Roaring Twenties' were over. From 1929 to 1933 the national annual income would fall from $87 billion to $40 billion (11.62 trillion to 5.35 trillion in modern terms) and the value of stocks bought in 1929 did not return to their previous values until 1954.

Yet in a climate of mass unemployment, poverty and social disintegration, there were several millionaires who wanted to build the world's tallest building.

New York was the natural home of the skyscraper for three reasons. Firstly, God hadn't notified anyone of any plans to increase the size of Manhattan Island, some of the world's most valuable real estate, so if central New Yorkers wanted to live there, they had no choice but to build up. Secondly, Manhattan Island is virtually a huge solid piece of granite, extremely stable geologically and little vulnerable to earthquakes or even minor tremors. It provides a great platform for building tall structures on firm foundations. Thirdly, New York had had a long-standing rivalry with Chicago and the plutocrats of both cities became involved in a game of architectural one-upmanship to build the world's tallest buildings, which may or may not have had even more obscure origins in their trying to compensate for, well, something. These combined factors would eventually result in a city where people travel further vertically in elevators, mile for mile, than they travel horizontally in cars, trains, taxis, buses and subways combined.

New York moguls succeeded various times in creating the world's tallest building:

The Singer Building, built on the back of the sewing machine fortune, on the corner of Liberty Street and Broadway, was the world's tallest building between 1908 and 1909 (187 metres, 612 feet and 47 floors).

The Metropolitan Life Tower, at 1 Madison Avenue, held the record from 1909 to 1913 (213 metres, 700 feet and 50 floors).

In 1913 discount store empire owner Frank Woolworth finished his construction of his 241 metres (792 feet), 57-floor Woolworth Building at 233 Broadway after spending $13.5 million ($4.75 billion today) which he paid in cash.

The Car Mogul versus the Bank

By 1930 the Great Depression was underway, but several rich men had already committed to enter the record books with their contribution to the world's biggest phallic symbols.

First up, automobile tycoon Walter Chrysler, previously the highest paid executive in corporate history and now a capitalist emperor in his own right, had planned to build the Chrysler building at 282 metres (925 feet).

Not to be outdone, the Bank of Manhattan planned to build a 70-floor tower 282.5 metres (927 feet) high, a full 41 metres (135 feet) taller than the nearby Woolworth Building but only a measly 0.5 metres (2 feet) taller than the proposed Chrysler building. By May 1930 the Bank of Manhattan Trust Building did indeed become the world's tallest building after a construction period lasting only 11 months.

In 1955 the Bank of Manhattan would merge with the Chase Bank to form the Chase Manhattan Bank and the Manhattan Trust Building became 40 Wall Street. Donald Trump would later buy the building at the

bargain basement price of only $8 million in 1995 and refurbish it to become the Trump Building in 1996.

But, knowing what the bankers were up to, Walter Chrysler and his architect-in-chief William van Alen had an ace up their sleeves. After the completion of 40 Wall Street, Chrysler got approval for and added a 38-metre (125 feet) spire to the Chrysler building and with its 77 floors and its full 319 metre (1047 feet) height situated at 405 Lexington Avenue, it became the world's tallest building on 27 May 1930. Erected with the frantic energy that characterised these projects, at one point the Chrysler building was going up at a rate of four floors per week. Yet in stark contrast to so many large projects throughout history, no workers died in its construction.

The rivalry for the world's tallest building was also a personal matter for the architect. William van Alen had previously enjoyed a prosperous partnership with H. Craig Severance, but the two had dissolved their working relationship on less than friendly terms. When Severance had been engaged for the design of 40 Wall Street the chance to spoil things for him must have been irresistible to his ex-friend. Van Alen's finishing spire remained a secret until the very last moment. The spire was delivered to the site in four sections and hidden within the framework of the Chrysler building while it was still under construction. On 23 October 1929 it took only 90 minutes to rivet the four sections into place at the top of the building. In so doing, it became the first man-made structure to surpass 1000 feet (305 metres).

It remains to this day the world's tallest

The Chrysler building from the air; still the world's tallest brick building, and likely to remain so. No other skyscraper says 'Art Deco' so spectacularly.

brick building—3 826 000 were used in its construction and with its distinctive crown, it's still considered a masterpiece of art-deco style.

But Chrysler's dream to have the world's tallest building was short-lived.

The Empire State Building

Former New York State governor and failed presidential contender Al Smith had already joined forces with a couple of the richest men in America to build the world's tallest building. Smith, Pierre S du Pont, head of the du Pont chemical empire and John Jacob Raskob, CEO of General Motors and the head of the Democratic National Committee, had already committed $50 million to the project when the crash came, but they weren't about to let a little thing like the Great Depression get in their way. With an extra $27.5 million loan from the Metropolitan Life Insurance Company they now had $77.5 million ($10.35 billion in today's money) to form the Empire State Corporation and engaged the firm of Shreve, Lamb and Harmon to turn the dream into a reality.

There's a story that John Jacob Raskob held up a square pencil to designer Lamb and asked, 'Bill, how high can you make it so that it won't fall down?'

The Corporation bought the site of the old Waldorf-Astoria and began tearing it down on 24 September 1929, forcing the relocation of the hotel to a 47 floor building at 301 Park Avenue—completed in 1931. By 3 February 1930 there was nothing left of the old building. The Empire State Building is now officially situated at 350 5th Avenue New York City but in actuality takes up a two-acre footprint of half the city block bounded by 5th Avenue, West 33rd Street, West 34th Street, Broadway and 6th Avenue, about 2 kilometres (1 mile)

south of Central Park. Demolition crews removed 24 321 loads of material from the site. The roughly 70 000 cubic metres (90 000 cubic yards) of remains of what was once the world's grandest hotel were dumped into the ocean, five miles off Sandy Hook, New Jersey. A further 20 000 cubic metres (26 000 cubic yards) of earth and rock had to be removed for the foundations of the Empire State.

Zoning laws required that the initial five floors would go to the edge of the property to allow for the main tower to rise with the proper set back from the street, but the Chrysler Building, and the 'dirty tricks' that Chrysler and van Alen had pulled to make it the world's tallest, determined the rest of the agenda. From an earlier plan to make the building 85 storeys high the designers finally settled on 'Plan K': a structure that would rise to 102 storeys—just over 1 million cubic metres or 36 million cubic feet—and that would weigh 365 000 tonnes.

The tower was designed from the top down; ensuring that floor 86 would have all the necessary elevator shafts and amenities to service the floors both above and below it.

Thoroughly modern materials

Like the pyramids of old, the Empire State would be clad in limestone, 18,580 square metres (200,000 square feet). Unlike the pyramids, the window trims and mullions also needed 300 tonnes of chrome nickel steel and a further 300 tonnes of cast aluminium spandrels. Interestingly, of all the many ethnic groups that were involved in building the steel framework, the ones with

The Empire State building—arguably the most revered skyscraper in the world— a fact that must be making Walter Chrysler roll in his grave.

the greatest skill were the Caughnawaga and Mohawk Indians who came to consider welding red-hot rivets hundreds of feet in the air as a rite of passage. They were the original 'skywalkers' and bystanders would watch in fascination as workers tossed burning bits of metal to each other across tens of feet overhead from girders not much wider than a couple of shoe widths. At lunchtime, they'd toast sandwiches on their rivet forges.

All in all, the workers in 60 trades that construction contractors Starrett Brothers and Eken engaged welded 57 000 tonnes of structural steelwork. The Pennsylvanian factories produced the beams so quickly and transported them so efficiently that they were still warm from the factory when they arrived on the building site.

Other workers poured 51 225 cubic metres (67 000 cubic yards) of concrete (from upstate New York) and laid 10 million bricks to create

EMPIRE STATE BUILDING STATISTICS

On completion the building contained:

- 1 886 kilometres (1 172 miles) of elevator cables for 63 elevators that used 1 232 doors
- 120 kilometres (75 miles) of main water pipes
- 80 kilometres (50 miles) of radiator pipes
- 400 fire hose connections
- Sockets for 350 000 light bulbs
- 610 kilometres (380 miles) of electrical wiring. In 1931 the building used as much electricity as the entire city of Albany NY.

a structure clad with 6 400 windows. Paul Starrett had got the job precisely because he didn't have any pre-existing equipment on hand. Everything was procured specifically for the project. Skilled workers were paid $1.92 per hour (an impressive $72.00 per hour in modern terms, which must have seemed like a real windfall in those years) and the weekly payroll came to $250 000 per week ($9.5 million).

The largest number of people working on it at any one time was 3 439, on 14 August 1930. The jobs were not without risk. Six people died during the building's construction, but it had taken 7 million man-hours to accomplish it.

The interior designers made extensive use of marble. The two-storey lobby has a variety veined with yellow and blue, while black Belgian marble forms the base courses. The names of the marbles are poetic—Est Rellante and Formosa Rose from Germany, Travertine and Red Levanto from Italy, Bois

Jordan from France. The ornamental panel that decorates the Fifth Avenue entrance uses no less than 80 patterns of marble just to depict the shore of Long Island.

The whole building is suffused with the sharp, sculptured lines of Art Deco. In contrast to so many more modern buildings with their stark anonymity, the impression of the Empire State is one of craftsmanship.

Nonetheless, when it came to the privately leased office spaces, the tenants generally opted away from Art Deco. Today the building houses over one thousand businesses taking up 208 880 square metres (2 248 369 square feet) of office space. The building is so large it has its own ZIP code.

At the very top of the building is a mooring mast incorporating 25 tonnes of polished steel. The roof of the Empire State reaches to 381 metres (1 250 feet) but the addition of the mast and the antenna on top of it brings the building's total height to 448.7 metres (1 472 feet). Originally the plan was to use the mast to moor zeppelins, but in reality the strong winds at that height made mooring impractical, and at any rate, it would have been rather unnerving to cross from a dirigible to a skyscraper over a hundred floors from the pavement below.

In the end the mast became a communications tower. At a cost of $3 million it was converted into one in 1950 and all nine TV networks in New York State transmit programs from there to five states. The mast is also crucial for traffic monitoring operations in New York.

Construction to completion —and the winner is...

The first steel columns were placed on 7 April 1930. Construction took all of thirteen months, the entire framework having taken only 23 weeks. It was a masterpiece of planning and execution that had employed prefabrication wherever possible and masonry work was finished, on schedule, on 13 November 1930. The total cost of the project was nowhere near the $77.5 million that the financiers had raised, the Depression being what it was. The land came in at $16,230,900 and the building itself only $24,718,00. Total $40,948,900 ($6.215 billion in today's terms).

When President Herbert Hoover turned on the building's lights on 1 May 1931 it was an event celebrated throughout the country.

In less than a year Chrysler had been trumped—spectacularly. Chrysler was so disgusted that he refused to pay the full balance of the architect's fee to William van Alen. The Empire State Building would hold its record as the world's tallest building until outdone by the World Trade Center in 1972.

In the end, though, Chicago was to beat the stakes for the world's highest building if measured to pinnacle height (a place it held until August 2007). The Sears Tower was completed in 1973. Its 108 floors (or 110 if you're the building's owners) and antenna spire rise to 527 metres (1730 feet) with 104 elevators servicing 418,064 square metres (4.56 million square feet)—more than double the usable space of the Empire State.

It was considerably cheaper to build too, reflecting changes in the economy and in the cost of manufacturing. Its cost of $150 million ($1.5 billion) is a quarter of the Empire State's. But for all its gleaming black efficiency it doesn't have a lobby with 80 different types of marble, and it doesn't quite have the Empire State's iconic status. But don't say that to any Chicagoans.

Modern Man-made
Mountains

The ongoing architectural Festival of Freudian one-upmanship to create the world's tallest building isn't likely to end soon, although the laws of physics, the principles of practicality and the reality of economics are putting some restrictions on human ambition and grand vision.

The Burj Khalifa

Formerly the 'Burj Dubai', the Burj Khalifa officially opened with much pomp, ceremony and fireworks on 4 January 2010 and is at the time of writing, the world's tallest building.

The Burj is the most prominent element of a $20-billion, 2 square kilometre (0.8 square miles) development called 'Downtown Dubai'. The brainchild of a number of very rich men led by the current ruler of Dubai, Sheikh Mohammed bin Rashid Al Maktoum, Downtown Dubai represents a considerable investment of the economy of the United Arab Emirates of which Dubai is a member state. The UAE had a registered GDP of only $104 billion in 2005, $37 billion of which came from Dubai itself, but its economy was growing fast. When completed, Downtown Dubai will comprise 30 000 houses, nine hotels, parkland, a mall and a 0.12 square kilometre (0.05 square miles) Burj Khalifa Lake. But the centrepiece is the Burj Khalifa itself.

Its architect, Adrian Smith, had previously been involved in the design of other prestige projects such as the master plan for the Canary Wharf development in London and General Motors Renaissance Centre in Detroit and would later be the architect for another grand vision, King Abdullah Economic City. This planned city 100 kilometres (62 miles) north of Jeddah is under construction at the time of writing—a $26.6 billion project comprising an area of 173 square kilometres (2 billion square feet).

Groundbreaking on the Burj started on 21 September 2004 and even before it was finished the tower was breaking records:

February 2007—surpassed the Sears Tower in Chicago as the building with the most floors.

13 May 2007—highest vertical pumping of concrete at 452 metres (1 483 feet).

21 July 2007—at 509.2 metres (1 671 feet) surpassed Taipei 101, the tallest building on earth.

12 August 2007—at 527.3 metres (1 730 feet) overtook the height of the Sears Tower antenna to become the tallest building as measured from base to top of spire.

The Burj Khalifa under construction. Named after the current President of the United Arab Emrates in a major gesture of fawning, the compliment may be short-lived. In light of the financial crisis of 2009, the Burj might remain largely empty for years.

12 September 2007—at 555.3 metres (1 822 feet) became the tallest freestanding structure on land, surpassing the CN Tower in Toronto. The CN tower was completed in 1976. If it were a 'building' it would be 147 storeys high. At this point it had also truly surpassed the projected height of Freedom Tower in Manhattan (541.3 metres or 1 776 feet).

Shortly after, the Burj also took the record for the highest vertical pumping of concrete for any structure—601 metres (1 972 feet), a record previously held in the construction of the Riva del Garda Hydroelectric Power Plant in Italy (in 1994, 532 metres or 1 745 feet).

7 April 2008—at 628.8 metres (2 063 feet) overtook the KVLY-TV mast 4.8 kilometres (3 miles) west of Blanchard, North Dakota as the world's tallest artificial structure.

A total of 160 habitable floors taking up a floor area of 33.4 hectares (82.5 acres). The world's tallest service elevator with a loading capacity of 5500 kilograms.
The world's highest observation platform at 442 metres, serviced by double-decker elevators capable of carrying 21 people per deck. These elevators are the world's fastest, travelling at a top speed of 18 metres per second (40 miles per hour). The elevator system is computer managed, and in the event of a fire or other major emergency scenario the system can guide a controlled evacuation of the whole building for up to 35,000 people.

Completed on 13 August 1963, the KVLY-TV mast is 18 metres (57 feet) shorter than the Warszawa Radio mast near Konstanynow, Poland was—the Polish tower collapsed on 8 August 1991.

1 September 2008—the Burj reached 688 metres (2 257 feet), becoming the tallest artificial structure ever built. With a topped-out height of 828 metres (2 717 feet) the Burj stands over half a mile tall.

However, the Council on Tall Buildings and Urban Habitat at the Illinois Institute of Technology refused to acknowledge the Burj's status until its official completion, requiring that it be 'clad and at least partially open for business'.

Given that, realistically, you can't expect people to walk down 160 floors, the designers have allowed for special pressurised air-conditioned rooms every 25 floors where people can rest or await rescue.

A peak electricity demand equivalent to 360 000 x 100 watt light bulbs all operating at the same time.

The general water supply is 946 000 litres (250 000 gallons per day) of which 10 000 tonnes of circulating chilled water flows through its infrastructure at peak cooling times.

All that cooling creates atmospheric moisture condensate collected in a separate system, stored in a holding tank below the basement car park and then pumped into the tower's gardens. Moisture reclamation alone provides 15 million gallons of water per year—think of it as about 20 Olympic swimming pools worth.

Total concrete used in the tower and immediate surrounding buildings (but excluding the foundations) is 230 000 cubic metres (300 000 cubic yards). If it were a solid mass, it would be a cube 61 metres (200 feet) to a side—the same weight as a hundred and fifty, 700-kilogram African bull elephants. Including foundations that include 192 50-metre-deep (164 feet) piles, the total concrete amounts to 330 000 square metres (431 600 cubic yards) with 39 000 tonnes of steel rebar reinforcement. Laid end to end, the steel rebar would stretch a quarter of the circumference of the earth.

The building's exterior curtain wall covers 83 600 square metres (20.7 acres) of glass and 27 900 square metres (6.8 acres) of framing metal—the equivalent of 17 soccer fields or 25 American football fields.

Within the tower is the 40 000 square metre, 175-room Armani Hotel and 144 Armani residential suites.

Slave labourers revolt

Creating the tower required up to 7 500 skilled workers to be working on site on any given day. Most of these workers who provided the 22 million man-hours to complete the project were illegal immigrants from Pakistan, India, Bangladesh, China and the Philippines.

Unskilled workers were labouring for only US$4.00 per day, while skilled workers were earning US$7.60. Given the low US dollar at the time and the cost of living in the UAE this meant that workers had been enduring both poverty and poor working conditions.

On 21 March 2006 they went on strike and rioted, causing $1 million in damage.

Workers building the new terminal at Dubai International Airport joined the strike. In June 2007 the government of Dubai offered free flights home, no questions asked, to the illegal workers and they could barely cope with the number of people wanting out.

Given the general tone of such projects, unless civilisation collapses or we enter at the very least into a totally crippling major worldwide economic recession, it's highly unlikely that the Burj Khalifa will remain the world's tallest building for more than a few decades, or even much less. Here's a shortlist of various contenders, in increasing height and perhaps increasing impracticality and fantasy.

Also given that there are frequent design (and height) changes to these projects, and the secrecy with which final plans are kept, this list could easily change.

Burj Mubarak al Kabir. Part of the 250 square kilometres Madinat al Hareer ('City of Silk') project in Kuwait. Proposed height: 1 001 metres (3 284 feet).

Murjan Tower, Manamah, Bahrain. Proposed height 1 022 metres (3 353 feet) and 200 floors.

Al Burj, Dubai. Proposed height: 1 400 metres (4 593 feet) with a top floor roof at 850 metres (2 789 feet) for a full floor count of 228 and a total floor area of 1.49 million square metres (16 038 200 square feet).

The Japanese
Aim High

Faced with the world's highest land prices and some of the world's highest population densities, but possessing some of the world's most advanced technology, the Japanese have been at the forefront of some of these cutting-edge grand visions. When you consider that in Japan a whopping 90 per cent of a building's budget can go on the land price alone, there comes a real economic incentive to build higher.

Sky City 1000

In 1989 Japan's biggest architecture, construction and engineering firm, The Takenaka Corporation, proposed Sky City 1000.

This megascraper would comprise three huge towers linked by a core centre. Each tower would comprise 14 units of 'Space Plateaus' each 14 storeys high, stacked one on top of the other, with spaces in between the plateaus to allow for air circulation and green spaces.

The building's 196 floors would rise to a height of 1 000 metres (3 281 feet) on a footprint 400 metres (1 312 feet) wide, housing 36 000 permanent residents and office/retail space for another 100 000 workers on a total floor area of 8 square kilometres (almost 2 000 acres).

Just to give you an idea of the scale, the lower three plateaus of a Sky City tower alone would be taller than the Eiffel Tower. The dampening mechanism for Sky City would make that of Taipei 101 look like child's play.

Sky City demonstrates that at a certain point we begin to move beyond the idea of a simple building and into the realm of a small town that just happens to be housed in a structure conceived as one integrated whole.

Mega City Pyramid

Going one step further is the Shimizu TRY 2004 Mega City Pyramid (MCP).

The MCP is so large and heavy that it can't be built with current materials and engineers are waiting for the development of carbon nanotube technology to provide the necessary strength without the unnecessary mass. Such material would be 100 times

The Tokyo skyline. Real estate prices are even higher than Manhattan and, unlike the granite island, Tokyo is built in an earthquake zone, necessitating innovative engineering.

lighter than materials of the same strength today.

If the MCP were built this is what it would be like: First set down 36 huge piers in a 6 x 6 square into Tokyo Bay, covering a footprint of 8 x 8 kilometres (5 x 5 miles).

Then build a first layer of 25 individual pyramids on an area 5 kilometres (3 miles) to a side (25 square kilometres, or 9 square miles). Each pyramid would be about the size of the Great Pyramid of Giza, but would be fully habitable. External trusses would create the main pyramid superstructure of eight layers. Within each layer or two above would be a series of 30-storey high skyscrapers supported above and below and connected by the trusses. Layers one to four would house

Towers, Pyramids & Skyscrapers

residential skyscrapers; five to eight would be for business, science and recreation. Each layer would be 250.5 metres high, giving a total height to the structure of 2 004 metres (6 574 feet or 1.24 miles).

The total floor space of the buildings would be around 88 square kilometres (21 745 acres), about the same size as the island of Manhattan. About 240 000 housing units would be home to 750 000 people. Offices and commercial facilities would employ 800 000 people.

The trusses and the buildings within them would devote a considerable proportion of their surface areas to efficient, photovoltaic cells to generate solar electricity in order to meet the huge energy demands of the Mega City Pyramid.

X-seeding Expectations

Yet even the MCP's grandeur pales in comparison with the vision of George Binder, Managing Director of the European firm Buildings and Data, and their Japanese partners in planning, the Taisei Corporation. The well-named X-Seed 4000 was fully designed in 1995 and is therefore the largest artificial structure ever envisioned. Rising to a height of 4 000 metres (13 123 feet or almost 2.5 miles) it would be almost 224 metres (735 feet) taller than Mount Fuji, which it resembles.

Like the Mega City Pyramid, the X-Seed would be built on the sea, on a 6 kilometres (3.7 miles) diametre base. Its 800 habitable floors would provide living and working space for up to one million people. This true human-made mountain would cost anything up to one trillion dollars to construct, effectively meaning an investment of one million dollars per capita to create the infrastructure to house and provide working facilities for every inhabitant. How could you justify this? Although, in the words of George Binder, it was 'never meant to be built', it may well be that one day it will be not only technologically and economically but also psychologically possible to build something very much like it—an arcology, a fully self-sufficient and sustainable artificial architectural ecology the size of a mountain.

The Mile High
Illinois

All of these proposals still fall short of an idea posited by no less an architect than Frank Lloyd Wright. In 1956 Wright suggested that a mile-high (1 609 metres, 5 280 feet) tower could be feasible even with the technology available at that time. The Illinois, aka The Mile High Illinois, aka Sky City was to have been over four times taller than the Empire State and to have comprised a whopping 528 storeys. In fact, Wright's foundations for the Illinois were to extend as deeply into the earth as the Empire state was high. Totalling 1.71 million square metres (18.46 million square feet) or almost 424 acres the megascraper would have comprised just over half the surface area of Manhattan's Central Park (843 acres) all in one building, serviced by 76 elevators.

There are major difficulties in building such tall structures:

The taller the building, the more elevators you need to service it. At a certain point, the surface area of the elevators exceeds the surface area of the lower floors, making the whole exercise of building taller pointless.

Tall buildings sway in high winds, especially those made primarily of steel. Although this may be sensible from an engineering point of view, psychologically it's difficult to live with a building that feels as if it's about to fall down any second.

The higher you go, the thinner the air and some people are sensitive to this. I live at an altitude of 1km (3 281 feet) above sea level and yet I experience some nausea every time I'm driven into town at sea level. If you start having to pressurise upper floors this is a further complication. Within an enclosed environment air-quality management and air-conditioner maintenance is crucial in smaller buildings, how much more crucial would it be in a megascraper?

Heating is another factor. Heating has to take into account the number of people within the building at any one time, as well as heat generated by the proliferation of modern electrical and electronic equipment. There are heat gains and losses throughout the day and through the year on account of seasonality, and regardless of the season there's also a significant temperature differential between the ground floor and the highest floors of a super tall skyscraper.

Safety, especially in the post 9/11 world, is a concern. How do you minimise fire danger and expedite evacuation?

There's the problem of commuting, how do you handle the flow of people in and out of the building on a daily basis. Where do you park the cars?

Finally, there's the building's interaction with the city it's situated in. Very tall buildings create large wind vortices around them and they cast long shadows. Not everyone relishes the idea of actually living next to one.

Troubleshooting tall problems

Wright came up with various solutions for some of these issues. The number of elevators is reduced if you introduce the idea of separate 'sky lobbies'. Here, few elevators go the whole length of the building with many being for local transport only, effectively turning the building into a series of smaller skyscrapers, stacked upon one another. Double-decker elevators for some runs also help.

You can counteract swaying by various means. The Taipei 101, at 509.2 metres (1 670 feet) and the tallest building in the world before the completion of the Burj Khalifa, has a 660 tonne steel pendulum centrally suspended between floors 88 and 92 that acts as a tuned mass damper. When the building sways one way, this damper and another two six-tonne dampers at the top of the building swing in the opposite direction. Effectively the two sways cancel each other out. The Taipei 101 also has 380 1.5 metre (5 feet) diameter steel piles going 80 metres (262 feet) into bedrock to reinforce the foundations.

On 31 March 2003, even while it was being built, the Taipei 101 survived a 6.8 magnitude earthquake. You can also construct a megascraper using concrete—a far less flexible material which is less prone to swaying. Unfortunately for Wright, in his day concrete mixes that could withstand the necessary loads didn't exist, so he suggested basing the Illinois' cross-section on a tripod design as this would be stronger than the usual rectangular cross-section. The Burj Khalifa uses both a tripodal cross-section and high load-bearing concrete mixes that engineers developed in the late 1990s and early 2000s.

Wright's building was a purely conceptual exercise, it was never really intended to be built, but technological advances in materials sciences, safety features and environmental regulations such as already exist in the Burj Khalifa mean that megascrapers are even more technologically feasible now than they were in the middle of the 20th century. This doesn't mean that people need them, but that hasn't stopped some visionaries from going even further, even beyond the realm of current science and using technologies that haven't even been invented yet, but that engineers comfortably predict are only a few decades away.

The Ryugyong
Hotel

Sometimes vision exceeds capacity. Such is the case with the Ryugyong Hotel in the Potong-gang district of downtown Pyongyang, capital city of North Korea.

Words almost fail to describe it, though many have tried. It has been called 'The Hotel of Doom', 'The Phantom Hotel', 'One of the most expensive white elephants in history' and 'The Worst Building in the History of Mankind'.

In any other place a building with the following statistics would be impressive:

- 330 metres (1 083 feet) tall
- 105 storeys topped by no less than 7 revolving restaurants
- 360 000 square metres (3 875 million square feet or 89 acres) of floor space
- 3 000 rooms in three wings each 100 metres (328 feet) long, and 18 metres (131 feet) wide.

It's the tallest building in the country and completely dominates the Pyongyang skyline.

The hotel's construction began in 1989 as a piece of one-upmanship to out-do the completion of the Swissotel Stamford in Singapore in 1986. The Stamford just happens to be the tallest hotel in Asia and was built by a South Korean company. Not to be outdone, Kim Il Sung decided that North Korea would have not only Asia's, but the world's tallest hotel.

Unfortunately, the estimated cost of the structure was about $750 million ($1.9 billion) and represented an estimated 2 per cent of the GDP of North Korea. By 1992, the money ran out and construction stopped. The nation now had the world's most expensive piece of concrete skeleton, but no habitable floors. It stayed that way for the next 16 years, exposing the core to the ravages of the North Korean climate.

Construction recommenced in April 2008, but remains a half-hearted affair. An Egyptian company, the Orascom Group, is fitting the upper floors with the infrastructure for a mobile telephone network for up to 100 000 subscribers, despite the fact that owning a mobile phone in North Korea is an offence punishable by death.

So the Ryugyong just stands there, waiting for its windows and fittings, waiting for at least $250 million in foreign investment to save it in a world where not even organised criminals want to invest in North Korea.

Search for 'The Ryugyong Hotel' in Google Maps' 'Satellite' option for a bird's eye view.

Part 02

Aqueducts, Canals & Sewerage Systems

I f you want to build a civilisation with a population large enough to maintain a long-term sustainable military dictatorship large enough to create anything that's worthy of the name of 'empire', you have to create a lot of infrastructure. Fundamentally, you have to control the water supply. You need drinking water, water for hygiene both in (baths) and out (sewers) and because water transportation is cheaper than land travel for large quantities of materials, it helps to know how to build canals for those times when nature hasn't conveniently provided a river.

Of course, not all civilisations or empires have placed importance on water management, but those that didn't really didn't last very long.

Arguably the best hydraulic engineers in the ancient world were the Romans. Not content with what nature had provided they went one better and created artificial rivers—aqueducts.

045

Other civilisations also appreciated the advantages of sound water management, but what they did ultimately depended on a combination of cultural priorities, economic necessity and technological feasibility.

Roman
Aqueducts

The Romans didn't invent these specialised water-carrying bridges and channels—the Greeks were building them in the 5th century BCE—but the Romans took the principle to its highest form.

Aqueducts were built all over the Roman world, but most impressive are those that fed the city of Rome. As time progressed, more and more water had to be carried from further and further away over increasingly difficult geography in order to satisfy the needs of the burgeoning capital of the empire.

Aqueduct building was a balancing act. Unlike modern water systems that supply water through underground pipes under pressure, aqueducts were gravity systems with covered channels above ground. The gradient at which the water fell was crucial. Too steep and the water flowed too fast creating inefficient turbulent flow and eroding the channel. Too shallow and the water flow would be too sluggish. Among aqueducts in the Roman world, gradients range from ratios as steep as 1 in 40 (a drop of one unit in height for every forty of length) for the first 3.6-kilometre (2.2-mile) stretch of the Carthage Aqueduct, to as shallow as 1 in 14,000 for a 10 kilometres (6 miles) stretch of the Nemausus (Nîmes) Aqueduct.

The Nîmes Aqueduct is particularly impressive. Because it's a gravity system, an aqueduct had to go downhill all the way, and over its 50-kilometre (31-mile) stretch the Nîmes had to tunnel occasionally as well as bridge. Six teams worked for two months to dig the 60-metre (197 feet) Serhac Tunnel and at the River Gardon the Nîmes builders had to construct a bridge nearly 49 metres (160 feet) high spanning 24.5 metres (80.4 feet).

The aqueduct system was certainly worth the trouble and expense. In Pompeii, for example, no household was more than 50 metres (164 feet) from a street fountain. But with the collapse of the empire the advantages of cleanliness would be lost on European cities for centuries.

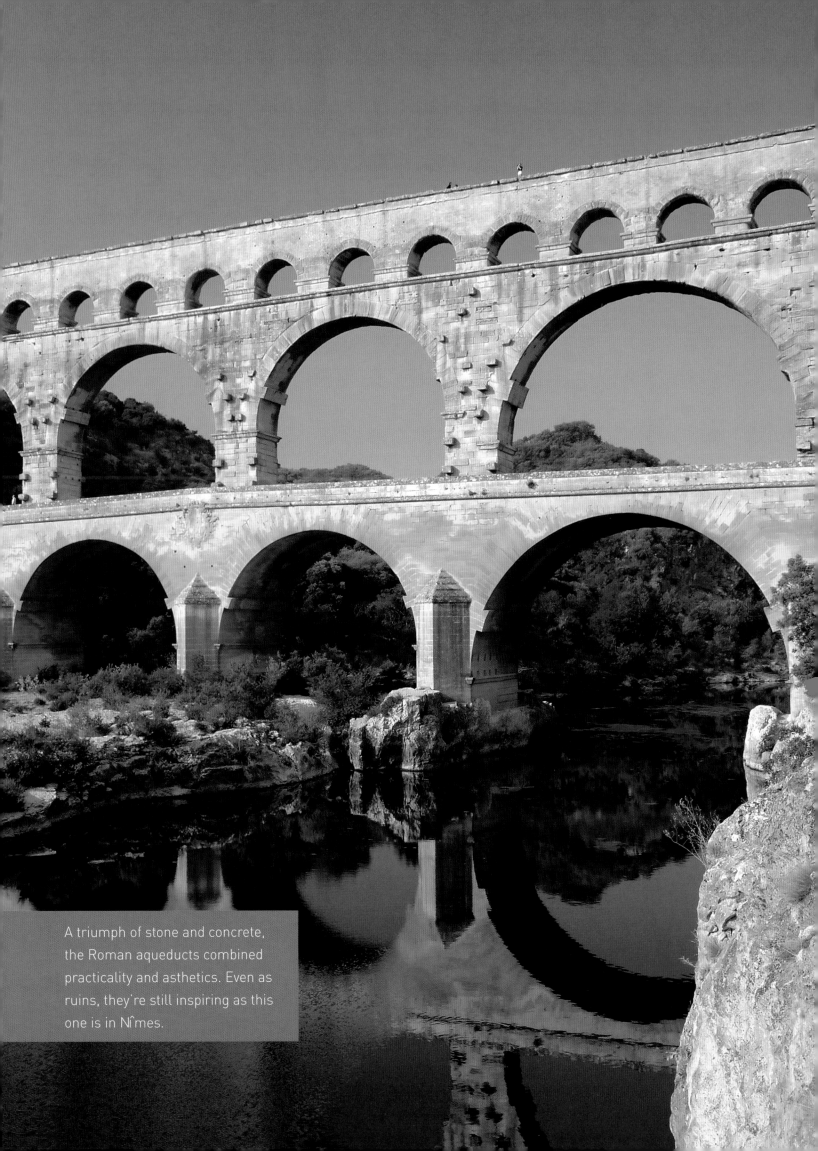

A triumph of stone and concrete, the Roman aqueducts combined practicality and asthetics. Even as ruins, they're still inspiring as this one is in Nîmes.

Aqueduct Name	Date Built	Estimated Capacity of Flow in Cubic Metres per Second	Estimated Total Length in Kilometres (Miles)	Estimated Length of Aqueduct on Arches and Bridges in Kilometres (Miles)
Appia	312 BCE	75,000	16 (10)	0.1 (328′)
Anio Vetus ac	272–269 BCE	180,000	81 (50.3)	None
Marcia	c. 140 BCE	190,000	91 (56.5)	10 (6.2)
Tepula	125 BCE	17,800	18 (11)	9 (5.5)
Julia	33 BCE	48,000	22 (13.6)	10 (6.2)
Virgo	22—19 BCE	100,000	21 (13)	1.2 (0.75)
Alsietina	2 BCE	16,000	33 (20.5)	0.5 (0.3)
Claudia	38—52 CE	185,000	69 (42.9)	14 (8.7)
Anio Novus	38—52 CE	190,000	87 (54)	11 (6.8)
Traina	109	Not Estimated	60 (37)	None
Alexandriana	226	Not Estimated	22 (13.6)	2.4 (15)

The Grand Canal of China

The Jintai Emperor of China Zhu Qiyu was very fond of building. In his eight-year rule, not only did he order a major refurbishment of the Great Wall but he was also responsible for the restoration of the Grand Canal.

Though it's far less well known than the Great Wall, the Grand Canal was arguably an even more impressive piece of engineering and it was certainly more important to the economic history of China than The Wall.

China is a huge country of considerable geographic diversity. The first thing you notice when you look at a physical map of China is that it's dominated by several large river systems, in particular the Huang Ho (the Yellow River) and the Yangtze. This is one of the reasons that China has traditionally been able to support a large population. Rivers also represent a cheap, ready-made transportation route; building roads of the length required in such a large country would be hugely expensive.

The problem from an imperial perspective is that China's major river systems all run west to east. There are comparatively few large river systems running north to south. The only

reasonable solution, and a very convenient one if you can pull it off, is to build an artificial river that could connect the east/west river systems, but also provide an alternative trade route between the large coastal and near coastal cities where a large proportion of the Chinese population have traditionally lived.

The Grand Canal is even older than the Great Wall. In the sixth century BCE, or possibly earlier, a canal was constructed linking the Yellow River near Kaifeng to the Si and Bai rivers. This canal came to be known as the Hong Gou ('The Canal of the Flying Geese').

Then in 486 BCE, Fuchai the King (or perhaps Duke) of Wu ordered a much larger canal to connect the Yangtze River to the Huai River to its north, which is situated about halfway between the Yangtze and the Yellow River. This canal came to be known as the Han Gou ('The Han Country Conduit'). The canal was large enough to allow the passage of military transport and the Jin Dynasty General Wang Jun was able to score a victory against the Eastern Wu in 280 because he was able to take a marine force up the Han Gou, attack the Wu capital of Jianye and force the surrender of the Emperor Sun Hao.

It was only a matter of time before there would be enough economic prosperity and political stability to link up the Huai with the Yellow River in a sustainable way. Although the Qi dynasty expanded the canal further, by the year 600 a change in the course of the Yellow River had caused a silt build-up that had made significant portions of the Hong Gou unnavigable.

The Emperor Wendi of the Sui Dynasty sought the advice of his chief engineer, Yuwen Kai. Yuwen recommended that rather than dredging the Hong Gou, a new canal be constructed parallel to the old one. Five million men and women laboured on this first section of the canal. The Emperor Wendi died in 604 and his son Yangdi took over, completing this section the following year. Then the work continued in a massive construction effort comprising the six years from 605 and 610 in which workers expanded the canal south as far as Hangzhou and as far north as Beijing.

Over such great distances the canal's waters underwent many changes of level, from 1 metre below sea level at Hangzhou to a highpoint of 42 metres (138 feet) in the mountains of Shandong and ending at Beijing at an elevation of 27 metres above sea level. Water locks controlled the levels somewhat but in some cases weren't quite enough. When it runs through the city of Gaoyou the base of the canal is at the same level as the city's streets and during wet years over the centuries, Gaoyou, has experienced massive flooding.

Further work on the canal under Emperor Yangdi included building several subsidiary canals, an imperial roadway parallel to the watercourse, the establishment of a postal and courier service and the planting of trees to maintain the integrity of the canal's banks.

Canal Benefits

All this work and its results had a major impact on China. Standing armies in the far north no longer had to depend entirely on the wheat- and millet-producing regions of the north. They could now gain fast and easy access to the produce of the rice fields of the south. As great an accomplishment as this was, the Sui paid the usual high price for a grand vision. It's estimated that at least half a million and as many as three million of the peasants recruited to do the work of digging the canal died in its construction.

It couldn't have helped matters either that while millions were dying, Emperor Yangdi had a habit of organising expensive and garish processions of conspicuous consumption up to 40 miles long, up and down the canal.

For all his accomplishments, history remembers Yangdi as a despot who was rightly strangled when the revolution came.

The Sui Dynasty was finished by 618, but China at last had its own version of the Nile, linking the north to the south but even more effectively linking the Hai, Wei, Yellow, Huai, Yangtze and Qiantang rivers through a connected system 1 794 kilometres (1 115 miles) long.

It was the Tang Dynasty that followed the Sui that really reaped the benefits of the work during their almost three centuries of rule (618–907) and the city of Yangzhou, close to the canal, became the economic hub of the Empire. By 745 almost 150 000 tonnes of grain was shipped along the canal every year, later peaking to as much as over 350 000 tonnes of grain per year.

Kaifeng, also a canal city, became the capital of the Song Empire (960–1279) and the canal's fortunes rose and fell with the dynasties that controlled the country.

Under the Yuan, with their capital at Beijing, the canal suffered considerable neglect and then between 1 411 and 1 415 the Ming undertook major repairs and renovations including redirecting the waters of the Wen River to feed the canal.

Under the Ming, 47 000 full-time labourers maintained the canal and in the mid-1400s records show that 121 5 000 soldiers were needed to operate 11 775 imperial grain barges.

The Manchu Qing dynasty maintained the canal for a while but in 1855, when the ever-difficult Yellow River once more flooded and changed its course again, the canal's course was cut off at Shandong. This effectively separated the north and south portions of the canal and large sections of it fell into disrepair. It wasn't until almost a century later, after the Communist takeover of the country, that the authorities started restoration work.

In spite of the canal's official length reaching as far as Beijing, today, of the seven sections in which the canal is divided, only the southernmost three sections, the portion from Hangzhou to Jining, are navigable. It's nonetheless still an extremely important thoroughfare. It's at least 100 metres wide going through cities and often 300 metres wide in rural areas and it handles traffic of around 175 million tonnes per year—a number that would have no doubt been inconceivable even to the Emperor Yangdi.

The Suez
Canal

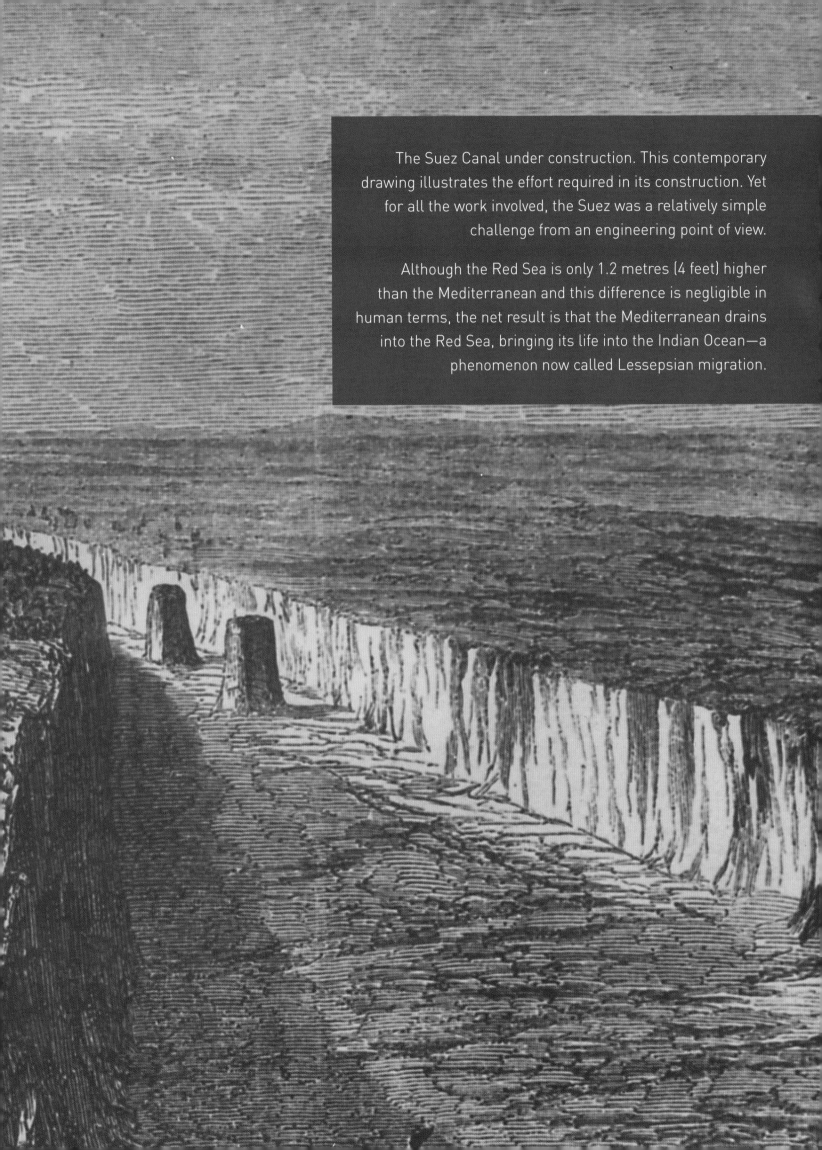

The Suez Canal under construction. This contemporary drawing illustrates the effort required in its construction. Yet for all the work involved, the Suez was a relatively simple challenge from an engineering point of view.

Although the Red Sea is only 1.2 metres (4 feet) higher than the Mediterranean and this difference is negligible in human terms, the net result is that the Mediterranean drains into the Red Sea, bringing its life into the Indian Ocean—a phenomenon now called Lessepsian migration.

The continents of earth have been creeping along its surface for eons and their recent configurations have had a profound effect on human history. The neck of land joining the continent of Africa to Asia is only about 130 kilometres (80 miles) wide at its narrowest, but since the beginning of seafaring and until relatively recently it's prevented easy access to the Mediterranean and Red Sea and by extension the Atlantic and Indian oceans. Human history would indeed have been very different without this barrier.

Ships from the Mediterranean were effectively blocked from the sea route to the east so for centuries merchants moved only the most valuable items for trade along dangerous, overland desert routes like the Silk Road. And it's not only silk, porcelain and spices that had to travel far. Ideas also moved, but more slowly by land than they might have by sea.

Digging the Ditch

The earliest record that we have of anyone trying to solve this basic transportation problem goes back to Pharaoh Senusret III (c. 1878 BCE–c. 1839 BCE), who may have dug a canal linking the ancient course of the River Nile to the Red Sea by cutting through what is now the Wadi Tumulat—a dry riverbed valley that only contains water for a short time after rainfall.

There is some evidence to suggest that either this, or a similar connection, existed until the reign of Ramses II (c. 1279 BCE–c.1213 BCE) and beyond, but by around 600 BCE the canal had fallen into disrepair as drifting sand and silt carried by the Nile built up. According to the Greek historian Herodotus, the Twenty-Sixth Dynasty Pharaoh Necho II (610 BCE–595 BCE) had wanted to create another canal joining the Red Sea and the city of Pelusium (Per-Amun), which was located at the easternmost point on the Nile, about 30 kilometres south east of the location of the modern city of Port Said. Necho squandered the lives of 120 000 in the attempt before giving up.

Darius I of Persia conquered Egypt in around 500 BCE and through better engineering, or perhaps just sheer brute force, succeeded in digging a canal from the Nile at Bubastis (near the modern city of Zagazig) to the town of Suez, on the very northern extremity of the Red Sea. Herodotus said that it was wide enough for two triremes to pass by each other with oars fully extended. With the characteristic redundancy of ancient despots, Darius had the following message inscribed for posterity near Kabret:

'King Darius says: I am a Persian; setting out from Persia I conquered Egypt. I ordered to dig this canal from the river that is called Nile and flows in Egypt, to the sea that begins in Persia. Therefore, when this canal had been dug as I had ordered, ships went from Egypt through this canal to Persia, as I had intended.'

Over the next thousand years or so various conquerors and rulers of Egypt neglected, ruined, rebuilt and repaired this canal until Caliph Al-Mansur of the Abbasids finally destroyed it sometime during his reign (754–775).

It wasn't until more than a thousand years had passed that someone decided to address the canal question again. During his ill-fated Egyptian 'expedition' Napoleon Bonaparte had the Isthmus of Suez surveyed, but the report concluded that the Mediterranean was 10 metres higher than the Red Sea. This would have necessitated a canal to be built with locks to take the ships from one water level to another, an undertaking too expensive for the French to consider, so Napoleon abandoned the project.

Unfortunately for history, but perhaps fortunately for those who might have had to work under Napoleon, the survey was conducted under war conditions, and the results were wrong. The canal could have been built then, but instead had to wait almost seventy years.

French Takeover

Ferdinand Marie, Vicomte de Lesseps (1805–1894) was the scion of a French noble family so well connected that he basically walked into a diplomatic job and in 1832 he became vice-consul at Alexandria. During his time there he read the accounts of Napoleon's surveyor, and a grand vision seized him. He also became friends with the future leader of Egypt, Said Pasha.

After a long and distinguished career, and after his retirement from the diplomatic service de Lesseps's wife and daughter died in 1853.

A year later his old friend Said Pasha became viceroy of Egypt and invited him back to Egypt. He arrived on 7 November and on 30 November 1854 Said signed a concession authorising de Lesseps to build the Suez Canal.

It took two years before an international panel of civil engineers approved a proposal by two French engineers based in Egypt— Louis Maurice Adolphe Linant de Bellefond ('Linant Pasha') and Mougel Bey.

In a bizarre twist, Said Pasha actually suggested dismantling the Giza Pyramid complex to provide masonry for the project. Linant had held the dream of the Suez Canal even longer than Lesseps, but he wasn't about to commit cultural sacrilege to do it. Appalled at the idea, but realising that he could be fired if he was too vocal in his opposition, Linant instead prepared an exhaustive financial cost benefit analysis and demonstrated that it would be cheaper to quarry new rock than to take apart the only surviving Great Wonder of the Ancient World.

The project met considerable opposition, especially from many in the English Government of the day, who were concerned about their imperial interests, and who seemed to object to anything French on principle anyway, but Lesseps wasn't the sort of person who could hear the word 'no' very easily once he'd made his mind up, and he also had the support of Napoleon III and the Empress Eugenie.

More importantly, de Lesseps had the support of the Egyptian Government who provided 80 million francs of funding, and the French public, who privately subscribed to 100 million francs worth of shares in the Compagnie Universelle du Canal Maritime de Suez established on 15 December 1858.

De Lesseps took a pickaxe and made the first symbolic strike at Port Said on 25 March 1859. The canal was finished almost eleven years later. As the canal was entering its last stages the 63-year-old de Lesseps would remarry and produce another 12 children, proving that canal building and marrying a woman almost 40 years younger than you can be invigorating.

Canal Opens

The Suez Canal was opened to shipping on 17 November 1869. A narrow body of water 163 kilometres (101 miles) long and 300 metres (984 feet) wide at its broadest point now separated Africa from Asia for the first time in 30 million years.

On 27 November 1869 Said's successor, Khedive Ismail Pasha, the de facto ruler of Egypt under the Ottomans and major shareholder in the Compagnie, officially opened the canal. Building the Suez had chiefly used the forced labour of some 30 000 Egyptians and the canal's final cost was around 400 million francs, double the original estimate.

Mounting debts forced Ismail to sell his shares in the canal to the British for £4 million in 1875—about $5 billion in modern terms.

In 1888 the Convention of Constantinople declared the canal a neutral zone under the protection of the British. Egypt wouldn't control the canal again until 1956, when Egyptian President Gamal Abdel Nasser nationalised it in order to use its toll fees to finance his own grand vision, the building of the Aswan Dam. On 26 July 1956, the codeword

that Nasser used to instigate the raiding of the offices of the Suez Canal Company was 'Lesseps'.

Nasser's seizure of critical real estate prompted the Suez crisis, which fortunately failed to materialise into full scale war between the British, French and Israelis against the Egyptians due to the diplomatic efforts of the Canadian Secretary of State for External Affairs, Lester Bowles Pearson. Pearson received the Nobel Peace Prize in 1957. Nonetheless, because Nasser had ordered the intentional sinking of ships in the canal, the U.N. had to be called in to clean out the wreckage and the canal was closed until April 1957.

The canal is flat and lockless. Ships of drafts up to 16 metres (53 feet) and 150 000 tonnes displacement can pass through it, and plans to increase this limit to 22 metres (72 feet) should allow the passage of fully laden supertankers. Ships too large to pass through the canal have to make the weeks long, over 20 000-kilometre (12 500-mile) journey around Africa, a journey that took months in antiquity.

In the first decade of the 21st century, the canal has averaged around 17,500 ships per year or 8 per cent of the world's shipping traffic. At an average transit fee of $150,000 per ship, the canal earns Egypt big bucks—from July 2005 to May 2006, $3.246 billion.

The story of the Panama Canal is actually the story of two canals—a French fiasco of corruption and incompetence that bankrupted a nation and a savvy, profitable piece of American know-how that changed the course of history.

THE PANAMA RAILROAD

On 24 January 1848, James Marshall discovered gold at Sutter's Mill in Coloma, California, inspiring 300 000 men, women and children to cross from the eastern seaboard and make their fortune out west. The Gold Rush had begun.

In response to the need to go west as soon as possible, the United States Congress decided to create two lines of mail ships, one from New York to Chagres, the other from Panama City to San Francisco. William H. Aspinall took charge of administering the shipping lines and after securing $1 million in funding (around $420 million in today's money) formed the Panamanian Railroad Company in May 1850. The Company then began the construction of a railroad to replace the roads that the Spanish had built to span the width of the Panama isthmus—old Camino Real and the Camino de las Cruces in May 1850.

The project encountered problems that were also a foretaste of the future. As the jungle cleared, soil erosion made the work difficult, and when the rainy season came workers found themselves labouring in water over 1.2-metre (4-feet) deep.

At midnight on 27 January 1855, after almost five years work starting from Aspinwall (later Colòn) on the Atlantic side, the company finished laying 60 kilometres (37 miles) of track up to the crest of the continental divide at Culebra and met with another team that had lain 11.25 kilometres (7 miles) of track from Panama, up the mountain. The first train crossed from station to station the next day.

The double-tracked railway's final cost had been $8 million ($3.36 billion in today's terms). Over 300 bridges had had to be built. Some swamps needed 30 metres (100 feet) of fill. The stifling heat, humidity and disease killed indiscriminately, and it's estimated that 12 000 people died building the railroad, among them Americans, Europeans, Chinese, West Indians and even African slaves—it would be another 20 years before slavery would be abolished.

The human toll at around 300 per mile to build a total of just over 77 kilometres (48 miles) of track had been considerable. It was also the most expensive length of track ever built but in spite of the cost the railroad was a tremendous financial success.

So many people used the railway that it carried the heaviest volume of freight per unit length of all the other railroads in the world.

Even death worked on the side of the Panama Railway. Universities and hospitals in Europe were always hungry for corpses to teach anatomy to the budding doctors and nurses of the future, and since so many of the workers who died building the railroad had come anonymously and without families, the company appropriated the corpses, pickled them and shipped them across the Atlantic. Sales of these cadavers fully funded the company's hospital to help those patients that did survive.

But as great an achievement and as useful as the railroad was, it wasn't enough.

The Panama Canal

The pre-Columbian civilisations of Central America were not averse to major engineering projects; however, we have no record of any of them ever attempting a canal crossing the Isthmus of Panama, even though at roughly 65 kilometres (40 miles) wide, the horizontal distance at its narrowest is shorter than the Suez. The geography of the region is complex and one particular peak, La Culebra, was to be of critical importance in the creation of a canal.

Although the natives may have been indifferent to the idea of a canal, the Europeans certainly weren't. On 25 September 1513, Vasco Nunez de Balboa reputedly became the first European to see the Pacific (the 'Mar del Sur', or Southern Sea) on its eastern side, and promptly 'took possession' of it on behalf of the Spanish, calling this specific part of it the Bay of San Miguel.

It took a while and a little more exploration, but eventually the Spanish realised that you could save yourself a 20 000-kilometre (12 500-mile) circumnavigation of South America around the hugely dangerous Cape Horn by building a canal through Panama and making the pillaging of what would later become Colombia, Ecuador and Peru even more efficient than it already was.

Unfortunately for the Spanish they had to abandon the idea once they realised that they didn't have the technology or the resources to make a canal happen. Several nations played with the idea of a canal at Panama before the late 1800s, most notably the Scots, in an ill-fated colonial enterprise called the Darien Scheme, which ended up bankrupting the Scots and costing them their economic and later, political independence. It was a foretaste of things to come.

Over a 120 years later history was conspiring to make the Panama Canal a more urgent proposition.

De Lesseps Takes Control

In 1879 at the age of 73, Ferdinand de Lesseps was possessed by an idea to top the Suez project that had made him famous. After a rousing speech from de Lesseps the Geographical Society of Paris voted to build the Panama Canal and he became the President of the Panama Canal Company.

The French had every reason to believe that they could build the canal, after all, hadn't they already built another and didn't they already have de Lesseps to make sure it would happen?

Compared to the Suez, the Panama was a nightmare to construct, necessitating the partial removal of a mountain.

After a preliminary survey of the site in December 1879 during which de Lesseps saw the Chagres River during the dry season and at its most well-behaved, the great Frenchman concluded that the canal would cost 658 million francs and take eight years to complete. This was the equivalent of about $214 million or $30 billion in today's terms.

De Lesseps had no trouble raising the cash. However, de Lesseps had goofed not only in not being thorough enough in his own survey, but he had relied too much on an earlier survey that assumed that the sea-level canal he insisted on building would follow the line of the Panama Railroad.

But a canal isn't a railroad. In reality, in order to have a sea-level canal at Suez, the builders would have to cut through the Culebra Mountain, through a crucial third that the faulty survey had ignored. The Culebra in fact rose to a height of 110 metres (360 feet) above sea level. Yet it was on the basis of this sea-level canal plan that de Lesseps convinced the French people to get behind him, lured by the promise of huge profits from passage tolls.

Over the next two years the engineers did their own surveying and gradually realised the enormity of the task before them—they would have to excavate a mountain. Then they realised that during the rainy season the placid Chagres became a raging torrent, rising as much as three metres in an hour, and that they'd have to divert the Chagres to build the canal.

And yet, back in France, de Lesseps blithely ignored geographic realities. One of history's great self-deceptions had begun.

The engineers discovered that although ocean tides only went up 0.75 metres (2.5 feet) on the Atlantic side of Panama, on the Pacific side the funnel-shaped nature of the Bay of Panama caused the high tide to rise to 6.5 metres (21 feet) and that they'd have to build a tidal lock. But the French still went ahead with the project without actually solving the problems.

The official groundbreaking took place on 1 January 1880.

Meanwhile, the engineers were discovering the same problems that had plagued the railroad builders 30 years before. Actual blasting of the Culebra didn't begin until 20 January 1882.

As they cut the forests and blasted through the mountains, they attempted to remove earth. But then the soil would destabilise, and landslides would fill the holes they'd already dug. When the rains came, the Chagres would flood, filling the excavations at that end with silt and the workers would have to labour in mud, slowing everything down.

The more dirt they removed, the shallower they'd have to cut on account of the landslides, and the shallower they cut, the more earth they'd have to remove. The war with the rain gods had begun.

Then there was the environment. A warm, soggy land dotted with uncountable still water pools made it a paradise for mosquitoes. The mosquitoes carried yellow fever and infected thousands with a disease that made people so sick that their vomit would turn black before they died. Six thousand people would fall in the first five years of the canal's construction.

People thought that the deaths were due to miasma—bad air. They had not yet made the connection to the mosquitoes, so they had no way of fighting the illness.

Yet in 1884 de Lesseps was still France's golden boy. As the head of the Franco-American Union he formally presented the Statue of Liberty as a gift to the United States on 11 June.

But by early 1885 anybody working on the Panama Canal project with any contact with the real world could see that de Lesseps' sea-level canal was an impossibility. De Lesseps himself, from the comfort of his French château, would hear nothing of modifying the existing plan.

In February 1885 two lieutenants from the U.S. navy stated that at the current rate of progress the work would take 26 years, require the removal of a further 180 million cubic yards of earth and cost a further $350 million (about $50 billion in modern terms). All this time de Lesseps had been paying for the canal by selling bonds, but insiders on the scheme were discreetly offloading their stocks.

By 1885 only 10 per cent of the work had been done at a cost of $250 million. By 1887 only 40 per cent of the work had been done. Where had all the money gone? The short answer is in having to do the same things over and over again, because nature had kept undoing the work. But the canal project was also riddled with wastefulness and corruption.

Management were paying themselves exorbitant salaries with perks, while labourers were dying of yellow fever, Chagres fever, a particularly virulent form of malaria also carried by mosquitoes, heat exhaustion and accidents. In one yellow fever outbreak in September 1884 there were 684 deaths out of a total workforce of 18 000. Later estimates concluded that unofficially the story was even grimmer.

Dr William Gorgas, who would later become the chief physician on the canal project, later retrospectively estimated that from 1881 to 1889 over 22 000 laborers died.

When the crash came in December 1888, the company declared itself bankrupt. For the almost $250 million that it had spent, investigators concluded that it was a case of 'one third work, one third wasted, one third stolen'.

Heads Roll

On 10 January 1893 de Lesseps and his son Charles were found guilty of fraud and each

ordered to pay a fine. They were further sentenced to five years prison, but neither Charles nor Ferdinand de Lesseps ever went to jail. By now the former hero was completely disgraced, a physical, mental and emotional wreck. He died in December 1894. The Scandal of the Canal brought down the French Government and it triggered a financial collapse that was to rival the Wall Street crash 40 years later.

The French, in an effort to salvage something, formed a second company, the Compagnie Nouvelle du Canal du Panama, which raised $13 million, mainly from people who knew that if they didn't invest they'd end up in jail.

Meanwhile, the Americans were considering digging their own canal in Nicaragua. The French realised that if the Americans went ahead and succeeded, then everything would be lost. So they kept working on their canal, investing just enough effort to keep the equipment in working order and to fulfill the terms of their concession with the Colombians, who controlled Panama at the time. The French were looking to sell out for $100 million, but the Americans were the only potential purchaser.

The U.S. then passed the Morgan Act of 1899 that said to the French, in effect: 'sell us your concession and the work you've done so far for $40 million or forget it, we'll go ahead with Nicaragua'. At this point the Americans still preferred the Nicaraguan option, but before President McKinley could sign it into law, he was assassinated and the plan stalled.

Burnau-Varilla

Engineer Philippe Burnau-Varilla had been working on the canal since 1894 and had become stranded there after the collapse of what was now termed the Old Company. He'd never lost faith in the canal, and actively worked with the U.S. to make it happen at Panama. He had a lot of money tied up in the new company and he'd be damned if he was going to let the project go to Nicaragua.

After much political finagling and a little US gunboat diplomacy, Panama proclaimed its independence from Colombia on 3 November 1903 and the United States was the first to recognise the new nation state.

For his efforts, the United States made Philippe Burnau-Varilla their Ambassador to the new nation. Panama handed over the 'keys to the canal' in a small ceremony on 4 May 1904.

Out of a total of approximately 59.75 million cubic metres (78.15 million cubic yards) that the French had cut to date, 14.26 million cubic metres (18.65 million yards) had come out of the Culebra Cut. Eventually, engineers estimated that only 23 million cubic metres (30 million cubic yards) was to be useful to the Americans—an effectiveness of about 38.5 per cent—not exactly 'one third wasted, one third stolen' but close enough.

In almost every sense that you can think of, both of the French canal efforts had been spectacular failures, in particular the first, which many still consider one of the world's great fiascos—a grand vision gone hopelessly wrong

The principal driving force for the American canal effort was 54-year-old Chief Engineer John Frank Stevens. He arrived in Panama on 26 July 1905. He devised a double-track system that functioned like a huge conveyor belt. One track dug the dirt, the other carted the dirt away. Stevens then began blasting away at the Culebra in earnest.

The workforce tripled and they went through about 181.5 thousand tonnes (400 000 lbs) per month and were setting excavation records. The Americans were soon removing more earth in one day than the French had in a month. In pure excavation terms the removal of earth was the same as building a Channel Tunnel every three and a half months. In fact, the Panama was the equivalent of excavating 35 Channel Tunnels.

Dr William Gorgas, the project's chief physician, and Stevens allocated a force of 4 000 specifically to mosquito control including mass fumigation, spraying and patient isolation. After six months of unrelenting warfare against the mosquito gods—the single biggest assault on a tropical disease in history—the incidence of yellow fever and malaria dropped to almost nothing. Things finally got so safe that expatriate communities started springing up, and more and more people were calling Panama home.

Then in May 1906 the rains came again and the Chagres flooded to unprecedented levels. The flooding did so much damage and undid so much good work that it completely killed the dream of a sea-level canal. Stevens convinced Roosevelt that a lock-based canal was the only way to go and the President relented. Stevens then set about working with the rain gods, rather than against them.

A New Plan

Steven's plan called for damming the Chagres where it met the Pacific. This would flood the river and create the Gatun—the largest artificial lake in the world—and it would require the building of several huge water locks.

In February 1907 President Roosevelt appointed Major George Washington Goethals to work under Stevens. Whether Stevens felt put upon, maybe out of basic unhappiness with the project, or because he realised that perhaps he wasn't the best man to oversee the building of the world's biggest canal locks, Stevens decided to resign suddenly the next month. Roosevelt was furious and appointed Goethals to succeed as Chief Engineer. Stevens returned to the States. He died in 1943, aged 90. Although his work on the canal was short and he had made crucial and correct decisions, he was not the man who completed the canal.

Overcoming Challenges

With military precision and doggedness, Major Goethals pushed 48 000 workers on the project through every obstacle but the challenges were still immense and the statistics impressive.

The Pacific Division, under the supervision of Sydney B. Williamson required the construction of a 4.8-kilometre (3-mile) breakwater in Panama Bay as well as the two-step Miraflores locks and single-step Pedro Miguel Locks and their dams.

The Atlantic Division under Major William L. Sibert, required a 5.6-kilometre approach channel to the three-step Gatun Locks and the construction of the Gatun Dam.

The Miraflores dams would comprise an earth dam 825 metres long (2 700 feet) at the west and a 150 metres (500 feet) concrete spillway dam to the east. Pedro Miguel's is another earth dam 430 metres (1400 feet) long.

The largest dam, and the largest earth dam ever built at the time, was the one at Gatun, 640 metres (2 100 feet) thick at its base and 2 300 metres (7 500 feet) wide along its top.

When the dam was finished in 1910, the Gatun valley had to be filled to form the Lake. This process alone took 3 years.

The side walls of the locks vary from 13.7 to 15.2 metres (45 feet to 55 feet wide at their bases tapering to 2.4 metres (8 feet) at the top. Each lock chamber is larger than the *Titanic* was, they had to be; by definition a lock has to be larger than the ships they are meant to hold—33.5 metres (110 feet) wide and 320 metres (1 050 feet) long. In fact the Panama has had a major impact on ship building in that the upper limit for a ship that can go through the canal is defined as a Panamax [see opposite].

Entry and exit to the locks are by means of huge gates. The largest are 25 metres (82 feet) high, 2.1 metres (7 feet) thick and each door (or leaf) weighs 662 tonnes but in spite of the weight, they're designed to float in the water they lock off. Each time they are used, the locks have to first fill with, or drain, 101 000 cubic metres (26.7 million gallons) of water, plus the weight of the ship in the lock.

Most impressive of all was the work on the continental divide and the Culebra Cut over the next six years under the supervision of Major David du Bose Gaillard of the US Army Corps of Engineers.

- Dynamite used: 21 670 million kilograms (61 million pounds)—up to 23 600 kilograms (52 000 pounds) in a single blast. 600 holes fired daily.

- Workers on the Culebra cut: 9 000

- Number of trainloads of material per day: 160 carted to dumps 19 kilometres (12 miles) away.

The Pedro Miguel locks were finished in 1911, the Miraflores in May 1913 and dry excavation of the Culebra Cut ended on 20 May 1913.

On 10 October 1913, diggers removed the Gamboa dyke, the final portion of earth separating the Culebra cut from Lake Gatun and the Pacific. President Wilson actually set off the first explosive charges for this by telegraph from Washington. At last, the Atlantic and Pacific oceans mingled at the points where the continents joined for the first time in 3 million years.

David Gaillard died on 5 December 1913 in Baltimore, of a brain tumour. He was too sick to attend the joining of the waters and he was already dead when on 7 January 1914, the old French crane boat *Alexandre La Valley* became the first ship to make the complete transit of the canal, eighteen months ahead of the estimated completion date of 1 June 1916.

On 1 April 1914 the Isthmian Canal Commission ceased to exist and George Goethals became the first Governor of the Canal Zone.

The elaborate festivities for the grand opening of the canal never took place. By the time people were ready to use the canal, World War One had begun, and the international community had more pressing concerns.

Doctor William Crawford Gorgas, became the 22nd Surgeon General of the United States from 1914–1918 and King George V awarded him an honorary knighthood shortly before his death on 3 July 1920.

George Goethals resigned as Canal Zone Governor in 1916 and continued his distinguished career, becoming the first consulting engineer of the Port of New York Authority. The Goethals Bridge that links Staten Island to Elizabeth, New Jersey, is named in his honour. It was completed in 1928, the same year as his death.

Seventy-five thousand people in all had taken a direct part in the construction of the Panama Canal, with 40 000 working on it at its peak, but it had taken the lives of more than 28 000 in its construction and had cost the US around $375 000 million—up to $40 billion or so dollars in modern terms if you consider the relative share of the GDP of the U.S.in 1914.

The single most expensive project in U.S. history up to that time nevertheless proved to be very profitable to the Americans. Then in 1977 President Jimmy Carter signed the Torrijos-Carter Treaty, beginning the process of handing over the canal to the Panamanians. The treaty came into effect on 31 December 1999.

Under the Autoridad de Canal de Panama the canal has become even more profitable—close to a billion dollars a year in profit. This goes some way to explaining how a nation of only 3.5 million has the third largest economy in Central America. Canal-generated hydro-electricity provides the country with four times the electricity needed to run the canal. Panama sells the excess.

Although David Gaillard never lived to see the modest grand opening or the completion of the project that he'd worked so hard for, on 27 April 1915 the Culebra Cut was renamed the Gaillard Cut in his honour. It is a pity that the 28 000 or so others who died in the construction of the canal could not be honoured in a similar way.

Expansion

For several decades the Panamax limit has placed an inconvenient limit on world sea trade.

The Panamax is defined as follows:

- length: 294.1 metres (965 feet)

- beam (width): 32.3 metres (106 feet)

- draft: 12.0 metres (39.5 feet) in tropical fresh water

- air draft: 57.91 metres (190 feet) measured from the waterline to the vessel's highest point

- the typical displacement of a Panamax is around 65 000 tonnes.

On 22 October 2006, 80 per cent of the Panamanians approved a project to expand the capacity of one of the world's busiest waterways.

The Gatun Lake would have to be deepened to increase the draft capacity of the ships. The lake is very wide, so the real bottlenecks are the locks, especially those at the Pacific end, limited as they are by the Gaillard Cut. Building a third and fourth set of locks would cost about $5.25 billion There would have to be improvements to the control towers that guide the 14 000 ships that pass through the canal annually in rather the same way as air traffic control towers guide the take offs and landings of airplanes.

Even now GPS guidance systems are revolutionising the control of canal traffic. Also needed would be improvements to the canal's locks to make filling and emptying them faster.

In the Panamax II-world the dimensions of the biggest ships will be as follows:

- length: 426.72 metres (1400 feet)

- beam (width): 54.86 metres (180 feet)

- draft: 18.29 metres (60 feet) in tropical fresh water

- air draft will depend on the final floor height of any spanning bridges. The typical displacement of a Panamax II would be well over 100,000 tonnes.

The London
Sewers

In 1800 London was vying with Beijing (then known as Peking) for the status of the world's largest city, but by 1825 it was winning with a population of 1.35 million and by 1850 it was the clear leader with 2.32 million inhabitants. In 50 years, London had doubled in size. It was the biggest, richest and most densely populated urban concentration on the planet. It had more Irish than Dublin, more Catholics than Rome and more excrement than both cities put together.

When the Metropolitan Commission of Sewers appointed railway engineer Joseph William Bazalgette as assistant surveyor in August 1849, he had just recovered from a nervous breakdown brought on by overwork. The city was completely ill-equipped to deal with its 'night soil' problem. The city stank. In response to this, in 1848 the Commission ordered the closing of all 200 000 of the city's cesspits and that all house drains should feed into the sewer system, that would then feed directly into the Thames River, from which, incidentally, London got a lot of its drinking water.

Unfortunately, the 'sewers' weren't sewers at all. They were drains designed to deal with storm water runoff, not sewage and certainly not the quantities of sewage that the increasingly popular water closets were producing. Backwater back-ups were common and it was nothing unusual for a combination of rainwater and excrement to come up through the floorboards of houses. Things got so bad that in the summer of 1849, 54 working-class people from East London wrote to

The sewers of London under construction. One of the grandest visions of the Victorian Era is hidden underground. Without them, London would be one huge, disease-ridden cesspit.

Aqueducts, Canals & Sewerage Systems

The Times about it. *The Times* faithfully reproduced their letter on 3 July:

'Sur – May we beg and beseach your proteckshion and power, we are Sur, as it may be, livin in a wilderness …'

The Commission then appealed to *Times* readers for ideas, and it was Joseph Bazelgette's unenviable task to sift through 137 ridiculous and impractical suggestions. While the Commission dithered, an 1848–1849 cholera epidemic killed 14 137 Londoners.

Deadly Diseases

Cholera is nasty. Its symptoms include diarrhoea and its concomitant dehydration leads to liver failure and causes your skin to go grey/blue. If you're malnourished and poor to begin with, it will kill you in 48 hours. People were dying of it faster than they had been dying of bubonic plague during the Black Death. There were riots to bury the dead in the East End, and if you couldn't get a burial you'd keep your loved one's corpse in the house and hope that you could afford enough onions to cut up to mask the smell of decomposition.

In the mid-1850s medicine still wasn't particularly advanced. In the middle ages it was thought that bad odours actually caused disease and during the Black Death people would wear masks filled with sweet-smelling herbs to avoid contagion. They even took to burning herbs in fire pits in the streets to 'purify the air'.

In the mid-19th century the theory of bad air, or 'miasma' as the cause of disease still held sway. People generally felt that miasma was equally to blame for influenza, scarlatina and even smallpox, even though people such as Benjamin Jetsy and Edward Jenner had proven that smallpox had nothing to do with miasma as far back as the late 1700s. No less a personage as Florence Nightingale even believed the miasma theory, as did William Farr, Chief Statistician of the Registrar General's Office, whose job it was to count the dead.

Nothing more substantial happened though, except that in 1852, after the Commission's Chief Engineer died of 'harassing fatigues and anxieties' Bazalgette took his place. Bazalgette knew that the answer lay in building sewers, not to deal with germs that he didn't know existed, but simply to carry the smell away. Yet no-one wanted to listen to him, even when another cholera epidemic broke out in 1853, killing 10 736.

In 1854 cholera made another comeback in the Soho district of London. Pioneering epidemiologist Dr Joseph Snow took the unusual step of actually talking to the people in the affected area and realised that the 'sweet' and delicious tasting water of the Broad Street pump was to blame. Snow insisted that the pump be shut down.

'I had an interview with the Board of Guardians of St James's parish, on the evening of the 7th inst (Sept 7), and represented the above circumstances to them. In consequence of what I said, the handle of the pump was removed on the following day.'

When it was, no-one drank from the pump anymore and the cholera went away. For Snow, it also killed the miasma theory. Why would one house get cholera when their next door neighbours didn't and they were breathing the same air? Unfortunately, this implied that cholera was transmitted because water was coming into contact with faeces and that people were drinking raw sewage. This was literally too much to stomach, and people continued to subscribe to the miasma theory. Ironically, though Snow drank boiled water all his adult life he died of a stroke in 1858, so he never lived to see his theory vindicated, and though he worked a few blocks away from Joseph Bazalgette the two men never met.

In 1856, the useless Metropolitan Commission of Sewers was disbanded, to be replaced with the marginally less useless Metropolitan Board of Works.

Bazalgette plans the plumbing

Bazalgette worked hard on his sewer plans. London is built on the slopes of the Thames Valley, so it was logical to build a sewer system that intersected the existing storm water channels and carried the effluvia far to the east of the City.

Just like in the case of the aqueducts, gradient was important. He calculated a slope of 2 feet per mile to induce an optimal flow of 1.5 miles per hour (96 centimetres per kilometre for 2.4 kilometres per hour). Once at a safe distance the sewage would have to be pumped up 21 feet (6.4 metres) to be held within huge reservoirs. If you got the timing right you could then pump the sewage out of the reservoirs and into the delta of the Thames, just as the tide was going out. As the tide ebbed, it would carry London's sewage with it.

Isambard Kingdom Brunel, the twisted genius behind the *Great Eastern* championed Bazalgette's appointment as Chief Engineer of this new body, and though Bazalgette got the job, it still didn't do much good.

On 18 February 1856 Bazalgette presented his plan to the Board. It called for a High Level North Sewer from Hampstead Hill and a Middle Level North Sewer from Kilburn. These sewers would

join at Wick Lane, Hackney to form the Northern Outfall Sewer. A Low Level North Sewer from Fulham would hug the Thames embankment before proceeding north to the Northern Outfall, which would then proceed to a pumping station at Abbey Mills and onto a proposed Sewerage Works at Beckton.

South of the Thames there would be three other sewers. The High Level from Herne Hill, a Middle Level from Balham Hill and Lower Level from Putney would eventually meet at Deptford to form the Southern Outfall Sewer. The Southern Outfall would proceed to a pumping station at Crossness Pumping Station that would pump its contents into a 27 million gallon reservoir before going into the Thames Estuary.

The sewers would be ovoid in cross section. If you take an egg and turn it pointy end down, then place it between your thumb and forefinger and squeeze, you notice that it requires considerable effort to break the egg. Bazalgette used the same idea so that the sewers could support the weight of earth above it. The shape also allowed fluid to flow in such a way that the sewers would be self-cleaning.

The plan was huge. It called for the city's existing 21 000 kilometres (13 000 miles) of sewers to feed into 1 770 kilometres (1 100 miles) miles of main sewers. It would require the excavation of 3.5 million tonnes of earth and the baking and laying of 318 million bricks using 670 000 cubic metres (880 000 cubic yards) of long lasting, but expensive and water resistant Portland cement.

The project would cost £3 million, or about 5 billion in today's terms.

After considering the project for almost five months, the Chief Commissioner of Public

Works wrote on 2 July 1856 that he was 'not convinced'.

Bazalgette would have to redraft his plans five times. It must have been galling to a man who believed that he could save lives, particularly as he himself had lost two sisters and two infant brothers to infectious disease.

The big stink acts as catalyst

Then in the unusually hot summer of 1858 came the Big Stink. Two years of abuse had turned the Thames into an open sewer. The smell became so bad that Parliament left en masse and sat in Hampton Court, while workers soaked the drapery of Parliament House with chloride of lime. Although heavy rain finally broke the stench, the government had had enough, and after a bit more dilly-dallying finally approved Bazalgette's plan. Thus proving that if you want to get anything done, you usually have to inconvenience politicians in a big way and force them to experience, first hand, the consequences of their incompetence.

Bazalgette got his money and ground-breaking started on 19 February 1859.

For a project of its size, there were remarkably few mishaps, but each one made front page news to the hypersensitive Londoners.

• On 8 December 1860 owing to a miscommunication the Royal Artillery decided to perform some shelling while sewer workers were building in their field.

• A bricklayers' strike successfully concluded with a raise from 5 shillings to 6 shillings a day (£100 to £120).

• 28 May 1862—a gas main fracture at Shoreditch caused an explosion that killed a pedestrian.

• 25 June 1862—a team of railway workers dug too close to the sewer and flooded the Clerkenwell underground. Even though it wasn't his fault, Bazalgette still got the blame.

• 28 April—the tunnel at Deptford collapsed, burying six workers alive of whom only three were rescued.

For all the trouble only nine people died during the system's construction—an excellent record in a time prior to any sense of occupational health and safety.

After over six years of work, and almost sixteen years from its first inception the Prince of Wales and future King Edward VII finally opened the Crossness Pumping Station on 4 April 1865. No-one had had time to test the pumps, so the Prince was actually the first person to activate them. Fortunately, the four largest steam engines ever built worked perfectly.

Further work on the system would take another ten years, and in the 1890s, two more sewers were built to supplement the needs north of the river.

But the stench was gone, leaving a future London to worry about the poisonous fog of the late Victorian era, and the traffic pollution of the 20th century.

Bazalgette became the hero of the day. Three months after the pump opening ceremony, the East London Water Company was found to be responsible for contaminating a water supply with untreated sewage from a pipe choked with a rotting eel. Even William Farr had to concede that the ensuing cholera outbreak had nothing to do with miasma, much to his, and no doubt, Joseph Bazalgette's amazement. On 26 July 1867 the equivalent of two months normal rainfall fell on London. Bazalgette's sewer held its own without incident.

Bazalgette would go on to build bridges at Putney, Battersea and Hammersmith. Joseph became Sir Joseph in 1875 and the Institution of Civil Engineers elected him President in 1883. Bazalgette died, a couple of weeks short of his 72nd birthday, on 15 March 1891.

His great-great-grandson, Edward Bazalgette, produced and directed the 2003 BBC documentary *The Sewer King* as part of the series *7 Wonders of the Industrial World*, while another great-great-grandson and BBC producer Peter 'Baz' Bazalgette once presented a documentary on *The Great Stink*. English actor Stephen Fry has noted that since Baz was the producer of *Big Brother*, the descendant is undoing a lot of his ancestor's good works by 'pumping shit back into our homes'.

The Crossness Pumping Station was in use until 1953 then abandoned and left to fall apart and decay. A restoration project is currently underway.

Part 03
Irrigation

For early civilisations there was a more fundamental need than hygiene or transportation. It was the need for a steady food supply to build up the population of workers. Before humans invented machine slaves, most of the work had to be done using human muscle. Muscle needs fuel and this fuel comes from food. Agriculture created a regular food supply but there was one catch; cultivated food needs a regular supply of fresh water allocated specifically for this purpose.

The trouble is that except in very few cases the fresh water supply isn't regular at all. Not only are there not enough rivers or enough rainfall in the world to provide for human ambition, many of the rivers that do exist depend on snow melt or intermittent rain cycles and this is a seasonal phenomenon. The result is literally feast or famine. Rivers are prone to drying out, or flooding. So you can't rely completely on rivers or rainfall for irrigation.

You can't tame the rain, but you can tame the river, and for that you need a dam. This effectively turns the river into a drainable lake, and then you can decide what to do with the water and when you're going to use it.

Now, in the modern world, dams continue to provide irrigation and water supplies for cities. We've even found a further use for them, generating electricity to power the machines that have replaced much, although not all, of the human work required to support other grand visions.

The Aswan High Dam was the structure that finally tamed the annual flooding of the Nile and ended thousands of years of natural cycles. In so doing it changed the character of Egyptian agriculture and the culture that went along with it.

Dams of the
Middle East

The Marib Dam

Although the earliest dams that we know of date from about 3000 BCE, a notable early dam was the Marib Dam that impounds the Wadi Dhana in Southern Arabia. Built and rebuilt over centuries between around 700 BCE and 580 CE, this dam was originally 16 metres (52 feet) high but would eventually comprise 150 000 cubic metres (196 000 cubic yards) of materials that varied over time. Rammed earth gave way to cut limestone, using unmortared blocks weighing one to two tonnes a piece, but later improvements used volcanic stone and cement, effectively creating a concrete dam.

The Marib Dam provided intensive irrigation over an area of 100 square kilometres (38.6 square miles or almost 25,000 acres) and helped to support a population of about 50,000 people in what was, and still is, a desert. But when Marib's political power declined in the early centuries of the Common Era, so did its capacity to recruit labour to maintain the dam.

Silt was constantly building up, forcing the dam keepers to build the dam higher. Remnant sediments are 30 metres (98 feet) high. Finally around 610, the waters breached for the last

time and no-one would rebuild the dam, but the event was notable enough for Mohammed to mention it in the Koran (Surah 34. 14–15).

Abu Simbel and the Aswan High Dam

Ramses II was one of the great builders among the Pharaohs. Three thousand two hundred years after he lived, it's difficult to make an exact count of all the building projects he initiated, but there are probably more statues of Ramses extant than of any other Pharaoh. He had plenty of time to build as his 66-year-reign is one of the longest in history, and he ruled at a time when Egypt was undergoing a golden age. He built a city, Pi Ramses, and destroyed another, Akhetaton, doing what he could to erase the rule of the Pharaoh Akhenaton from history and in this he was almost successful, but mostly he built, and on a grand scale.

The dating of Ramses' reign is uncertain although we can assume a birth date of 1303 BCE for him. His father, Seti I, made Ramses Prince Regent when the young man was 14, in 1289 BCE. Abu Simbel must have been on the prince/king's mind for some time, because in the mid 1280s BCE he ordered the construction of one of the great temples of history. Abu Simbel was dedicated to no less than three major state gods of Egypt—Amon-Re, Ptah and Re-Horakhty, but mostly it was to be dedicated to Ramses himself.

The timing of the building of Abu Simbel may be significant. Ramses was anticipating perhaps that in 1249 BCE he would be at the 30-year mark of his reign and would undergo the Sed festival, in which Ramses would be ritually transformed into a living god, a feat that few Pharaohs before or after him would ever achieve. Building the temple would take about 20 years, so the Pharaoh obviously believed in thinking ahead. Ramses didn't doubt that he'd make godhood in his lifetime and Abu Simbel would be one more prop to confirm his divine status.

Construction of Abu Simbel didn't really begin in earnest until 1285 BCE and proceeded over the next 20 years. It was originally built on the side of a mountain in what was then Nubia. Aside from its religious purpose its political one was to intimidate the Nubians with Egyptian power.

A temple fit for a king and queen

The main temple was finished in regnal year 25 (1265 BCE). Its most impressive feature is an entrance facade 35 metres (115 feet) wide and 30 metres (98.5 feet) high. Four 22-metre high statues of the seated king flank the entrance. Smaller statues at the feet of the king's images represent Ramses' chief wife, Nefertari, the Queen Mother Mut-Tuy and his first two sons and five daughters

from both Nefertari and his second wife, Isetnofret, are also depicted. Both the facade and the temple interior were hollowed out directly from the living rock. In all, workers excavated some 11 000 cubic metres (14 400 cubic yards) of stone.

Ramses and his principal queen, Nefertari, thus inaugurated the temple in 1265 BCE, six years before Ramses' official deification. Ramses was also quick to deify his beloved wife and had dedicated a smaller temple to her and to the goddess Hathor right next to Abu Simbel. Nefertari thus joined her predecessor Queen Tiy (c. 1398–1338 BCE) as the only Egyptian queen to become a goddess in her lifetime. Unfortunately Nefertari died ten years after the dedication in 1255 at the young age of 35. True to his optimism, Ramses would live to undergo the Sed festival in 1249, then every three years after that for a total of 14 in his lifetime.

At an uncertain date, but within Ramses' lifetime, an earthquake damaged the second of the Great Ramsian statues and the face and torso now lie at its feet. For the most part, the temple's remote location helped to preserve it and later peoples virtually ignored it. Abu Simbel would lie buried under Egyptian sand for three thousand years.

It was rediscovered to western awareness in 1813 by Johann Ludwig Burckhardt, the same man who had 'rediscovered' Petra, but the building was covered in so much sand that no-one could get inside it until Paduan explorer Giovanni Battista Belzoni excavated enough of it to gain access, finally on 4 August 1814.

Abu Simbel's front facade as you would see it if you walked right up to it.

Harnessing the Nile

In the 1880s, the British, who controlled Egypt at the time, wanted to build a dam to control the Nile's annual flooding. Construction of this first dam lasted from 1889 to 1902. Although 1 900 metres (1.2 miles) long and 54 metres (177 feet) high, it wasn't high enough. Builders raised the dam from 1907 to 1912 and when this wasn't enough, again in 1929 to 1933.

Then in 1949, the Nile threatened to overflow the dam again, so the British decided to build a new dam, the Aswan High Dam. The original plan called for construction to start in 1952, but in that year Gamal Abdel Nasser and the Free Officers led the Egyptian Revolution and the British postponed. When Nasser took over in 1956 the British cancelled the plans permanently.

Then in 1958 the USSR offered to finance and help build the Aswan High Dam to support Nasser's regime. Construction began in 1960.

At this point the United Nations Educational, Scientific and Cultural Organization (UNESCO) stepped in and completed a survey of 24 major sites of historical significance that were going to end up underwater once the dam was finished. UNESCO decided to move the sites to safer locations.

Abu Simbel became the showpiece of the restoration project. Between 1964 and 1968 both temples were dismantled and relocated 65 metres (205 feet) above their original site. The Great Temple itself was cut into 807 blocks, weighing on average 20 tonnes a piece. The temples were reassembled onto a reinforced concrete skeleton inside artificial mountains expressly constructed for the purpose. The total cost of the project: $40 million (about $500 million today).

And just in time too. The first stage of the Aswan High Dam finished in 1964 and the project was completed on 21 July 1970.

The Aswan High Dam contains 43 million cubic metres (56.24 million cubic yards) of material. It's 980 metres wide at its base (0.6 miles), 40 metres (131 feet) wide at its crest and reaches 3830 metres (2.38 miles) in length. The reservoir behind the dam, Lake Nasser, is 35 kilometres (21.75 miles) wide at its broadest but an incredible 550 kilometres (341.75 miles) long. With a surface area of 5250 square kilometres it holds 111 cubic kilometres (26.63 cubic miles of water). By 1976 it had taken 12 years to fill to capacity. The electricity the dam generates accounts for about 10 per cent to 15 per cent of the total Egyptian power grid.

The Americas

Hoover Dam

From its origin in the Poudre Pass Lake, high in Rocky Mountain National Park and west of the North American Continental Divide, the 2330 kilometres (1 450 mile) long Aha Kwahwat, better known to most non-Americans as the Colorado River, had been winding its way through what is now the southwestern United States and a small part of northwestern Mexico for 12 million years before the European Americans showed up. In that time the river had unobtrusively carved the Grand Canyon. Depending on rainfall, the river could dump anything into the Gulf of California from a measly 113 cubic metres (4 000 cubic feet) per second during droughts to 28 000 cubic metres (1 million cubic feet) per second during floods into the Gulf of California.

In May 1869 Major John Wesley Powell made the first recorded trip down what was then called the Grand River and Green River and followed that journey with a more extensive survey in 1871. It was apparent even then that the river had potential.

The first step to realising that potential was in 1902 when President Theodore Roosevelt signed the Newlands Reclamation Act, specifically to provide funds for irrigation projects in the dry American west. In 1905 a major flooding of the Grand River created damage in the Imperial Valley in Southern California that took $3 million dollars ($500 million) and three years to fix but it wasn't until 1920 that the Secretary of the Interior started looking for a long-term solution.

On 25 July 1921 the river was officially renamed the Colorado (Spanish for 'Red') and in February 1922 Arthur P. Davis submitted his Fall-Davis report suggesting that the river be dammed, and that it would pay for itself through the sale of hydro-electricity.

In January 1928 Secretary of Commerce Herbert Hoover under President Warren Harding started negotiations with the Governors of Arizona, California, Colorado, New Mexico, Utah and Wyoming to work out what to do with the river. The result was the Colorado River Compact, signed on 24 November, but it wasn't until 21 December 1928, under President Calvin Coolidge, that the Boulder Canyon Project was finally approved and even then initial appropriation for the Project didn't start until July 1930, when Herbert Hoover finally became president.

The taskmaster takes over

In March 1931 the Six Companies were under the directorship of Francis Trenholm Crowe, better known as Frank 'Hurry Up' Crowe. Crowe was a real innovator. In 1911, while working on the Arrowrock Dam in Idaho he refined the method of transporting large quantities of cement using an overhead cableway system that had been so useful in the construction of the Panama Canal. But he also developed the technique of pouring cement pneumatically through pipes to deliver the material exactly where it needed to be—quickly and efficiently.

Crowe was famous for being a harsh taskmaster who cut corners wherever he could. It was his accounting acumen that led to the Six Companies getting the gig for $48 890 995 (around $5 billion) a mere $24 000 under the estimate of the US Bureau of Reclamation, the government agency commissioning the dam.

Crowe's chief engineer Walker 'Brig' Young, whom Crowe called affectionately 'The Great Delayer', was in contrast a much more cautious man. In early 1921 he led a team of 58 from the reclamation bureau to do a preliminary survey of the river and it was he who had made the decision to place the dam at Black Canyon on the border of Arizona and Nevada.

Groundbreaking began on 20 April 1931. In the midst of the Great Depression the project was a huge boon to an economy suffering 20 per cent unemployment. There were 12 000 written applications and 2 400 in person for 3 000 jobs. Former Wall Street brokers and people with PhDs were applying to work tunnelling and driving dump trucks. Men were working for $5 ($250) per day—great money under the circumstances—with an extra 60 cents ($30) a day danger money paid to high scalers.

These men had to work from 250 metres (900 feet) above the river floor and abseil down the sides of the canyon walls, smoothing them down with drills and pick axes to prepare the surfaces for the 3.3 million cubic metres (4.36 million cubic yards) of concrete that would have to be poured. The work was so dangerous that workers pioneered the use of crude hard hats—baseball caps dipped in tar. In the first three months of building there would be four deaths from falls.

Construction and conditions

The ultimate shape of the Hoover would be an arched gravity dam. Using similar eggshell force distribution principles that Joseph Bazalgette had used for the cross-sections of the London Sewer, the dam would make gravity and the water pressure behind it work for it. The more forces acting on it, the stronger it would become.

But before any concrete could be poured, infrastructure had to come first. Fifty-three kilometres of road had to be constructed from Las Vegas to the work site. The contract also called for the building of Boulder City, 13 miles from the site to house workers, but 'Hurry Up' Crowe accelerated the construction timeline to a point where dam construction started before any work on Boulder City. As a result shantytowns of tents sprang up in the desert. Conditions in 'Rag Town' (population 1 000) and others like it were so primitive that people were dying of heatstroke in temperatures of 49° Celsius (120° Farenheit) in the shade.

Conditions at the site weren't much better. Before the dam could be built the plan called for the digging of four miles of diversion tunnels—two inner and two outer—flanking both sides of the river. Begun on 16 May 1931, these tunnels would eventually be 17 metres (56 feet) in diameter, but narrow guide tunnels had to come first. Installing ventilation would have cost money and time, so temperatures in the tunnels in June and July were reaching 60 degrees Celsius (140 degrees Farenheit).

One worker was dying every two days. Trade unions were banned on the site, but activist Frank Anderson of the Industrial Workers of the World snuck in and after calculating that providing the workers with minimal sanitation, water, ventilation and housing would cost the company $2 000 a day, convinced the workers to go on strike. They downed tools on 7 August, 10 weeks after construction commenced. But with queues of others lining up for jobs the workers didn't really have anything to bargain with.

Crowe didn't stand for it. The strike lasted five days, then he fired the strikers and brought in new workers who worked for less pay to subsidise the provision of water coolers and worker shelter. Even when work recommenced the housing still didn't show up.

In October 1931, Crowe commissioned the construction of four specially built trucks. These 'drill jumbos' carried teams of 50 men at a time to drill the diversion tunnels. With 1 500 men working on the tunnels, progress came at the rate of almost 14 metres (45 feet) per day. But exhaust fumes and heat exposure were as bad as ever. Later lawsuits from labourers claiming carbon monoxide poisoning came to nothing.

The company successfully argued that the men were suffering from 'pneumonia'. Eventually, Brig Young managed to convince Crow to fulfill his contractual obligations and build Boulder City. It would accommodate 658 families. Three houses were going up every two days and when the families moved in the workers were docked 25 per cent of their wages for the privilege of living in them.

This indifference to welfare and even basic decency continued. When the spring floods of 1932 saw the waters of the Colorado rise over 5 metres (17 feet) in two hours, work came to a halt until the waters subsided and the workers were laid off without pay.

On 13 November 1932 diggers finally blasted through the last barriers in the tunnels. The Colorado was diverted and the riverbed was exposed one year ahead of schedule.

By mid-1933 the Six Companies were ready to pour concrete. As much as Frank Crowe would probably have liked to, he couldn't pour all of the concrete at once. Crucial to sound integrity is that concrete cure evenly. As it does, it generates heat and uneven heat can cause cracking. Union Carbide handled the production and mixing of ice into the concrete to ensure evenness.

A further complication is that concrete retains heat and the larger the mass the more heat it retains. It was estimated that if they'd poured all the concrete at once the dam would have taken 125 years to cool down. So the concrete had to be poured into rectangular moulds 1.5 metres (5 feet) to a side. Each mould took three days to set. Nevertheless, a combination of pipe distribution and logistical genius meant that between 6 June 1933 and 7 January 1934 the United States Department of Interior Bureau of Reclamation Boulder Canyon Project poured 1 million cubic yards

Boulder City still exists. Over 16 000 people live there now. It's one of only two locations in Nevada where gambling is illegal but it now has two golf courses among its other diversions and every year it holds a festival of short films called the 'Dam Short Film Festival'.

(765 000 cubic metres) of concrete. At the height of the project 5 251 men were working on the site and in the next six months they poured a further 3 million cubic yards (2.3 million cubic metres) of concrete.

On 1 February 1935 concrete pouring was complete. The 900-tonne doors that would block the diversion tunnels were closed and the dam began to fill.

Electrical generation began on 26 October 1936. The dam's 16 turbines generate up to around 2000 megawatts of power and provide electricity for 50 million people in 7 states. Almost 19 per cent of the power the dam generates goes to Arizona, 23 per cent goes to Nevada while 28.5 per cent of the power goes to Southern California, with the City of Los Angeles alone taking a 15.5 per cent share of the dam's total power output. By the time the water reaches the plant it's travelling at 137 kilometres per hour (85 miles per hour).

Almost all the flow of the Colorado passes through the turbines, the dam's spillways have hardly ever opened.

Hoover Dam facts and figures

The dam created Lake Mead, named after Elwood Mead, the Commissioner of the Bureau of Reclamation from 1924 until his death on 26 January 1936, barely five weeks before the final construction of the dam and hydro-electric generators finished. To date, Lake Mead is still the largest artificial reservoir in the United States. 177 kilometres (110 miles) long, it covers an area of 640 square kilometres (248 square miles or 158 147 acres) and holds 35.2 cubic kilometres of water (about 9.3 trillion gallons). The City of Las Vegas draws nearly all its water from the lake.

The dam holding this great body of water back is 200 metres (660 feet) thick at its base, 15 metres (50 feet) thick at its crest.

Between 13 000 and 16 000 vehicles cross over the dam's 379.2 metres (1 244 feet) length using it as a bridge across the river. It reaches a height of 221.4 metres (726.4 feet). In the US only the earth-fill Oroville Dam that impounds the Feather River in Butte County California is taller, at 235m (771 feet).

Aside from its purely practical value, Hoover Dam hosts 8 to 10 million visitors each year making it the fifth busiest National Park in the U.S.

Frank Crowe had whipped the workforce into finishing the Dam two years, one month and twenty-eight days ahead of schedule.

On account of Crowe's speed, the Six Companies walked away with a $4 million

($250 million) bonus. 112 deaths are directly attributed to the construction of the dam—96 on site. One weird story relates that the first person to die was J.G. Tierney, a surveyor who drowned during Brig Young's 1922 survey. The last person to die was Tierney's son, Patrick W. Tierney, who died on the construction site 13 years *to the day* later.

The Six Companies would eventually go on to be the builders behind such projects as the Bonneville Dam (1933) and Grand Coulee Dams (1942) on the Columbia River and the foundations of the Golden Gate Bridge in San Francisco (1937).

Although the dam was originally called Boulder Dam, on 14 February 1931 an act of Congress formally recognised it as Hoover Dam. Hoover lost his bid to re-election in 1932 to Franklin Delano Roosevelt. When FDR appointed Harold Ickes as Secretary of the Interior, Ickes issued a memorandum to the Bureau of Reclamation that the dam be referred to again as Boulder Dam. Politics being what it was, Hoover wasn't even invited to the dam's dedication ceremony in September 1935. It would take 12 years and both the death of FDR in 1945 and the retirement of Harold Ickes in 1946 before President Harry S. Truman signed Public Law 43 on 30 April 1947 to confirm the name Hoover Dam officially. Herbert Hoover died in 1964.

The Itaipu Dam

The largest hydro-electric scheme in the world in the first decade of the 21st century was the Itaipu Dam, impounding the river Paraná on the border of Brazil and Paraguay.

The two countries signed the Itaipu Treaty on 26 April 1973 and work commenced in January 1974. Engineers completed rerouting the Paraná on 14 October 1978, allowing the construction of the dam proper. It took almost 13 years to finish the 7 700 metre (4.8 mile) long and 196 metre (643 feet) high dam but when the reservoir began to fill on 13 October 1982 rainfall and flooding was so heavy that the water level climbed 100 metres in just two weeks, reaching the spillways on 27 October. Electricity generation began eighteen months later on 5 May 1984.

The dam has 20 separate units generating 700 megawatts each. They were installed over a period of more than 20 years with the last two commencing operations in September 2006 and March 2007. The total of 14 000 megawatts of electricity is 7 times the peak of the Hoover Dam. Itaipu provides 20 per cent of the electricity used by Brazil's 187 million people and a whopping 93 per cent of the electricity needs of Paraguay's 7 million.

The Pacific and Asia

Snowy Mountains Scheme

In 1949, when its parliament passed the Snowy Mountains Hydro-Electric Power Act, Australia was a nation of only 8 million people. The Chifley Government knew that in the long term the populations concentrated in the south-east of the continent would need irrigation and electricity. The Snowy Mountains Scheme would do both.

Governments had been considering using snowmelt from the Australian Alps for irrigation for about 60 years but it wasn't until the middle of the 20th century that economic necessity, technological know-how and political will would meet to make it happen. Even then it required the ingenuity of the Minister for Works and Housing, Nelson Lemmon, to create the Snowy Mountains Authority under the Defence Act to make it legally possible, as the Australian Constitution didn't assign the Commonwealth any rights to build a project like The Scheme.

Once the bill went through, it took four years for Edward F Rowntree, Engineer for Major Investigations, just to complete the survey and design the project. The Snowy Mountains Scheme was Ted Rowntree's grand vision.

His plan was radical. It required diverting the flow of the Lower Snowy River to the Tumut River for hydro-electric generation and to the Murrumbidgee River for irrigation. O T Olsen, an officer of the State Electricity Commission of Victoria further suggested diverting the Upper Snowy River to the Murray River for hydro-electrics and irrigation.

The two ideas combined in the final plan that would encompass 5 124 square kilometres (1 978 square miles), three quarters of the 6 750 square kilometre (2 606 square mile) Kosciusko National Park, south west of Canberra. The scheme called for the creation of 16 dams, 80 kilometres (50 miles) of aqueducts and 145 kilometres (90 miles) of tunnels.

It would be, and still is, the most complex engineering project ever undertaken in Australia; so intricate that it even required the use of Australia's first transistorised computer, dubbed Snowcom.

The scheme created profound changes in the nation's character and culture. The project needed workers, 7 300 at a time at its peak, and labour shortages necessitated immigration. More than 100 000 people from over 30 countries came to live and work in Australia as a direct result of the scheme. For many it was an opportunity to escape the ravages of a Europe still recovering from World War Two and to make their fortune, and many of them later did.

Seventy per cent of the workers were migrants and even after the project ended they continued to come. Within a generation a predominantly white Anglo-Saxon country would become one of the most cosmopolitan on earth.

Trying conditions for workers

Ninety-eight per cent of the project was underground. The work was hard, noisy, dirty, humid, hot and smelly. As the work moved from one area to another the workers dismantled the towns they lived in and rebuilt them at the new worksite.

As a result, there's hardly any evidence left of the communities that existed to build the scheme. Some still survive though. Cabramurra NSW (Wiradjuri 'crooked hand'—population 60), for example, which houses some of the staff of the Tumut 2 power station and the Tumut Pondage Dam, at 1475 metres (4839 feet) is the highest town in Australia.

Seven power stations were built. In chronological order of completion they were: Guthega—1954; Tumut One—1958; Tumut Two—1961; Murray One—1967; Blowering—1967; Murray Two—1969 and Tumut 3—1974.

By the time the Snowy Mountains Scheme was fully completed in 1974, Australia and many of its newest citizens had devoted 25 years and lost 120 lives to it.

It cost $AUS 800 million, equivalent to about $AUS 6.5 billion today. The scheme generates 3 800 megawatts of power or 3.5 per cent of Australia's total electricity grid. It's repaid its investment many times over and now provides 2.1 million litres of water to the Murray-Darling Basin for an irrigated agriculture industry worth $5 billion a year.

Three Gorges Dam

Begun on 14 December 1994 and due for completion in 2011, the Three Gorges Dam will be the biggest hydro-electric scheme in the world. Spanning a length of 2 335 metres (7 661 feet) at Sandouping, Yichang in Hubei province, China, the dam will impound no less than the mighty Yangtze River. The river that's now officially called the Chang Jiang ('long river') flows 6 300 kilometres (3 914 miles) from a 5 042 metre (16 542 feet) highpoint in Qinghai Province in China's extreme north west to its delta in Shanghai on the coast of the China Sea.

At the point where the Three Gorges dams its flow, the river has already crossed about 4 830 kilometres (3 000 miles) of Chinese territory.

The dam takes its name from the Three Gorges area that it's situated in, comprising about 200 kilometres of the Yangtze course.

The gorges and their lengths are:

Qutang Gorge—from Baidicheng to Daxi—8 kilometres (5 miles)

Wu Gorge—from Wushan to Badong—45 kilometres (28 miles)

Xiling Gorge—from Zigui to the Nanjing Pass at Yijiang (where the dam is located)—66 kilometres (41 miles).

The dam is a comparatively recent idea. Sun Yat Sen only proposed it in 1919. It's unlikely that if any previous ruler had considered the dam that he would have pursued the thought. Megalomania notwithstanding, the sheer scale of the task is daunting even today. It took China's fourth Premier, Li Peng, to push the project through.

The dam is 101 metres (331 feet) high, 115 metres (377 feet) thick at the bottom and 40 metres (131 feet) thick at its top. When water level reached maximum in late 2008 the surface was 175 metres (574 feet) above sea level.

The project used 27.2 million cubic metres (35.6 million cubic yards) of concrete and 463,000 tonnes of steel. That's 63 times the amount of steel used to build the Eiffel Tower.

The workers removed 102.6 million cubic metres (134.2 million cubic yards) of earth, about half of the effective removal for the Panama Canal. Although the Itaipu Dam created a reservoir of water behind it of 1350 cubic kilometres (324 cubic miles), the 600 kilometre (375 mile) long reservoir behind the Three Gorges has a capacity of only 632 cubic kilometres (324 cubic miles). Yet the Three Gorges is a much more controversial project.

A major focus of the dam has been its demographic effect. By 2008 the government had had to relocate 2.3 million people, with an estimated further 4 million more displacements by 2020. The dam will also flood about 1 300 archaeological sites and unlike Abu Simbel, many of them can't be moved.

The $30 billion price tag of the dam will be offset from the sale of electricity which began on 18 October 2006. When fully operational, the dam's 34 x 6 000-tonne generators will provide a total 22 500 megawatts, 50 per cent more than the Itaipu. Originally the planners expected that the dam would provide 10 per cent of China's total needs, but with the explosion of the capitalist Chinese economy and its increased need for energy, experts have now revised that figure to 3 per cent, so the Three Gorges hasn't turned out to be as proportionally productive as its visionaries had hoped.

One positive point is that the dam reduces greenhouse gas emissions by 100 million tonnes but reckless deforestation compromised even these gains somewhat, until flooding and erosion forced the Chinese government to realise that trees weren't a luxury and commenced a serious reforestation process. Flood control is one of the main reasons for the dam to exist, any silt erosion would block the dam and make it less effective for hydroelectricity.

Ecological lessons like this one demonstrate that people can harness nature, but they still have to do it on its terms.

But the absence of silting may cause its own problems. Shanghai may be 1 600 kilometres (1 000 miles) away, but it rests on a bed of silt that has relied historically on the Yangtze's flow to replenish it. Without the silt top-up, the very foundations of Shanghai may be at long-term risk.

It may take decades to determine the end result of the cost/benefit equation of the Three Gorges Dam.

The Three Gorges Dam, for all its massive size, will only be able to provide 3 per cent of China's electrical needs after having displaced more than 6 million people and drowning 1 300 archaeological sites.

Part 04
Beaten Tracks & Bridges

Since all empires to date have been military dictatorships in one form or another, it's important that when you're building and maintaining an empire, you are able to transport your military as quickly and as easily as possible. How else can you crush the inevitable insurrections from ungrateful populations who don't appreciate the civilisation that you've brought them?

As anyone who has ever walked through wild country can attest, making your way through untamed wilderness is heavy going. First you have to cut through inconveniently placed vegetation, or you have to walk over loose rocks and gravel. You can always build a dirt road, but they have the unfortunate habit of turning to mud when it rains.

Walking on paved road makes things much easier so your bully boys will be in tip-top shape when they arrive in the far-flung corners of your empire to smash a few heads in. As a side effect, a good road makes trade much easier too, so you can grow rich enough to afford some of your bigger and perhaps less practical civil engineering ideas.

Pathways
Ancient and Modern

The pre-eminent builders of roads in the ancient world were the Romans, and they got in early, even before there was an Empire. The Via Appia—the famous Appian Way—was finished in 312 BCE. It originally stretched 196 kilometres (128 miles) from the Eternal City to Capua, an Etruscan city that Rome subjugated in 338 BCE. By 268 BCE the Romans extended The Way a further 48 kilometres (30 miles) east to Benevento and then a further 286 kilometres (178 miles) south east to Brindisi, right on the heel of the Italian peninsula on the coast of the Adriatic, giving a total length to Rome of 530 kilometres (about 330 miles). In ancient times, travelling from Rome to Brindisi took two weeks.

The Via Appia was a real road. The road itself averaged a width of 14.4 metres (47 feet) and had side pavements almost three metres (10 feet) wide. If all the paving materials were placed in a square, rather than in a straight line, it would have covered an area of about 11 000 square kilometres (over 27 million acres), or to put it another way, about 2000 times larger than the surface area covered by the ancient walled city of Rome itself. The road has to go over marshy and solid terrain,

and since the Romans liked straight lines where possible, they were prepared to build bridges spanning hundreds of metres, remove hillsides or tunnel through mountains.

The Appian Way was a major engineering achievement, but it was nothing compared to what was to follow. Modern estimates are that up to 20 000 kilometres (12 400 miles) of major roads serviced the North African provinces alone and at the height of the Empire major roads circumnavigated the entire Mediterranean Sea.

The Romans weren't the only great road builders. Across the world in North America, in about the year 1000 CE, the Anasazi Indians of Chaco Canyon New Mexico, were building their own extensive roads. Though unpaved, this 650 kilometres (400 mile) system of roads linked Chaco to over 70 settlements dispersed over an area of more than 65,000 square kilometres (25,000 square miles). One stretch of road follows a straight line for 63 kilometres (39 miles). One unusual feature of this system is that many of the roads lead nowhere.

We don't know if this is because they did once lead to places of which no traces remain, or if there is some obscure cosmological reason having to do with religion or sacred geometry. Whatever the reason, the whole Chaco region suffered a massive 50-year drought from about 1130. It couldn't have helped that the Anasazi had probably deforested a lot of their marginal ecosystem in order to build the Pueblos for which they are famous. In any case, their grand visions came to an end when the region was finally abandoned around the year 1200.

At its height, from about 1450 until the Spanish destroyed their civilisation in 1532, the Inca had arguably the most impressive road system of all, if you factor in that they had a lower population base than the Romans, and much more difficult terrain. Around 25 000 kilometres (15 500 miles) of Inca roads linked the capital, Cuzco, with 20 million citizens in Inca dominions spread out over a total area of 2 million square kilometres (772 204 square miles).

Compare this to Rome's 88 million citizens spread out over 5 million square kilometres (1.93 million square miles) at their height in 117 CE. The Inca had to do a lot more, with far less. The roads had to negotiate mountains, valleys and rivers. West of Cuzco a rope bridge of braided cabuya plant fibres had to cross the 45-metre (150 feet) span of the Apurimac gorge, 35 metres (115 feet) above the raging waters of the Huinchiri River. The descendants of the Inca still make and maintain such bridges even today, a team of about 72 can build such a bridge in about 20 days.

The showpiece of the Inca road system was the Quapaq Nan (Quechua 'Opulent Way') a dual road running both inland and on the coast between Cuzco and Quito. Relays

of couriers running on foot could cover this distance of almost 2 000 kilometres (1 230 miles) in just five days about 2.5 times faster than the Roman average using horses.

The Sapa Inca Emperor in Cuzco could eat fish still fresh from the coast, 320 kilometres (200 miles) away. And yet, for all the work the roads represented, Inca society was so regimented that most of its citizens never used the highway system. The network was reserved for official state business alone.

Technology has of course continued to improve over the centuries and over time the concept of roads, tunnels and bridges has expanded to encompass roads of steel for iron horses too.

The First Transcontinental Railroad

By the early 1860s a generation had passed since the Americans had annexed Texas (1845) and won California from the Mexicans (1848). The West was wild, but unwon and even before he became President, Abraham Lincoln wanted a nation united not only north to south, but east to west. He dreamed of a transcontinental railroad, and he might have lived to see it if it hadn't been for the rude interruption of the not-so-civil War Between the States and the even ruder interruption of his assassination on 15 April 1865, barely a week after the war's end.

But although the Civil War (1861–1865) occupied a great deal of attention, it wasn't the only matter on the mind of the American government. On 1 July 1862 Lincoln signed the Pacific Railway Act authorising the financing of what was to be the major engineer achievement of the decade.

The Act was a potential gold mine for anyone who could take up the challenge of building the railroad. Among the enticements were generous loans that could later be repaid from the profits of the railroads:

Payment of $16 000 per mile of tracked grade completed west of the base of the Sierra Nevada Mountains and east of the Rocky Mountains.

Payment of $48 000 per mile of tracked grade completed over and within the two mountain ranges.

Payment of $32 000 per mile of tracked grade completed between the two mountain ranges.

A 26 kilometre (10 square miles or 6 400 acres) land grant on each side of the tracks for every mile laid except where railroads ran through cities or crossed rivers. This was the biggest carrot of all.

All that money! All that free real estate up for grabs! The potential was huge, but so were the risks. And there was one catch. Whoever did the work had to prove that they were viable by first laying down 40 miles of track.

Two companies took up the task, one laying track from west to east, another from east to west.

The Central Pacific Rail Road

Four Sacramento shopkeepers became 'Associates'. Charles Hopkins and Collis Huntington ran a hardware store. Leland Stanford was a grocer and Charles Crocker was a draper. The 'Big Four' incorporated the Central Pacific Rail Road of California (CPRR) on 21 June 1861. Their task was formidable. There was no industrial infrastructure in California at the time to build a railroad. Everything had to come from the east coast and in the days before the Panama Canal this meant a risky and horrendously expensive four-month journey around the tip of South America.

The overland route was equally unattractive. Tens of thousands of settlers travelling in wagon trains had already died in the previous decades crossing the deserts of Colorado, Utah and Nevada before having to climb the 2 150 metre (7 000 feet) pass through the Sierra Nevada Mountains. Stories of death by exposure, Indian attacks, starvation and cannibalism were no exaggeration.

Given these challenges, Charles Crocker, who'd been designated Head of Construction, hired New Yorker Theodore 'Crazy' Judah as Chief Engineer.

Judah had already built the first railroad west of the Mississippi River—the Sacramento Valley Railroad—and he was the best man for the job. Actually he was the only man for the job.

There wasn't anyone more qualified. Judah had a huge emotional investment in the Transcontinental. He'd tried to get the initial financing for the railroad himself in San Francisco, but failing that, he'd managed to convince the Big Four to form the CPRR and it was Judah who had lobbied in Washington for the Pacific Railway Act. So in a real sense he was the granddaddy of the project and it was he who surveyed the route through the Sierra Nevada that the railroad would eventually take.

Judah concluded that to get to the 7 000 feet pass, the CPRR would have to build 120 miles of railroad. This doesn't sound like much, but to get to the high point they'd have to build 50 bridges over gorges and rivers and 14 tunnels through mountains in weather that could be fine one moment, blizzard the next.

Groundbreaking began on the railroad on 8 January 1863 in Sacramento. By then, former grocer Leland Stanford had managed to get himself elected Governor of California, but supply problems meant that the first rail wasn't laid until 26 October.

Then, having completed his survey, Crazy Judah grew dissatisfied with the way the Big Four were handling the railroad and he decided to go to New York to see if he could get funding to buy out the Big Four and wrest control of the CPRR.

He went by way of Panama, but caught yellow fever and died there on 2 November 1863. He was only 37 and never lived to see the railroad he'd worked so hard for.

A few days after his death, the CPRR's modestly named locomotive *Governor Stanford* made its first test run over the railroad's first 500 feet of track.

The 40-mile target finally reached

Charles Crocker had also hired one-eyed James Harvey Strobridge as foreman to hire and oversee the work gangs who'd do all the actual building and digging. Unfortunately, there was a labour shortage. Fifteen years earlier the California gold rush had started and was still going strong. Although this too provided a strong incentive to build the railroad and 300 000 people would eventually come to California, most of the immigrants figured 'why bother with back-breaking work building a railroad when there was a fortune to be had in the goldfields?' So although the CPRR had work for over 4 000, Strobridge could barely hold on to 800 at a time. And the turnover was constant.

093

Then along came the Chinese. They too had come seeking gold, but being more stoic, and perhaps more realistic, they looked for other opportunities and compared to what they were used to back home, even railroad work seemed an attractive proposition. Strobridge at first hated the Chinese, but their work ethic impressed everyone else. The *New York Times* even commented that they were like 'a great army laying siege to a nature in her strongest citadel—tunnelling, wheeling, carting and drilling and blasting the rocks and earth.' Progress through and up the mountains was painfully slow.

By 13 May 1865 the railroad had only gone 36 miles (58 kilometres) to Auburn, California, and it wasn't until July that they passed their 40 mile (64 kilometre) target. At last, after two and a half years the CPRR could get their government money. Even then it would take another 18 months until 3 December 1866 to reach the 92 miles (148 kilometres) to Cisco. Experiments with nitro-glycerine as an explosive proved to be disastrous, and the CPRR had to make do with the much less powerful gunpowder. Avalanches took their toll too, and work in winter could hardly proceed at all. At times the CPRR was making just 12 inches (30 centimetres) a day in progress.

The Union Pacific Railroad

Meanwhile, 2 000 miles to the east another company, the Union Pacific Railroad (UPRR), was getting its act together. Although incorporated on 1 July 1862 under its controlling stockholder Doctor Thomas Clark Durant, the UPRR didn't start laying track until mid-1866 because of the American Civil War. Durant chose General Grenville Mellon Dodge to oversee construction of the eastern portion of the Transcontinental.

Dodge was one of the youngest generals ever in United States history and was still only 35 when he headed the UPRR team.

Durant and Dodge went way back. During the Civil War they'd made a lot of money together smuggling confederate cotton and this turned out to be the seed money for the UPRR.

Laying track on the plains of Nebraska was easy. With military precision Dodge's Irish teams were able to lay one length of track every 30 seconds, and in the first six months the company laid 250 miles (400 kilometres)

of track and received $5 million dollars. But the UPRR had problems of its own.

In 1866 Dodge got himself elected congressman for Iowa, so he was effectively working two jobs. The building of the railroad also attracted all sorts of low-life 'whoring and brawling' squatters.

There were four deaths from shootouts for every death due to accident. Dodge was disgusted and lamented the railroad's reputation. He wanted the railroad to lease its land grants to 'decent, god-fearing Christians'. So Dodge hired Jack 'The Cossack' Casement, who created a 200-strong team of enforcers to exercise a sort of lynch law to keep everyone on the straight and narrow.

Then there were the Indians. On 28 August 1867, four miles (6.5 kilometres) from Plum Creek, Nebraska, a group of Cheyenne derailed an advance train and set fire to it. Of the 12 crew members, 7 died and 4 were rescued.

The engineer showed up the next morning at Plum Creek holding his scalp. Plum Creek was already infamous for the Plum Creek Massacre of 8 August 1864 when an organised attack of Cheyenne, Sioux and Arapaho Indians killed settlers. The locomotive attack caused a panic that halted track work.

Dodge decided that there was no room for 'us and them' and brought in William Tecumseh 'Burn Atlanta' Sherman, who promptly set up a program of genocide to prevent any further incidents, and the work continued.

Two years on...

After almost two more years of work building 13 miles (21 kilometres) of track from Cisco, and having survived 44 snowstorms in the winter of 1867–68, 50-feet snow drifts and 24/7 work weeks, the Chinese were living in tunnels and had had enough.

They went on strike. James Strobridge, who'd been so against them in the beginning, was on their side, but Charles Crocker wouldn't stand for it and starved them into submission; the work recommenced.

Finally on 1 December 1868, after tunnelling through almost half a kilometre (1 600 feet) of solid granite, the CPRR opened to the summit of the Sierra Nevada—105 miles from Sacramento.

On the plains of Nevada and Utah not long after, spring thaws, minus 40°F winds and rain and frost were destroying hundreds of miles of tracks and Dodge had to lay thousands of sandbags to preserve what he had.

Just when things couldn't get worse for the UPRR, freelance journalist Charles Adams discovered an interesting fact. Under contract the UPRR was supposed to tender sub-contracting work to get the best possible price.

However, what was really happening was that all the work was going through a company called Credit Mobilier, owned in part by Thomas Durant.

Along with Durant's ordering of extraneous track and other dubious practices, the Credit Mobilier scam meant Durant was really raking it in. Cost overruns amounted to an extra $20 000 per mile of track totalling $10 million.

Dodge was disgusted—he was a shareholder in Credit Mobilier. It was one thing to cheat the South, another to cheat your fellow Yankees.

The ensuing scandal forced Durant to resign from UPRR and Dodge 'retired' to Texas only to come back soon to finish the railroad he started.

Now that the worst part was over for the Californians and Chinese, the race was on to see who would get to the designated track meeting at Promontory Point in Utah.

The race to the finish

The Chinese worked like demons. After six years of work the teams were only 50 miles (80 kilometres) apart.

On 28 April 1869, the CPRR laid 10 miles (16 kilometres) of track, a record that stands today. They were the first to reach the finishing post two days later on 30 April 1869.

Ten days later, the UPRR teams arrived. On 10 May 1869 a team made up of workers from both companies laid the last section of track. The CPRR's locomotive *Jupiter* and the UPRR's *No.119* faced each other on the railroad. There are estimates that 3 000 people were there to witness the historic joining of the tracks.

Leland Stanford tapped a golden spike into the track with a silver ceremonial hammer. The CPRR officials cheered the Chinese. The ceremonial spike was removed and a regular iron spike replaced it at exactly 12:47pm.

Reporters telegraphed the event throughout the country. The Golden Spike now resides in the Cantor Art Center in Stanford, California. Dodge said at the time that 'we have finished the job that Christopher Columbus started'— seven years ahead of the government's schedule, one might add.

The construction of the Transcontinental created a 3 200 kilometres (2 000 mile) link that reduced a six-month journey to just seven days. It had cost upwards of $70 million. This amounts to $16.5 billion if measured proportional to the GDP per capita of the US at the time, but the amount varies depending on whether or not you count the graft and corruption. The price tag also included about 2000 lives, more if you include 'collateral' slaughter of Plains Indians.

Although this was the end of the beginning, passengers wanting to use the full length of the Transcontinental coast-to-coast still had to cross the Missouri River by boat until 1872, when the first Union Pacific Missouri River Bridge was completed, linking Dodge's home town of Council Bluffs, Iowa to Omaha, Nebraska.

Ironically, the first coast-to-coast rail link came into being in 1870 when the Denver extension of the Kansas Pacific Railway met the Transcontinental at Strasburg, Colorado.

The Brooklyn Bridge as it stands today.

The Brooklyn
Bridge

The story of the Brooklyn Bridge is very much the story of the Roebling family. The precocious Johann Augustus Roebling had qualified as an engineer in Germany at the tender age of 14, writing his graduation thesis on suspension bridges. Then in 1831 he, his brother Karl and 40 other friends left for the USA.

There, in 1832 the group bought 64 hectares (1 582 acres) of land in Pennsylvania and founded the town of Saxonburg. The town still exists and Saxonburg borough had a population just under 2 000 in the early 21st century.

The 1830s were great years to immigrate to the USA. The new nation had an infrastructure lag and President Andrew Jackson had freed up almost $100 million (almost $60 billion in today's money) for public works. His early projects involved canal building and railroad surveys. By 1841 the man now known to all as John Roebling was producing his main innovation: high-quality wire rope that he originally developed to replace hemp ropes

that were used to pull railroad carriages up steep inclines.

In 1845 he built his first suspension bridge over the Monongahela River in Pittsburgh. From 1848, when he moved to New Jersey and for the next 19 years he built more suspension bridges, culminating in the world's longest suspension bridge to that date, the 322 metre (1 057 feet) Cincinnati-Covington Bridge, later named the John A. Roebling Suspension Bridge.

This body of work, and the Roebling wire cable rope that his factory produced, made him the most qualified man in the country to build a bridge over East River Bridge in New York—a project for which Roebling had been campaigning for 15 years.

The bridge would replace the existing ferry service and connect Manhattan to Brooklyn. Design work started in 1867. Then on 6 July 1869, only three days after he'd received final approval on his design, Roebling was doing a routine site inspection when a ferry crashed into the Brooklyn Fulton Ferry slip he was standing on. Roebling's right foot was crushed.

With the stubborn arrogance of many men who have a great talent in one area and therefore believe that they are authorities on everything, Roebling refused conventional treatment even after the amputation of three toes (which he insisted be done without anaesthetic). Instead, he insisted on 'water therapy', continuous washing of the injured area with a stream of water. Tetanus set in on 16 July and he died, aged 63, on 22 July.

Of Caissons and Concrete

The only man that the Bridge's Board of Trustees could trust to fill the role of Chief Engineer was Roebling's eldest son, Washington. Although Washington had learned the family business and helped his father on many of the elder Roebling's major projects, critic's observed that the 32-year-old had never built a bridge the proposed size of the New York and Brooklyn Bridge. Washington simply replied that no-one else had either. Aside from expertise, obsession and a passion for detail, Washington also brought military discipline to the job. He'd served with distinction during the Civil War and had ended his service with the rank of Colonel.

Construction began on 2 January 1870. The colonel's chief engineering challenge was laying the foundations for the bridge's two main towers. For this he had to build two caissons of unprecedented size.

The caissons were large, lidless, thick-walled, airtight wooden boxes, 49 x 30.5 metres (160 x 100 feet), with sides sloping upwards to a height of about 5 metres (16 feet). The lips of the boxes were lined with sharp, iron-cutting edges and the boxes made waterproof and reinforced with iron, tin plating and pitch. The boxes were then turned upside down and connected with air hoses and air locks, and let sink into water while granite blocks and masonry were piled on top until they touched bottom. Air was then pumped into the caissons to force the water out and keep it out.

Unlike the construction of the Golden Gate Bridge (pictured), the Brooklyn Bridge was built without safety netting and many workers died during its construction.

Now, men can go into the caisson from the surface through the airlocks and dig into the riverbed. As they dig deeper, and as surface workers pile on more masonry and granite, the caisson sinks ever further until it reaches bedrock. At that point the caisson is filled with concrete and it becomes the base of the foundation for the bridge tower.

It's simple in theory, but hard in practice. The lower you go, the more water pressure builds up and the more air you have to pump into the caisson to keep the water out.

For the men working under high atmospheric pressure the experience could be bizarre and uncomfortable. The sense of vision and sound becomes distorted. Heat from working bodies and illuminating flame couldn't escape so your upper body is sweltering while you're up to your knees in ice cold water and mud.

Pay, progress and problems

Pay rates for caisson workers reflected both the risks and the practical limitations of the job. Surface workers were getting $2.50 ($300) for an eight-hour shift. Caisson workers were getting $2.10 ($240) for a four-hour shift. But if you were struck down with caisson's it could take you anything from three days to three weeks to recover.

Progress was initially slow, a rate of 6 inches (15 centimetres) per week, and workers were only 25 feet below the surface when they reached a concentration of boulders. Pickaxes were no longer working effectively so the Colonel decided to try dynamite. This was risky as no-one had ever used dynamite in a compressed air environment, but the risk

paid off and at two blasts per watch the new technique tripled the rate of progress.

The project faced a major crisis when a fire from a burning candle too close to the caisson ceiling broke out into the interior of the caisson's wooden roof structure.

The Colonel worked tirelessly to put the fire out, but it took 20 hours to get it under control. When he reached the surface, the Colonel suffered a severe attack of caisson's. After a few hours while recovering in bed, the Colonel learned that they hadn't gotten the fire under control, so he went back.

The fire was feeding off the compressed air and wood deep into the fourth course of the caisson's roofing. Taking the air out wasn't an option, and it took the work of 30 fire engines and 3.8 million litres of water pumped over five hours to quench the blaze finally. When the Colonel finally got out, caisson's disease struck him again even more severely.

It took another nine weeks for the Brooklyn caisson to hit bedrock at 13.5 metres (44.5 feet), then in February 1870, just before they were ready to fill the caisson with concrete, negligence caused an escape of air from the caisson, flooding it with water and nearly killing the workers inside before the situation was under control again. Fortunately they managed to avert disaster and the first foundation was ready.

The Roosevelt Street, Manhattan caisson proved to be even more problematic. Investigations showed that the caisson wouldn't hit bedrock until it reached a depth of over 32 metres (106 feet), almost three times further than the Brooklyn caisson—an unprecedented depth. But at the rate of progress the Manhattan caisson was already deeper than the Brooklyn after two months' work.

At this point, the rate of caisson's disease grew worse. Doing heavy manual tasks in an atmosphere of 30 pounds per square inch, the workers were labouring at double normal atmospheric pressure. The cases grew more severe and the first caisson disease death occurred on 22 April 1872. Two others soon followed.

On 18 May 1872 the Colonel made one of the great decisions of his life. The Manhattan caisson had reached a depth of 24 metres (78.5 feet). The Colonel estimated at the time that if he went further, as many as 80 more men would die and he wouldn't bear that on his conscience.

Although the caisson hadn't reached bedrock it had reached a layer of sand that had been compacting for millennia and was as hard as concrete. The Colonel judged that the compacted sand would bear the weight of the Manhattan tower. History proved that he was right.

Caisson's Disease

Bridge company physician Dr Andrew Smith had noted that lean wiry men fared better than large, stocky men. Today we know why, the lower body mass and higher volume to surface area ratio of thin bodies allows quicker diffusion of nitrogen out of the body tissues.

It probably helped Washington Roebling a great deal that he was a thin, wiry man,

The Grecian Bends

A major limiting factor to working in caissons was medical. Workers were coming down with 'caisson's disease', which seemed to get worse the deeper the caisson went. Caisson's symptoms included a rise in blood pressure, giddiness, vomiting, paralysis and pain so severe that men would curl up into foetal positions—a symptom called the 'Grecian Bends'. American doctors didn't know the cause of the disease at the time, but today we do.

Our breathable atmosphere is almost 80 per cent nitrogen. It's inert in our bodies—so inert in fact that although nitrogen is essential for making proteins, only bacteria have the trick of taking protein out of the air to build amino acids. But it's not the chemistry of nitrogen that's the problem—it's physics.

Under pressure nitrogen is forced to dissolve into the bloodstream and body tissues. When the pressure lifts, the nitrogen begins to dissolve out of the body, forming bubbles, damaging tissues and causing severe pain. The only way to alleviate this is to decompress slowly, allowing the nitrogen to leave the body as gradually as it first came in.

but even his body could only take so much punishment and he soon became bedridden, his nervous system damaged from the chronic effects of repeated decompression sickness.

Ironically, the English and French had known about the benefits of slow decompression for years. English natural philosopher Robert Boyle had demonstrated that reduction in air pressure could cause bubbles to form in living tissue as far back as 1670.

To add insult to injury, the chief physician on a St Louis bridge project, Dr Janimet and the Chief Engineer, James Eads, both had encountered similar problems with compression sickness in 1867, and had made progress in mitigating its effects with controlled slow decompression. But Eads had had a falling out with the Colonel, and didn't share his knowledge, and no-one in Europe thought to tell the Americans anything either.

Now that the Colonel was in his sick bed in the family mansion in Trenton, New Jersey, it was his wife, Emily Warren Roebling, who came to the fore.

Always her husband's staunchest supporter and an engineering genius in her own right, Emily took it upon herself to teach herself higher mathematics and civil engineering. She became, simultaneously the Colonel's chief nursemaid and de facto chief engineer of the Brooklyn Bridge.

The Woman Behind the Man

While Washington continued to write detailed instructions and plans for the bridge, it was Emily running the show, liaising with junior engineers to implement her husband's grand vision, and impressing everyone with her authority and expertise.

The Bridge Towers took four years to build. On 14 August 1876, the Roeblings received this telegram:

'The first wire rope reached its position at eleven and one half o'clock. Was raised in six minutes.'

On 25 August, Master Mechanic Farrington rode the full length of the first guide rope, swinging in a bosun's chair, 92 metres (300 feet) above the waterline, demonstrating the safety of the task to workers and pulling a crowd-pleasing publicity stunt at the same time.

He became the first man ever to cross the East River by bridge. The Colonel had been too sick to attend.

Construction proceeded and then a scandal. Vocal opponents of Roebling on the Board of Trustees argued that any Roebling company's supply of wire cable for the Bridge constituted a 'conflict of interest'. They successfully sought to engage another supplier, a Brooklyn man, J. Lloyd Haigh, whom Roebling called a 'cheat and a rogue'.

Coincidentally, some of the board members had 'financial connections' to Haigh. Then on

14 June 1878 a cable snapped. The whiplash it created killed two men and injured three others before the cable was lost in the waters of the East River. Roebling's worse suspicions were revealing themselves to be fact.

The four suspension cables that held the bridge up were 3 578.5 feet long (1 091 metres), 15.75 feet (4.8 metres) thick and each contained 5434 wires that had to be woven in, strand by strand. If the cables were being made of inferior wire they wouldn't be able to support the load of almost 15 000 tonnes.

The whole project was in jeopardy. Roebling launched an investigation and discovered that the Brooklyn contractor was substituting approved wire with inferior wire after inspectors had approved samples of superior wire.

Fortunately, Roebling had designed the cabling to be six times stronger than necessary, so even though the compromised cabling made the bridge 33 per cent weaker, it was still four times stronger than necessary, but 250 extra cables would have to be put in. For those who might consider this overkill, consider that the Bridge is still standing more than 120 years later, while many of its contemporaries have since fallen down.

So the Colonel got the contract for the cabling wire but he'd made powerful enemies. These enemies then started a smear campaign and journalists began to report that a feeble minded madman was running the project.

By late summer, 1882 and with less than a year to go for the Bridge's completion, certain trustees were motioning to dismiss the Colonel as chief engineer.

So Emily came to the fore again to help recruit friends. At an extraordinary meeting of the American Society of Civil Engineers, she argued the Colonel's case. Quoting from her husband she said:

'If I live long enough to direct the important work still to be done I know it will be finished cheaper and better than if left to some engineer who has not had my experience.'

She was the first woman ever to address the Society, and she won their support. When the Board of Trustees met on 11 September 1882 they voted to retain the Colonel's title as Chief Engineer—10 to 7.

Success at last

The opening ceremony on 24 May 1883 was a nationally publicised event.

After 15 years of lobbying and 13 years of construction, the New York and Brooklyn Bridge was officially open for business (it wouldn't be the Brooklyn Bridge officially until 1915).

At 1 825 metres (5 989 feet) it was by far the longest suspension bridge in the world and would remain so for 20 years until another Manhattan to Brooklyn Bridge, the Williamsburg Bridge, opened on 19 December 1903—a far cry from the first trans-East River service, the rowboat ferry run by Cornelius Dicksen in 1642.

On the first day of the Roebling's great project the Colonel was again too sick to attend, but Emily Roebling became the first person to cross it. Around 150 300 people and 1 800 vehicles followed. Many would have been gazing down the 41 metres (135 feet) to the waters of the river below and looking up to the top of the towers 84.5 metres (276.5 feet) above the waterline.

The bridge had cost $15.5 million ($3.15 billion) and had claimed 27 lives, but it became one of the great iconic structures of the world. Emily Roebling considered it a work of art.

Emily would die in 1903, but the Colonel, as tough as invalids often are, lived to be 89. He amassed a collection of 16 000 geological specimens that are now on display at the Smithsonian Institution. Washington died on 21 July 1926—one day short of 57 years after his father's death. Every year the Rensselaer Polytechnic Institute in Troy, New York, awards the Emily Roebling Scholarship to the most gifted female Engineering student.

Compared to the 13 years it took to build the Brooklyn Bridge, the Yichang suspension bridge in China that crosses the Yangtze River took a mere three years, from 1998 when construction began, to 2001 when it was open for traffic.

The Sydney Harbour
Bridge

Yes, it looks somewhat like a coat-hanger, but it's also one of the most iconic bridges in the world and it certainly has a nice setting. Sydneysiders had dreamed of connecting the south and north shores of their harbour since 1815 when Francis Greenway first suggested it, but it wasn't until a Royal Commission in 1890 that anyone took the idea any further.

Even then there was no official request for design proposals until 1900, then everyone got distracted because of Australian Federation (1 January 1901) and it wasn't until 1911 that John Bradfield received his appointment as chief engineer. He travelled throughout the world and finally settled on New York's 310 metre (1 017 feet) Hell Gate Bridge as his inspiration, with maybe a touch of the 389-metre (1 276 feet) Tyne Bridge in Newcastle as well.

Bradfield completed his designs in 1916 but then everyone got distracted with the closing years of World War One and no-one did anything again until 1922, when the New South Wales Parliament finally passed the laws to make the bridge possible. By then, Bradfield was also building Sydney's underground railroad, the City Circle line,

The Hell Gate Bridge in Queens, New York— built in 1916, it is considered one of the strongest in the world and inspired the design of the Sydney Harbour Bridge.

The Sydney Harbour Bridge; under construction in mid-1930, one of a number of public works built during the depression that kept hundreds of men employed and hundreds of families from starvation.

The two halves of the Sydney Harbour Bridge were constructed separately, a month apart, but were finally sealed together on 19 August 1930.

Sydney Harbour Bridge Facts

Length, width and height: At 1 149 metres (3 770 feet) with a span of 503 metres (1 650 feet) it's not the longest steel arch in the world. Even when the Sydney Harbour Bridge was opened the span of the 1931 Bayonne Bridge over the Kill van Kull dividing New Jersey and New York was longer by a metre (3 feet). But at 48.8 metres (160 feet)—8 traffic lanes, 2 rail tracks, 1 pedestrian lane and 1 bicycle lane—it's still the widest and at a height of 134 metres (429.6 feet) it's still the tallest.

Weight of steel arch: 39 000 tonnes.

Weight of bridge: 52 800 tonnes.

Number of rivets holding everything together: 6 million —all manufactured at and imported from the Park Bridge Iron Works in England.

The two pairs of 89 metre (276 feet) high concrete and granite pylons that frame the arch perform no structural purpose whatsoever. The designers originally put them there just for show and to give a sense of psychological security, but the south east pylon is now a museum, the south west pylon houses the NSW Road and Traffic Authorities local surveillance unit and the two northern pylons are venting chimneys for the Sydney Harbour Tunnel.

so the two projects became each a part of the other's design. The final tender to build the bridge finally went to Dorman Long and Company of Middlesbrough England, since the Australians at the time didn't trust themselves to do the work properly, so we can credit the final detailed design of the bridge to Consulting Engineer Sir Ralph Freeman.

Work began in 1923. Eight hundred houses and a high school were demolished before the actual construction, which commenced with a 'Turning of the First Sod' ceremony on 28 July. Excavations of abutments and approach spans took another six years and construction of the arch didn't start until 1929.

Two halves make a whole

The Sydney Harbour Bridge's arch was built in two halves, with the southern half being constructed a month ahead of the northern half, so that if any problems showed up in the south, they'd be corrected for the north.

The two halves finally met on the afternoon of 19 August 1930 and were permanently sealed together at 10 pm. Building the road, tram and train tracks took up 1931, and the first test train, a steam locomotive, crossed the bridge on 19 March 1932.

The bridge had cost $10 million (close to $1 billion today), but maybe because the Depression and then World War Two were so distracting, the bridge wasn't paid off until 1988.

Seventeen workers had died during its construction. Yet for the most part people were overwhelmingly positive about a project that kept so many people alive during the Depression that they called it 'The Iron Lung', although sadly because of the economy many people would also use the bridge as a convenient way to commit suicide. The suicide death toll currently stands at 40.

Left-wing Premier Jack Lang was all set to cut the ribbon and open the bridge on 19 March 1932 when right-wing fanatic Francis de Groot, protesting that neither King George V or the Governor General Sir Isaac Isaacs had been invited, came charging on the back of a chestnut horse named 'Mick' and slashed the ribbon shouting: 'In the name of His Majesty the King and all the decent and respectable people of New South Wales.'

After someone retied the ribbon, Jack Lang cut it and there was the usual 21-gun salute and RAAF fly past. After de Groot's arrest, the court found him sane and fined him 5 pounds (about $1 000). De Groot later returned to his birthplace, Dublin, and died there in 1969, aged 81. The sword he used to cut the ribbon is now on display at the Bridge.

The
Golden Gate

Another great iconic bridge was also a child of the Great Depression. At a total length of 2 737 metres (1.7 miles) with a long span of 1 280 metres (0.8 miles) the Golden Gate held the record for the longest suspension bridge span for 27 years until the completion of the Verrazano-Narrows Bridge between Staten Island and Brooklyn, whose span is only 18 metres (59 feet) longer.

Not only is it beautiful, but the Golden Gate is extremely practical. Although the north opening of San Francisco Bay is a relatively narrow

2 024 metres (1.27 miles), at 120 metres (400 feet) deep it's also a relatively deep strait. Strong currents and high tides drive 2 billion cubic metres (528 billion gallons) through the strait every six hours, making the passage dangerous. Tall cliffs leave few landings and make the pass even less attractive to ferries. The ferries travelling from Hyde Street Pier to Sausalito have to travel further to avoid the currents and still take 27 minutes.

The experts said it couldn't be done, citing the city's frequent fog and almost constant 96

kilometres per hour (60 miles per hour) winds across the gap. But that didn't deter Joseph Baermann Strauss. Although people rejected his original 1916 design for a cantilever bridge as ugly, eventually, after much consultation, local authorities agreed on a suspension bridge.

But to get his bridge built, Strauss had to fight. The Department of War didn't want the bridge to interfere with shipping. Labour unions wanted guarantees that local workers would build the bridge. Southern Pacific Railroad sued because the bridge threatened their ferry fleet so the citizenry responded by boycotting the ferries and Southern Pacific caved. But the automobile industry was on Strauss' side, and in 1927, after ten years of fighting, Strauss got the go ahead for his bridge.

Then, just when the money was getting organised, the 1929 Wall Street Crash came and Strauss had to wait another four years for a bond issue to raise the estimated $30.1 million ($3 billion). It almost didn't happen, but the Bank of America bought the bonds and work finally started on 4 January 1933.

After all that, in the delegated hands of local architect Irving Morrow, and the collaboration of Senior Engineer Charles Alton Ellis with Leon Moisseiff, the bridge building was relatively easy. Amazingly, Ellis was entirely self-taught. He didn't have an engineering degree, but although Strauss was the driving force, Ellis was largely responsible for turning Strauss' vision into a reality.

Although Strauss took the credit for the bridge when he should have spread it around, it was he who pioneered the use of safety netting to protect workers. Only 11 men died building the bridge; ten in one accident when the safety net failed under the weight of a collapsed scaffold. The 19 men who were saved by netting over the course of the construction formed the 'Halfway to Hell' club.

The Golden Gate Bridge opened on 27 May 1937, $1.3 million under budget. It had achieved the unprecedented spanning of an ocean harbour mouth. One temporary pier had had to be planted right in the middle of the span, 335 metres (1100 feet) from shore, to do it.

Two hundred thousand people walked over it that day. The day after, President Roosevelt pushed a button in Washington at noon California Time to signal the official start of vehicle traffic. San Franciscans celebrated for a week—a cultural event

The Golden Gate's distinctive profile and colour make it instantly recognisable.

they dubbed 'The Fiesta'. Strauss even wrote a poem. Find it at www.goldengatebridge.org/research and search for 'the mighty task is done' poem.

The bridge is 27 metres (90 feet) wide and 227 metres (746 feet) high—as high as a 62-storey building. Traffic runs 67 metres (200 feet) above the water every day on six lanes on two levels, suspended from 129 000 kilometres (80 000 miles) of wires spun into cables. The two main cables weigh 11 000 tonnes each, each comprising 27 572 wires. Given the wind forces it has to endure, the bridge sways up to 8.4 metres (27.7 feet) to compensate. The south tower's foundations extend 33.5 metres (110 feet) below the water line. The first coat of International Orange paint that gives the bridge its lovely colour used 37 850 litres (10 000 gallons) of the stuff.

Joseph Strauss died in 1938, only a year after the Golden Gate's completion. Today 120 000 vehicles cross the bridge and pass his statue at the Golden Gate's southern end.

The Longest Bridge in the World

Although there's no official, internationally recognised standard for measuring a bridge length, especially if the bridge is a multi-spanned bridge, the longest bridge in the world is considered by most to be the Akashi-Kaiko Bridge linking Awaji Island Shikoku and the City of Kobe in southern Honshu, Japan. Completed in 1998 at a cost of $8.5 billion, its full length is 3 911 metres (2.43 miles) with the longest span 1991 metres (1.24 miles).

A Bridge To Jump From

For a bridge that was built with such safety consciousness in mind, it's ironic then that suicides from the Golden Gate bridge have so far exceeded 1 500. In the first decade of the 21st century the official average was one every ten days or so, but it may be much higher. For a variety of technical and engineering reasons no authority has erected a barrier, or is likely to.

The bridge is closed to pedestrians at night, but cyclists can still be buzzed through security gates, thus limiting potential suicides at night to people who can afford a bicycle. Only one person to date has survived the jump without serious injury—a sixteen-year-old wrestler landed in the bay on his buttocks, then swam ashore. His first words: 'I can't do anything right.'

Tunnels

The Chunnel

The English have had a long-running debate: are they or are they not Europeans? If joining the European Community in 1973 didn't settle the matter, then the Channel Tunnel has certainly helped to erode any sense of separation that the English Channel (34 kilometres or 21 miles at its narrowest) might have provided.

The Chunnel is another one of those long-standing dreams that only came to fruition in the late 20th century. Most of the early suggestions came from the French. In 1802 French mining engineer André Mathieu proposed a tunnel for horse-drawn carriages that would have required building an artificial island in the middle of The Channel.

Other French overtures happened with a serious survey in the 1830s and a proposal in 1856. The English then made their moves in 1865 and 1867. The English and French then decided to work together in 1876, and the two countries even dug test tunnels in 1881 before the English got cold feet, citing 'national security concerns'.

They came close in 1973–5, before the English pulled out yet again. Then Prime Minister Margaret Thatcher and President François Mitterrand considered several options with names like 'The Mousehole

Project' and 'Flexilink', but nothing came of those either. It wasn't until private industry got involved in the mid-1980s that the Chunnel looked like becoming a reality.

On 2 July 1985 The Channel Tunnel Group, a consortium of two banks and five construction companies and France-Manche (three banks and two construction companies), formed a joint venture supervised in turn by TransManche Link. The English bored from Shakespeare Cliff in Folkestone, Kent and the French from Sangatte, Coquelles in Pas-de-Calais.

The Chunnel was hugely expensive. When construction began in 1988 the projected costs were 2.6 billion pounds. By the time construction ended in 1994, the cost had overrun by 80 per cent to 4.65 billion pounds. With the addition of the Channel Tunnel Rail Link—now called Highspeed One—the cost was a further 5.8 billion pounds. The equivalent cost today for the whole project would be around $72 billion.

Tunnelling wasn't too difficult—most of the Chunnel bores through chalk—but it was still hard work. At its peak 15 000 people were involved in its construction, and it claimed 10 lives.

One major ongoing issue is air quality. The three tunnels that the Chunnel comprises—two rail tunnels and a central

The Channel Tunnel opened on 6 May 1994 and did wonders for Anglo-European travel, but the engineering marvel hasn't been as profitable as its visionaries hoped it would be. A cost-benefit analysis even concluded that the British economy would have been better off if it had never been constructed in the first place. Eurostar, the Chunnel owners, didn't post a profit until 1999. The Chunnel has seen several fires, one in 2008 cost 60 million Euros in damages, but snow and ice seem to be the Chunnel's biggest enemy. The extreme winter of 2009 created such a contrast between outside and inside temperatures that on 18 December 2009, five London-bound trains simply broke down inside the Chunnel, stranding thousands of passengers and ruining their Christmas plans. The next day a Paris-bound train broke down outside the Chunnel. Eurostar services didn't recommence until 22 December.

service tunnel—have walls 1.5 metres (5 feet) thick. The cavities require the continual conditioning of 6000 tonnes of air. Trains travelling through the Chunnel also create pressure differentials at the front and rear, producing drag effects.

To reduce these problems the Chunnel incorporates 2-metre (7 feet) diameter piston relief ducts—four per kilometre. 483 kilometres (300 miles) of cold water pipes line the tunnels to cool down the heat generated by air friction.

The opening on 6 May 1994 was an international affair. Queen Elizabeth II rode to Calais from Folkestone and François Mitterrand rode from Paris to Calais where the two trains met nose to nose. The next day, the two heads of state did it all over again, meeting in Folkestone.

On Highspeed One you can now travel from London, under the Channel and on to Paris at 300 kilometres per hour (186 miles per hour) in a journey lasting 2 hours and 15 minutes of which 27 minutes are actually spent in the 50.5 kilometres (31.4 mile) long Chunnel itself.

The Cheriton Station at Folkestone and the Coquelles in Calais can transfer vehicles directly onto trains at a rate of 700 cars and 113 heavy vehicles per hour. The double-decker trains they ride on are the broadest ever built at 4.26 metres (14 feet).

Although it's an impressive achievement, the Chunnel isn't as well patronised as its designers originally thought it would be, and there are no plans currently to build a similar road tunnel.

The Seikan

Although surveying began as early as late April 1946, the Seikan Tunnel linking Honshu to Hokkaido in Japan did not begin until 1971. Opened on 13 March 1988, at 53.85 kilometres (33.49 miles) the tunnel is longer than the Chunnel but its portion underwater is shorter—23.3 kilometres (14.5 miles). The Seikan boasted the world's first undersea railway stations—for emergency use only. Like the Chunnel, the $3.6 billion (now $8 billion) Seikan is also underutilised because air travel in Japan is relatively cheaper and faster.

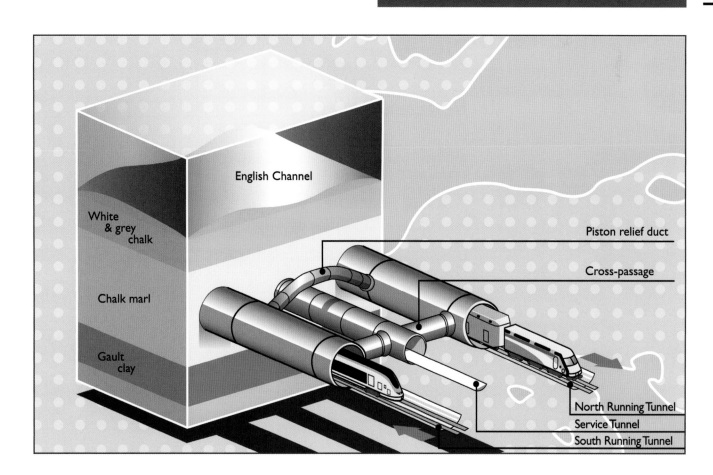

English Channel

White & grey chalk

Chalk marl

Gault clay

Piston relief duct

Cross-passage

North Running Tunnel

Service Tunnel

South Running Tunnel

Part 05

Buildings That Move — The Great Ships

With the exception of electronic equipment, ships, like everything else, have gotten bigger over time. After all, why should grand visions be confined to land? But there are fewer big ships in the world than there are buildings and other engineering projects, so there are fewer opportunities to practise building big ships.

This can mean that things are more likely to go wrong when you're experimenting with the design of what are essentially moving buildings that need to survive conditions unlike anything on land.

Surviving historical accounts and politics being what they are, as well as there being no easy definition of what 'largest' means, makes working out what was the largest all-wooden ship ever built a tough job. Traditionally, it's supposed to have been Noah's Ark. Its biblical measurements in modern terms are 137 x 22.9 metres (450 x 75 feet) but can a floating barn that couldn't even be steered be properly called a ship?

The largest true ships predating the modern era may have been some of the Chinese Treasure Ships that Admiral Zheng He used during his seven voyages of exploration in the early 1400s. If we take the surviving and fragmentary Ming Dynasty accounts as accurate these ships were huge for their time—or for any other time for that matter. At 137 x 55 metres (450 x 180 feet) the treasure ships were 40 per cent longer and 65 per cent wider than any other historical wooden ship ever built. With up to nine masts and four decks, they could have taken anything up to 1000 passengers and cargo.

The Vasa

In the early 1600s Sweden had long abandoned the disorganised raping and pillaging of its Viking past and had filled its coffers by means of trade and organised warfare. Its citizens would one day look back on the 16th century and call it the 'strormaktstiden'—the 'age of great power'.

But from 1625 young Protestant King Gustav II (1594–1632, ruled from 1611) of the Vasa Dynasty was embroiled in the fourth and final stage of a war with Catholic Poland that had been going on and off since 1600.

The war wasn't going well for Sweden. The Poles had won numerous battles in the Baltic and were destroying many of the smaller Swedish ships, which would eventually include the particularly humiliating sinking of the Swedish Admiralty flagship *Tigern* ('Tiger') in the Battle of Oliwa (1627).

The Swedish Navy was in a mess. To control the Baltic and secure their interests, the Swedes needed bigger ships. So they hit upon a plan to build five ships that would be bigger, heavier and meaner than anything else in their day. The *Applet*, *Gota Ark*, *Kronan*, *Scepter* and *Vasa* would be those ships, and the *Vasa* was originally planned to be the foremost and grandest of them all.

Dutch-born ship builder, Henrik Hybertsson, and his brother Arendt would build these ships at Stockholm shipyard.

If anyone knew how to build ships, it was the far trading and seafaring Dutch.

On 25 January 1625 they signed a contract to build the first four, two with 41-metre (135 feet) keels and two with 33-metre (108 feet) keels.

But after the Baltic disasters the king wanted Henrik to rush the building of the two smaller ships, but stipulated that the keel should be remade larger, at 37 metres (120 feet). The shipyard had already cut the planks for the smaller keels and the government wasn't giving them any additional money.

Then Henrik Hybertsson got sick and had to delegate the work to his assistant, also from Holland, Henrik Jacobsson.

Hybertsson died in 1627, before the *Vasa*'s lower hull was completed and launched in the spring. When it was, it was a compromise and when the upper decks were built, they really belonged on a larger ship with a deeper keel. The problems were obvious even then.

Top heavy and too small

The stability test for a ship was to have 30 sailors run from one side of the upper deck to another. After only three runs, the ship showed significant rolling. Amazingly, none of the chief shipbuilders were there for the test.

Admiral Klas Fleming who was there reputedly said: 'Had they run more times, she would have keeled over.' He rationalised any concerns away by observing the track record of the Dutch.

It was true that the Dutch could build ships, but what the Dutch couldn't cope with was a constant stream of dispatches from the Polish front from a king who knew nothing about naval architecture but kept insisting that they hurry up and do things his way.

The king had originally wanted 72 24-pound cannons for the ship on a single gun deck. What he got was 48 24-pound guns on two decks, with an additional 16 guns of smaller sizes. With all the compromises, the *Vasa* was neither the biggest ship ever built, nor did she have the most guns, but she did have the biggest broadside.

This meant that in a single, coordinated shot the *Vasa* was conceived to fire a weight of 267 kilograms (588 pounds) of cannonballs.

The *Vasa* was not only top heavy, but at 1 200 tonnes and only 69 metres (230 feet) long too small for this much firepower and arguably too small for the 145 sailors and 300 soldiers she was supposed to carry.

Then, because the *Vasa* was supposedly a showpiece, the shipbuilders had to build a high stern, rich in heavy ornamentation and statues—almost 500 of them. This work took two years to complete.

Reproductions of the ship show a stern that looked more like a jewel box than the rear of a warship. All this additional top weight made the stability problem worse, and 120 tonnes of ballast wasn't enough to make up for it.

In the spring of 1628 the *Vasa* underwent her final fittings and arming. On 10 August 1628, Captain Sofring Hansson had the ship towed to the southern end of Stockholm Harbour. There, the gunports were opened in preparation to fire a salute as the Ship left Stockholm harbour. The ship set sail and in the lightest of breezes from the southwest she began to move.

A disastrous end

After travelling about 1.2 kilometres (0.75 miles) she reached the southern tip of Beckholmen Island. In a gust of wind she keeled heavily to port and righted herself.

Then in another gust she leaned so far to port that water began to flow through her lower gun ports and she sank in minutes, in front of thousands of witnesses, finally resting on the bottom of the harbour 32 metres below. She took up to 50 lives with her. It was a huge and very expensive public relations disaster for a small nation.

Captain Hansson survived to be arrested and tried. He swore the crew had been sober and the guns properly secured. Crews and contractors blamed each other, but in spite of the desire for a scapegoat the inquest committee couldn't find any one person at fault.

Henrik Jacobsson said he was following the orders of the conveniently dead Henrik Hybertsson, who had followed the orders of the king. Arendt Hybertsson said 'Only God knows' and the inquest agreed with him. In the end no-one was found guilty or punished.

It was easier to blame God than the king who had approved every step of the project and browbeaten everyone to get it done. Within a few years the king would be dead anyway, killed in the Battle of Lutzen fighting the Holy Roman Empire and the Catholic League as part of the Thirty Years War. The Swedes had learned their lesson, and the other ships planned at the same time as the *Vasa* went on to become very successful warships that helped Sweden build her golden age.

In 1664 a team using a simple diving bell recovered 50 of the *Vasa's* expensive guns, but the ship itself was lost to history until its rediscovery in 1956. Recovery took a further five years and raising the ship took a slow two years.

At last, on 24 April 1961, under the gaze of the world's media the *Vasa* broke the surface after 333 years under water. A combination of cold water and pollution had inhibited organisms from destroying the material structure of the *Vasa*. Even so, full preservation of the old wood took 26 years and yet it's possible that nothing can stop the ship's eventual deterioration. She is still on show at the specially built *Vasa* Museum in Stockholm.

The hull of *The Great Eastern*, easily dwarfing anything else in the water at the time.

Great Eastern

Isambard Brunel was one of the world's big thinkers, but what else can you expect from a man whose middle name was 'Kingdom'? The son of famed engineer Sir Marc Isambard, the younger Brunel took to the family business with extreme gusto.

Today we'd call Isambard a compulsive workaholic. He smoked cigars continuously (40 a day), survived on four hours of sleep a night and generally ignored his family. But his career demonstrates a love of continuous innovation that he no doubt got from his father.

Marc Brunel had invented a tunnelling shield that made possible the world's first major sub-river tunnel. Built between 1825 and 1841 the Thames Tunnel—11 metres wide, 6 metres high, 396 metres long and 23 metres below river surface level at high tide (35 x 25 x 1300 feet and 75 feet)—succeeded where no other tunnel had ever before and it was still in use over 150 years after its completion.

Isambard had worked as assistant engineer on the tunnel since 1826 when he was twenty and he learned a lot from his father, but his later career seems to show a need to outdo his old man.

Brunel's solo work included the Maidenhead Bridge of 1838. It was so well built that it's now carrying trains 10 times heavier than Brunel ever anticipated.

But in his day he became really famous for his work on the Great Western Railway, originally running from London to Bristol. He pioneered the use of a new, wider broad gauge (2.14 metres or 7 feet and 0.25') and specially designed stations along the route which included the Box Tunnel, the world's longest railway tunnel at the time.

He also designed the Avon-Gorge-spanning Clifton Suspension Bridge (1862–4), which at 214 metres (702 feet) was the longest suspension bridge in the world at the time. But Brunel never lived to see it completed, because his grandest vision of all would be his undoing.

His ultimate failure began, as so many of these things do, with great success. Using the kudos that he'd built up from the Great Western Railway, Brunel decided to get into shipping.

His dream was that people could go from London to New York on a single ticket—London to Bristol by rail, then Bristol to New

York by ship—so he convinced his employers to build the ship.

The Great Western

The *Great Western* was the first steamship specifically designed for the Atlantic crossing. At 72 metres (236 feet), it was the largest paddle steamer of the day, built to carry 148 passengers.

In 1837 people still didn't really trust steam, so the *Great Western* had four masts for sails too, to provide supplementary propulsion and stability, but the hybrid worked and on its maiden voyage between 8 April and 23 April 1838 it set the record for the fastest Atlantic crossing. It would make 45 crossings in 8 years before becoming a mail ship, then a Crimean War troopship before getting scrapped in 1856.

Brunel then built the *SS Great Britain*, now considered to be the world's first modern ship—iron hulled and with a screw propeller. 98.15 metres (322 feet) long, 15.39 metres (50 feet) wide at the beam she was the largest vessel afloat at the time of her launch in 1843. Designed to carry 360 passengers, she would eventually be capable of carrying 730 passengers.

Unfortunately, she was so big that she couldn't make it through the locks at Floating Harbour in Bristol, so she had to wait a year before conditions made it possible for her to be towed to the Thames for her final refit. She made her maiden voyage on 26 July 1845 and reached New York in 14 days.

Then in November 1846 the *Great Britain* ran aground on Dundrum Bay, Ireland. Although she was refloated and repaired, the salvage bankrupted the Great Western Steamship Company, and liquidators sold her. She became an immigration ship and made her first such journey in 1852, carrying 630 passengers to Melbourne, Australia. After a long and varied career she ended up back in England in the 1970s and after extensive work in the 1990s is now one of the most valued 'Heritage Buildings' in the world. You can see her on display in dry dock in Bristol.

The *Great Eastern's* Impressive Specifications were:

Length: 211 metres (692 feet)

Beam: 25 metres (82 feet)

Fully laden draft (portion of ship below the surface of the sea): 9.1 metres (30 feet)

Displacement: 32 000 tonnes

Propulsion: 4 engines (four stories high) for 17 metre (56 feet) high side paddle wheels with an additional engine for a 7.3 metre (24 feet) screw propeller. She also had 6 masts for 1 686 square metres (18 148 square feet) of sails although she couldn't set sail at the same time as the paddles were running because exhaust would have set the sails on fire.

Top speed: 13 knots (24 kilometres per hour or 15 miles per hour)

Passenger capacity: 4 000

Crew complement: 418

A Massive Proposal

Now the *Great Western* had worked well but despite the *Great Britain* being impressive from an engineering standpoint, it was not all that great from an economic one. All this rather equivocal success with shipping should have raised a few concerns about Brunel, and it did, but not enough. So when he proposed the *Great Eastern* in 1852, people didn't know whether Brunel was a visionary, far ahead of his time, or a madman. In retrospect, he was a little of both.

The *Great Eastern* would be bigger than Noah's Ark, in fact the largest man-made movable object ever. It would carry 15 000 tonnes of coal to circumnavigate the world without refuelling and need 200 stokers to feed the 8 000 horse power engines.

It would require 8 600 tonnes of iron. It would incorporate 30 000 hull plates each 2.2 centimetres (0.875 inches) thick and weighing up to 0.3 tonnes. Each plate would need six men to carry them into position.

Two hundred gangs of hand riveters (bashers) would then put them into place with 3 million rivets. The hull would be double-plated, with a 90 centimetre (3 foot) gap between each layer. Because the space was so tight, most of the bashers were boys, handling white-hot rivets and working for only a few pennies a week. Double-plating wouldn't be a design feature of another ship for 100 years.

Around 12 000 men would work for five years to build the *Great Eastern* and its

original cost was estimated to be 125 000 pounds ($188.5 million).

Critics argued, momentarily forgetting Archimedes' Principle, that a ship of such a weight would inevitably sink, or that given the weight versus strength ratios of the building materials that it would snap with any substantial storm stresses, but such was Brunel's reputation as the 'Napoleon of Engineers' that he actually got the Eastern Steam Navigation Company (ESNC) to approve the project—just. (If only someone had posited a few economic arguments!)

The Ship Wouldn't Move

Work commenced under the supervision of naval architect John Scott Russell at his shipyards on the Isle of Dogs in London's East End in May 1853. Things went well initially until a fire broke out on 10 September. In two hours 1 000 tonnes of deck planking went up in smoke along with plans, models and templates. Russel neglected to tell anyone he wasn't insured. He borrowed heavily to continue and work halted for five months until February 1854.

Over time, Brunel got suspicious of Russell. Always a control freak, he insisted on approving and micromanaging everything and then began to argue with Russell about a 900-tonne iron shortfall on the books. Brunel suspected that Russell was selling off iron to pay interest on his debts. Then in May 1855 Russell's creditors foreclosed on the shipyard and work halted. At this point the ESNC had already paid half the costs of the ship but only a quarter of the work on the hull had been finished and they hadn't even started on the engines yet. Work didn't recommence until September 1855. Russell was kept on but Brunel was watching his every move.

It took two more years until beaters put in the last hull plate in September 1857. Brunel then announced the launch for 3 November, but there were arguments between him and Russell even about that. Russell favoured the traditional free launch, Brunel wanted a controlled chain launch, easing the ship gradually into the water. Brunel won the argument mainly because Russell had lost too much credibility.

Brunel also wanted silence and strict discipline on the day of the launch, but it was not to be. The ESNC wanted to recoup some money so they invited Prince Albert and the Prince of Wales, sold 3 000 tickets and turned the launch into a circus.

It became a tragic farce. At the last minute they changed the name of the ship to Leviathan. Brunel didn't care what they called it, but when the time came to launch the ship one of the cables on the drum heads that controlled the launch chains snapped and killed two workers. Then the ship simply stopped moving. The crowds left, disappointed and Brunel was humiliated.

For the next month the ship moved only four feet. *The Field* newspaper called the ship a 'great monument of folly' and people started calling her the 'Leave her high and dry-athan'. Brunel borrowed hydraulic rams and winches from the Royal Navy to bash the ship an inch at

a time into the water. The rams would routinely explode from the strain. After two months work, finally at high tide on 31 January 1858 the ship floated.

The next 18 months were spent fitting the ship out. No expense was spared to give the ship the most luxurious appointments available. But by now the budget had blown out to four times the original estimate. The final cost would be over £500 000 (over $750 million) and Brunel paid for a lot of the shortfall out of his own pocket. Failure was not an option, but by now Brunel was dying from a chronic kidney disease and he didn't have much time left anyway.

With the fit out complete, on 5 September 1859 the engines were activated. Brunel posed for a photograph to mark the occasion. Shortly after, he suffered a severe stroke and became bedridden. The following day the *Great Eastern* left without him to Holyhead. On 9 September at 6pm a safety valve failed and the resulting explosion of the front water tank blew the forward funnel off. Six people died.

Three days later, on 12 September, after hearing about the accident, Brunel died. He was 53. He left behind a widow and three young children. His second son, Henri Marc Brunel, would eventually team up with Sir John Wolfe-Barry. The Blackfriars Railway Bridge in London is one of their projects.

John Scott Russell never built another ship again, but he did publish highly regarded technical books on naval architecture and made significant contributions to knowledge about the transmission of energy in waves. He was a far better scientist than he was a businessman and he died in 1882.

The Great Eastern Curse

As a passenger ship, the *Great Eastern* was a commercial disaster. There simply wasn't the demand to move 4 000 people at a time to the United States, or even to Australia. It never carried more than 1 200 passengers at a time and on some trips it only managed 100.

In mid-1861 she served as a troopship during which time it carried 2 617 people and 120 horses. She was amazingly safe. On 27 August 1862 she scraped an iceberg and suffered a 26-metre (85-foot) gash—longer than the hole that sank the *Titanic*, but the tear didn't puncture the inner hull. In fact, the passengers didn't even know there'd been an accident.

Then in January 1864, the bankrupted ESNC sold the *Great Eastern* for a tenth of what it cost to build. It would have been a complete failure, but fate intervened and the *Great Eastern* became one of the most important ships in history, beginning the whole era of modern, intercontinental telecommunications.

Its extraordinary propulsion combining screw and paddle wheel, made it highly manoeuvrable. In May 1865 she made the first attempt to lay the transatlantic cable that would initially link Europe and the Americas by telegraph.

On 2 August 1865, at the halfway mark, the cable was lost, but hope wasn't. On 14 July 1866 they tried again and this time Sir James Anderson and his crew were successful, arriving at Heart's Content, Newfoundland, Canada on 27 July, having laid 4 200 kilometres

(2 600 miles) of cable. They were even able to recover the cable lost in 1865.

Over the next few years Anderson and later Robert Halpin and crew used the Great Eastern to lay a further 48 000 kilometres (almost 30 000 miles) of submarine cable including links from France to Canada and Aden to Bombay.

Reconversion to a passenger ship in 1885 failed to make the ship viable, and she suffered various indignities, at one point even becoming a floating billboard. Then, in 1888, she was sold for scrap.

During the 18 months it took to take her apart there were unconfirmed rumours that the workers found the skeletons of two riveters, a man and a boy, who had somehow been trapped in the hollow between the layers of hull plating. No-one ever worked out how they died. Perhaps this was the origin of the curse that dogged the *Great Eastern*.

It's a great story, but although there are reports that workers found one skeleton, the rumour that two skeletons showed up goes back to an earlier report that a riveter and his apprentice mysteriously disappeared during the construction of the ship. Whether even this rumour was based on fact, is something we'll never know.

You can still see part of the *Great Eastern* today. Visit Liverpool Football club. The ship's topmast is now their Kop end flagpole.

The Titanic

On 18 January 1868, Thomas Ismay, one of the directors of the National Line shipping company, bought the trade name, logo and goodwill of a bankrupt steamship company and established a working relationship with the shipbuilding firm Harland and Wolff to build vessels that would specialise in the North Atlantic run from Europe to the United States.

The American Civil War had ended less than three years earlier and the renewed nation was experiencing a surge of immigration and commerce. The time was ripe for a new player to challenge the supremacy of the Cunard Line for this lucrative and ever-increasing trans-oceanic trade in people and merchandise. Thomas Ismay had calculated that the thousand pounds (about $1 million in modern terms) he paid for the White Star Line would be well worth it.

On 30 July 1869 Harland and Wolff received orders to build four ships, whose names would establish a pattern that White Star would maintain for all 90 of the vessels it would build between 1870 and 1932. The sister ships were called *Atlantic*, *Baltic*, *Republic* and *Oceanic*.

The *Oceanic* was the first. On her maiden voyage on 2 March 1871, its 64 passengers would have noted several innovations. First class cabins were positioned toward the bow of the ship, away from the engines, leaving the third-class passenger the discomfort of vibration noise at the ship's stern.

Most of the first-class cabins had running water and electric bells to summon stewards. Even the portholes were bigger. When you're competing for passengers, details are important. So is speed. So is volume.

So important were these three factors operating together that Cunard, White Star and other companies servicing the route embarked on a decades-long Atlantic crossing record and luxury appointments 'arms race' that dictated that crossing from Europe to the States would be an ever faster, and ever more sumptuous experience—especially for the very rich—on ever larger ships.

Profits were one thing, but what the competing companies seemed to really prize was The Blue Riband, awarded for the fastest trans-Atlantic crossings in two categories—westbound, and the faster eastbound. So fast was technology developing that ships set records every year, sometimes several times in the same year.

In 1889 White Star set another precedent. With the launch of the *Majestic* and the *Teutonic*, the company introduced the first truly modern steam-driven vessels—ships without sails.

By 1907 White Star had built the Big Four—the *Adriatic*, *Baltic*, *Cedric* and *Celtic*—24 000-tonne ships that could each carry up to 400 passengers in first and second class, over 2 000 in third, and up to 17 000 tonnes of cargo.

The 'bigger but slower, more comfortable and more reliable' formula was bound to be a winner during what would later come to be known as the 'golden age of immigration'.

But even while the Big Four were pressed into service Cunard was going one better. In 1905, White Star's big rival built the *Lusitania*. Launched the following year at over 31 550 gross register tonnes it was over a quarter bigger than the 'Big Four'. Her sister ship, *Mauritania*, was even larger at 31 938 tonnes and she was fast, designed for a cruising speed of 25 knots (46.3 kph or 28.8 mph).

A Class of Their Own

With the *Lusitania* and *Mauritania* on line, something had to be done.

So in mid-1907, J. Bruce Ismay and his wife Florence had dinner with Lord James Pirrie, a partner in Harland and Wolff, and Lady Pirrie and together they discussed the creation of the Olympic class of ships. They

Average *Olympic* Class Specifications:

Weight: 46 000 gross tons

Displacement: 52 500 tons

Length: 269.1 metres (882.75 feet)

Beam (Width at widest point): 28.2 metres (92.5 feet)

Height: 18 metres (60 feet) above water line

Draught: 10.5 metres (34.5 feet)

Power to drive these behemoths would come from 24 double-ended, 5 single-ended Scotch boilers serviced by nine furnaces which drove two four-cylinder engines each producing 15 000 horse power to drive two triple-blade outer propellers at 75 rpm. In addition, one low pressure turbine generating 16 000 horse power would drive a central, four-bladed propeller.

Cruising speed: 21 knots (38.9 kph or 24.2 mph)

Number of decks: 9 labelled A to G with two boiler decks below.

would vary only slightly from each other in detail and would be 50 per cent larger than the *Lusitania* class. Their names were to be the *Olympic*, *Titanic* and *Gigantic*.

Building each ship would require Harland and Wolff to undertake extensive modification of its shipyards. Builders laid the *Olympic's* keel in December 1908, launched her on 20 October 1910, and spent eight months on her final fittings before her maiden voyage on 14 June 1911.

Then on 20 September 1911 the *Olympic* collided with the British warship *HMAS Hawke* off the Isle of Wight, flooding two of her compartments and twisting a propeller shaft.

Repairs to *Olympic* necessitated moving the *Titanic*, still under construction, from dry dock. *Titanic*'s keel had been laid on 31 March 1909. She'd been launched on 31 May 1911 but the *Olympic* accident delayed her final outfitting until 31 March 1912. It was an expensive accident, delays meant that the ships would take longer to pay for themselves.

Each ship had cost approximately $7.5 million (in modern terms almost a billion dollars). White Star had a lot riding on them.

The Ship of Dreams

The *Olympic* and the *Titanic* were virtually identical but the *Titanic* was an improvement on her and represented the pinnacle of passenger ship design of its time. It boasted the finest first-class state rooms and even the second and third class accommodation was better than first-class aboard many another ship. The forward promenade 'A' deck, open on the *Olympic*, was enclosed on the *Titanic*, allowing for more comfort in winter along the cold North Atlantic route and accounting for a slightly higher registered gross tonnage than the *Olympic*.

Electricity was available throughout the ship—a first. The *Titanic* also had its own post office and hospital. Most importantly, the designers—Alexander Carlisle, William Pirrie and most notably Thomas Andrews—had divided the ship's hull into 15 sealable compartments. Four compartments could flood below the waterline and the ship would still remain afloat.

Since the designers perceived the possibility of an accident that would flood four compartments would be extremely unlikely, the press widely reported that the *Titanic* was unsinkable.

But while the technology and infrastructure were impressive, it was the appointments, the luxurious surface details, that people focused on.

First and second class male passengers had their own respective barber shops, so that gentlemen could always look their best, but for the most part it was the first-class that the *Titanic* was designed to spoil. The *Titanic* was one of the first luxury liners ever to have its own (indoor) swimming pool but it also had a gymnasium and Turkish Baths.

First class also had access to a ladies parlour suite, a gentleman's smoking room, an a-la-carte dining room, a lounge, a verandah and palm court and the Café Parisien.

All classes had their own separate dining salons, but the First Class Dining Saloon was over 30 metres (100 feet) long and was the largest room afloat. Passengers dined off blue, white and gold specially designed china. The First Class menu for 14 April 1912 included oysters, consommé Olga, cream of barley soup, filet mignons lili, sauté of chicken Lyonnaise, vegetable marrow farcie, minted lamb, roast duckling, roast squab, cold asparagus vinaigrette, and for dessert, peaches in chartreuse jelly, Waldorf pudding and chocolate and vanilla éclairs.

On modern air travel there's little to do except read, eat and sleep, and transatlantic ship crossings in the early 20th century weren't much different, but at least on the *Titanic* you could eat and sleep in rooms with lead crystal light fittings, walls lined with intricate panels carved from expensive woods and you could tread on finely woven woollen carpet. The pinnacle of fine living on the *Titanic* were the four parlour suites. Each had two bedrooms, two wardrobe rooms, its own sitting room, private bath and lavatory.

On the *Titanic's* maiden voyage, J. Bruce Ismay occupied one of the two parlour suites that also had a private 50-foot promenade. If he hadn't been the company director, he would have had to pay the full fare for a one-way passage of $4350, in modern terms close to a whopping $100 000 for the privilege.

Titanic's maiden voyage began on Wednesday, 10 April 1912. On her way out of Southampton her wake was so large and powerful she caused the liner *City of New York* to break from its moorings and float towards her. The *City's* stern missed crashing into the *Titanic's* bow by barely over a meter (4 feet) and the incident delayed *Titanic's* departure by an hour. If the *Titanic* hadn't been delayed, would it have made a difference to her final fate?

Superstitious seamen or passengers brushed aside whatever forebodings that they may have had. The White Star Line couldn't afford to lose face. The list of rich and famous on the *Titanic* included John Jacob Astor IV, whose family owned the site on which the Empire State Building would later be built, Isodor Straus, owner of Macy's Department Store in New York, and their wives and although the ship wasn't fully loaded, it was still carrying a respectable 2 223 passengers in its 840 state rooms and 40 open berthing areas.

Toll of the Titanic

First Class total: 329
Men lost: 119
Men saved: 54
Women and children lost: 11
Women and children saved: 145
Total lost: 130
Total saved: 199

Second Class total: 285
Men lost: 142
Men saved: 15
Women and children lost: 24
Women and children saved: 104
Total lost: 166
Total saved: 119

Third Class total: 710
Men lost: 417
Men saved: 69
Women and children lost: 119
Women and children saved: 105
Total lost: 536
Total saved: 174

Crew total: 899
Men lost: 682
Men saved: 194
Women lost: 3
Women saved: 20
Total lost: 685
Total saved: 214

Total passengers and crew: 2 223
Total lost: 1 517 (68.2%)
Total saved: 706 (31.8%)

The Ship of Nightmares

The voyage of the *Titanic* proceeded normally until the night of Sunday 14 April. Captain Edward John Smith had steered his ship along a heading slightly south of the original route on account of earlier warnings of sea ice, but on that Sunday radio operators, overworked with transmitting telegraph messages on behalf of passengers, neglected to report more serious warnings of large icebergs in the vicinity.

At 11:40 pm, after the captain had gone to bed and the *Titanic* was around 640 kilometres (400 miles) south of Grand Banks, Newfoundland, lookouts spotted a large iceberg directly ahead of the ship. First Officer William Murdoch immediately ordered the ship to steer hard to starboard. It's been almost a century since the accident and analysts have been debating the wisdom of Murdoch's decision ever since. It's arguable that if the *Titanic* had hit that iceberg dead on it would have crippled her, but she would have remained afloat.

As it was, the ship grazed the great hunk of ice. Contrary to popular misconception, the iceberg didn't tear a hole in the ship. The quality of iron manufacture at this time and the effects of the near-freezing water made the ship's structure brittle, and the pressure of the ice scraping against the starboard hull caused the bulkheads to cave in, popping them out of their rivets and opening a seam below the waterline some 90 metres (300 feet) long. Four compartments flooded, then a fifth, causing a chain reaction that as more compartments flooded, more fell below the waterline and over the compartments' seals further along the length of the ship.

Alexander Carlisle had designed the *Titanic* to carry 48 lifeboats and had even installed state-of-the-art davits to handle the loads to put them into the water, but the White Star Line's directors had overruled him and in the end the ship carried 20 lifeboats with a total capacity of 1 178 people.

Although this was criminally negligent, White Star had actually exceeded regulations at the time, which required lifeboats for only 962 people out of its potential full load of 3 511 passengers and crew.

And yet even then in the combination of confusion and complacency by 1:20am six lifeboats had left the Titanic, none of them filled to capacity. By that time the ship was listing heavily to starboard, her bow dangerously close to the waterline. The crew had fired signal flares, but if any other ship had seen them, they failed to respond. The radio operators likewise, failed to get a response from any nearby vessels.

The last lifeboat—collapsible 'D'—left the ship at around 2:00 am. By 2:15 the ship's bow was sinking. As the first half of the ship sank, its rear half lifted out of the water. Then as the ship's structure underwent stresses that it was never designed for, the hull broke in two. The front section began its downward plunge, levelling off and sinking relatively gently. It would eventually reach the sea bottom at a depth of 3 800 metres (12 460 feet).

The stern's sinking was much more violent. As water rushed in, compressed air in the stern's many chambers caused explosions that broke the structure apart. The stern section of the ship would eventually settle 600 metres (1 970 feet) away from the bow.

One ship had heard the *Titanic*'s distress call and was close enough to come to the rescue as fast as it safely could over the calm ice-mottled sea, in a dark night without moonlight. The *Carpathia* began rescuing survivors at 4:10am, by 8:30 she'd picked up the last of those who had managed to get into a lifeboat. Of those who'd been left in the water, only a handful were rescued alive. Almost all the others had died of hypothermia in the freezing water—comparatively few had drowned outright.

Truths, lies and consequences

The sinking headlined around the world and caught the public imagination in the way that few other events have before or since. The American inquiry into the event was scathing, the British inquiry considered a whitewash. The British Admiralty was in no position to admit that its antiquated laws were largely responsible for the sinking of the ship.

What did emerge from the examination of evidence and consciences was that after the *Titanic* sinking, all ships were required to carry enough lifeboats to accommodate all the passengers.

Radio operations had to continue around the clock. Shipping lanes were moved south to avoid the worst of the ice and a special internationally funded surveillance operation was established to watch for the sort of hazard that had brought the *Titanic* down.

The sinking of the *Titanic* was a disaster for the White Star Line and the company had suffered a blow from which it would never recover. The *Gigantic* was renamed the less hubristically sounding *Britannic*, but the *Olympic* and *Titanic*'s sister ship would never operate as a luxury liner.

Its launch was delayed while White Star redesigned it, giving it a double hull. World War One started and the *Britannic* was converted into a hospital ship just as the luxury interiors were being completed. She served until 12 December 1916, when she struck a mine in the Kea Channel in the Aegean Sea. The mine blew a huge hole in her port bow. It took her only an hour to sink, but of the 1 100 aboard only 30 died. Resting at a depth of 107 metres, she is the largest liner wreck on the ocean floor.

And what of the *Lusitania*, the ship whose very existence had goaded J. Bruce Ismay's rivalry? Unlike the *Olympic* and *Britannic* it remained a merchant vessel, and, in spite of certain war modifications to reduce its fuel consumption, it remained the fastest passenger transport on the sea.

Then, on 1 May 1915 it departed New York for its 202nd crossing of the *Atlantic* with 1 959 aboard. On Friday 7 May it was just 70 kilometres (43.5 miles) from Queenstown, Ireland when, at 2:10pm she crossed the path of German u-boat U-20. The u-boat torpedoed her. Immediately she began to tilt heavily to starboard, making the launch of lifeboats from both sides of the ship difficult. Of its 48 lifeboats, only six were successfully launched.

Captain William Thomas Turner stayed with the ship until he was washed overboard and survived by clinging to a floating chair, unconscious, for over three hours. But the *Lusitania* had taken only 18 minutes to sink and 1 198 people died with her, including almost 100 children. Eight-hundred-and-eighty-five bodies would never be recovered.

The American public were so incensed at the German attack of a virtually unarmed civilian vessel that the ensuing outcry played an important role in forcing the later participation of the United States in World War One.

The *Olympic* would have a much different fate. She was converted into a fast troop transport and survived the war. Refitted and modernised, she became a commercial passenger ship again in 1920 and continued in that capacity until 1935. By then the Great Depression had set in, and demand had declined. White Star had merged with its old rival Cunard the year before and the directors sold the ship that people had come to call 'Old Reliable'. In 1937 she was sold for scrap, but her interiors were auctioned off, piece by piece.

If you want an inkling of what the *Titanic* was like, go to the White Swan Hotel in Alnwick, England and take a look at some of its fittings. Or visit the RMS Olympic Restaurant on board the Celebrity Cruises cruise ship *Millennium*. Visit the Titanic Museum in Branson Missouri

where you'll find a first class cabin from the Olympic that serves as an example of its sister ship's counterpart or go to the Southampton Maritime Museum to see the clock taken from the Olympic's grand staircase to get a feel for the one on the Titanic.

If you want the real thing, go to 41°43'57" N, 49°56'49" W, in the North Atlantic and hire a deep sea submersible to see the wreck of the *Titanic* itself and what's left of J. Bruce Ismay's grand vision gone horribly wrong.

Heroes and villains

Many stories of heroism would be born out of the tragedy of the *Titanic*. The *Titanic*'s band played on for as long as it could, doing what it could to keep passengers and crew calm. None of the band members survived.

Second Officer Charles Herbert Lightoller was the ship's senior surviving officer and took charge of an overturned lifeboat for several hours, constantly getting around 30 survivors to redistribute their weight to compensate for the swelling sea so that the lifeboat wouldn't sink.

Fifth Officer Harold Godfrey Low was the only crewman to take charge of a lifeboat that actually went back to seek survivors in the water. All the other lifeboat survivors had feared that if they returned they would have been swamped from overloading as desperate swimmers sought to climb into the boats.

Crew Member Gareth Brown was said to have helped save more than 50 women and children before he died, and survivors reported that the ship's designer Thomas Andrews unstintingly helped people to the lifeboats before he went down with his ship, as did Captain Smith.

Arthur Henry Rostron, captain of the *Carpathia*, was honoured all his life for his role in rescuing the survivors of the *Titanic*. He was knighted in 1919.

The most notorious of the survivors was J. Bruce Ismay. In his defence he later said didn't go into a lifeboat until he believed that all the women and children had been safely accommodated. In fact, 157 women and children died in the accident although all would have easily survived if the lifeboats had been properly filled.

As it was, the press and public hounded Ismay mercilessly, and although he would continue to be involved in maritime work for many years, two inquiries and media pillory would ruin his reputation and he lived as a virtual recluse until his death in 1937.

Two other crew members are worth mentioning. The 23-year-old crewman John Coffrey was so spooked by the *Titanic*'s near miss of the *City of New York* in Southampton that he jumped ship, stowing himself among the mailbags that were headed for Queenstown (now Cobh) as the ship made a stop in Ireland.

Stewardess and later nurse Violet Constance Jessop was on board the *Olympic* when it collided with the *HMS Hawke*, she survived the *Titanic* sinking and she survived the sinking of the *Britannic*. She thus had the dubious honour of surviving all the accidents of the ill-fated Olympic-class ships.

The worst recorded maritime disaster happened on the night of 30 January 1945 when Soviet submarine S-13 shot the German hospital ship *MV Wilhelm Gustloff* with three torpedoes. It took only 45 minutes for the ship to sink and with her died 9 343 people, including German soldiers and civilian evacuees escaping from East Prussia. This is equivalent to over six times the number of people who died aboard the *Titanic*.

The H-4

Howard Hughes is better known nowadays as the obsessively compulsive mentally ill billionaire who died in reclusive paranoia. But in his heyday he achieved a great deal, particularly in the field of filmmaking and aviation. He established the Hughes Aircraft Company in 1932 and on 19 January 1937 he set a transcontinental airspeed record.

Flying non-stop between Los Angeles and New York City in 7 hours, 28 minutes, 25 seconds, the Hughes-designed H-1 was one of the first ever airplane whose rivets were set flush to the fuselage and to feature retractable landing gear, radically improving streamlining.

On 10 July 1938 he established a round-the-world record flight of 91 hours.

Such were his accomplishments that when the U.S. government wanted a very large flying boat to use as a troop carrier in World War Two, director of Liberty Ships Program, Henry J. Kaiser, thought of Hughes.

Originally called the HK-1 and contracted in 1942, the plane that would ultimately be realised as the Hughes H-4 *Hercules* took so long to develop that the war had been over for two years before it took its first flight.

'The Spruce Goose'

Restrictions on the availability of metals meant that the *H-4* was built out of wood. The press dubbed it 'The Spruce Goose,' a name that Hughes hated. It wasn't even accurate, as the flying boat was mostly made of birch. It was hugely controversial, having cost so much and taken so long to realise that several senate enquiries sought to establish if Hughes had defrauded the government. Why all the fuss?

The *H-4* was simply impossible to ignore. It was and is still the biggest flying boat ever built. Its wingspan is the largest of any aircraft in history, at 97.54 metres (319 feet and 11 inches), it's longer than a football field. It's also the tallest aircraft ever, at 24.18 metres (79 feet and 4 inches) from ground to the top of its tail. Even the Airbus A380 is 8 centimetres shorter.

Eight three-thousand horsepower Pratt and Whitney Wasp Major engines with propeller spans of 5.23 metres (17 feet, 2 inches) were meant to power the plane at a cruising speed of 354 kilometres per hour (220 miles per hour) for a range of 4 800 kilometres (3 000 miles).

But the H-4 never got anywhere near fulfilling its brief. After two test taxi runs on 2 November 1947, Hughes, his co-pilot, two flight engineers, sixteen mechanics, two crew, three reporters and four industry representatives flew on a maiden flight off Cabrillo Beach, near Long Beach California, where the H-4 reached a height of only 21 metres (70 feet) for a distance of 1.6 kilometres (1 mile) at a top speed of 217 kilometres per hour (135 miles per hour).

The H-4 was in the air for less than thirty seconds. It was the first and last flight. Hughes' grand visions remains a footnote in aviation history.

In 1980, four years after Hughes's death, the California Aero Club acquired the H-4, but in during the second half of 1992 it was dismantled.

It finally arrived in McMinnville, Oregon, on 27 February 1993, after a 138-day, 1 700 kilometres (1 055 mile) barge journey. Restoration work took eight years and the H-4 is now on display as a prize exhibit at the Evergreen Aviation and Space Museum.

In yet another link between Hughes, filmmaking and grand visions gone awry, the hangar in which the H-4 was built is now a sound stage in which portions of James Cameron's 1997 movie *Titanic* were filmed.

Monster Cru

One way of measuring the size of ships is the Bruto Register Tonnage. This gives one type of measure of the ship's dry weight. The *Great Eastern* had a BRT of 18 195. No other ship would surpass that until the White Star Line's *RMS Celtic*, built in 1901 at 21 035 BRT. The *Titanic*, famously sunk in 1912, had a BRT of 46 329; its sister ship, the *Olympic* was 46 439.

Before air travel became fast and cheap, passenger ships became bigger and bigger very quickly. The 1914 *Bismarck's* BRT was 56 551. Then there was a sudden leap to what was arguably the classiest ship ever built, the 1935 *Normandie*—79 280 BRT.

The *Queen Elizabeth* wasn't much bigger at 83 676 BRT but at least the British had beaten the French, and the *QE I* held the record for 35 years until she was scrapped in 1975. Even then no-one would surpass the *QE I* until the United States built the bizarrely named *Carnival Destiny* in 1996—101 509 BRT.

Now the builders of the world's biggest ships are the Norwegians working in cahoots with the Americans.

Cruise Ships

Not withstanding the British with their contribution of the 2004 *Queen Mary II* at 137 308 BRT, the Norwegians, and in particular Royal Caribbean International, is making super big ships.

The Freedom Class ships *MS Freedom of the Seas* (2006), the *MS Liberty of the Seas* (2007) and the *MS Independence of the Seas* (2008) all have gross tonnages of 154 407. Sure, in the past 150 years or so ships have got bigger, but they've also become more efficient and therefore more luxurious.

There's more room to play in them, and triple the crew to tend to your whims and desires, but they haven't gotten much faster. That's because they're not in a hurry to get you anywhere—cruising has become an end in itself.

The next generation up from the Freedom Class is the Oasis Class, with gross tonnages of 220 000 displacing 100 000 tonnes of water. Eight 17 500 horsepower engines power them.

At 360 metres (1 181 feet) long these ships aren't much shorter than the Empire State Building is tall—at least if you're just counting

to the roofline of the top floors. These ships are big—16 decks high.

They even have their own 'neighbourhoods'— seven of them to be exact—separate enclaves to cater to a variety of different tastes and moods and at $6 million a day to run, they're going to have to cater for as many different tastes and moods as possible to keep occupancy up.

The Oasis Class ships feature a boardwalk and carousel, a bar that's actually a giant elevator platform that continually rides up and down between four decks, promenades and even garden space and parks.

These giant ships carry 5 399 passengers accommodated in 2 700 roomy state rooms and 28 two-level loft suites with floor to ceiling windows.

Part 06
Planned Cities

The development of agriculture (helped by dams) requires settlement. Settlement leads to villages, towns and cities. Usually there's a regular supply of water nearby and the city grows around wherever the government happens to sit. Government, until relatively recently, meant whichever strong man could squeeze the most peasants and the peasants could usually be squeezed to build the strong man a very nice, very big house on the best real estate in the area.

Most cities grow organically. They're made up as they go along in response to the immediate needs of the people living in them. In the past, the result was often a haphazard arrangement that had to be purposely torn down and updated unless a war or a sacking of the city achieved the demolition work.

But occasionally, a people and their rulers are organised enough to think ahead. The vision of the place in which they are going to spend their lives springs up as a singular image—a combination of practicality and propaganda. These are the planned cities.

Harappa and
Mohenjo-Daro

Two of the earliest planned cities were Harappa and Mohenjo-Daro. The Harappan culture began before 3300 BCE and later developed into the Indus Valley civilisation. It sprang up on the banks of the Indus River on the border of what we now know as India and Pakistan. Although much of the area is bleak and desolate today, at the time it was much lusher and spectacularly beautiful.

The Harappans were Dravidians, the people who once inhabited all of India until the Aryan invasion that filled the northern part of the sub-continent with what we usually think of as Indian culture. At their height, between 2500 and 2000 BCE, they dominated an area of over 1 million square kilometres (386 000 square miles) and were the world's largest Bronze Age culture. And yet after their final decline about 1300 BCE the whole civilisation was lost to history.

In the mid-1800s the British builders of the East Indian Railway Company virtually demolished the ruins of two ancient Harappan cities to provide ballast for a 150-kilometre (93 mile) stretch of railroad from Karachi to Lahore. It also hasn't helped that we are yet to decipher their language. But what has survived gives us some idea of Harappan sophistication.

Mohenjo-Daro—a city of 200 hectares (494 acres) and 40 000 inhabitants—included dockyards, granaries, warehouses and complete encirclement with protective walls. Both Harappa and Mohenjo-Daro show planned regular streets in a grid pattern, serviced by the world's first urban sanitation systems.

All houses drew water from either their own wells or communal wells. The houses had special bathrooms and wastewater left to an integrated system of covered drains. The fact that everyone had similar facilities is evidence of considerable egalitarianism.

Mohenjo-Daro had over 700 wells. Near its 10-hectare (25 acre) citadel it even had a large bath, 12 x 7 metres and 2.4 metres (39 x 23 feet and 9 feet) deep within a bathhouse complex the likes of which the world wouldn't see again until Roman times. The city was constructed out of baked bricks, many of uniform size with regular, precise proportions, evidence of highly organised mass production. The overall effect is that the city was built by people with exacting standards and attention to detail—a city of hygienic engineers.

Persepolis and the
Apadana

It was Cyrus the Great (c 590 BCE–530 BCE) who conquered the Medes, the Lydians and the Babylonians to earn himself the right to the title of Shahansha, king of kings. As the first emperor of the Achaeminid Dynasty and the founder of the Persian Empire, he wanted a capital city that would be an enduring monument to his glory, so in about 546 BCE he started building one, Parsagadae, but he died before finishing it, and his sons and successors Cambyses and Bardia didn't live long enough to make much more of it because Darius the Great killed everyone who stood in his way to become Shah himself.

In 515 BCE Cyrus had founded another city, near the Pulwar River, 70 kilometres north-north east of what is now the modern city of Shiraz. The ancient Persians called it Parsa—City of the Persians—but we know it by its Greek name, Persepolis, which means the same thing.

Parsagadae reminded people too much of the earlier kings so Darius decided that Persepolis would be his capital of choice—a monument to his own enduring glory. In his newly acquired territory of Egypt he re-dug the ancient canal from the Nile to Suez, and he laid an extensive road network throughout his empire, including a royal road from Sardis, in what is now Western Turkey, to Susa in Western Iran and then on to Persepolis—a distance of over 2 500 kilometres (1 553 miles). But it was in Persepolis itself that he really gave himself free rein.

He built walls around the city, 18 metres (60 feet) feet high and 11 metres (36 feet) thick. The highpoint of the city is a terrace, around 450 x 250 metres and up to 20 metres high (1 476 x 820 feet and 66 feet), partly artificial and partly cut out of a mountain on its east side. A wall 27 metres (88.5 feet) high surrounded the almost 125 000 square metre (31 acre) area.

The main features of the terrace are Darius' palace, the 12 100 square metre (3 acre) Apadana and the Throne Hall. Situated on the west of the terrace, the 3 844 square metre (0.95 acre) inner room of the Great Ceremonial Hall dominates the Apadana. 36 20-metre (66 feet) high columns once held up the Hall's central roof. To the east, Xerxes began the Throne Hall, or Hall of 100 columns. But the 70 x 70 metre (230 x 230 feet) hall wasn't finished until 480 BCE, during the reign of Darius' son, Xerxes I.

But the most striking feature of Persepolis, aside from the amount of gray limestone and granite needed to build it, are the carvings. Over 3 000 shallow relief carvings of human

The relics of Persepolis, carved as if living supplicants weren't enough, so that the Persion kings had a permanent procession of them in stone

figures have survived. They decorate the base platforms upon which stood the buildings and they must represent only a small fraction of the artwork that would have decorated the buildings when they were in use. The carvings show an almost mathematical identity, as if they weren't carvings at all but huge plaster tiles all cut from the same mould. Perhaps the message was 'Compared to me you are all the same, interchangeable and disposable.'

Persepolis was one of the great cities of antiquity. But it didn't last. In 480 BCE, after the Battle of Thermopylae during the second Persian invasion of Greece, Xerxes burned the city of Athens to the ground. In 331 or 330 BCE, when Persepolis was only about 185 years old Alexander the Great captured the city. After a

few weeks of celebratory drinking someone suggested that now would be a good time to set fire to the city in retribution for the burning of Athens, 150 years before. Alexander began the fire himself with a few well-placed torches. Although he changed his mind soon after, by then it was too late and the fire consumed the palace and a considerable portion of the city.

Although the burning of the Apadana and the city was one of the great acts of vandalism in antiquity, the debris that would have fallen around the lower courses of the buildings probably helped to preserve them. Today only a few of the terrace's 872 columns still stand to suggest the former magnificence of the place, and in that part of the world Alexander's name is still reviled.

The Forbidden City

T**he** Chinese like a sense of discipline in their architecture. Feng shui principles favour the square as an architectural ideal in the ground plans of houses and even of cities. In fact, many ancient Chinese cities have a planned look about them. When you have cities like Chang'an, which in 750 had about 1 million inhabitants, you can understand this need for regularity—chaos and large populations make for urban planning nightmares.

Chang'an is now the modern city of Xian ('Western Peace'). The history of the cities in the area now covered by the modern city of Beijing ('Northern Capital') is complicated, but it's safe to assert that Beijing first became the capital of China under the Yuan Dynasty. The city was then called Khanbalic (Mongol 'City of the Khan'), and Kublai Khan finished it in 1293, the year before his death.

Hardly any of the Khan's city survives in modern-day Beijing. The Beijing of today is really the product of the Ming Dynasty (1368 –1644). The first Ming Emperor relocated the capital to Nanjing ('Southern Capital'), when he died but when his son Zhu Di became Emperor in 1402, Zhu Di promptly moved it back. Maybe he didn't like the humidity of the south.

A City Within a City

The following year Zhu Di began construction of a palace complex right on the site of the old Yuan capital that his father had razed. The Zi Jin Cheng ('Purple Forbidden City') takes its name from the symbolism of the 'Purple Star', what Westerners call the Pole Star, believed by the old Chinese to be the abode of the god known as the Celestial Emperor. The 'Forbidden' part of the name is literal. No-one could enter it without the express permission of the emperor.

It was to be both a city within a city and a palace worthy of one of the most politically powerful men in the world. It was meant to represent not only China, but to be the earthly counterpart of heaven.

More than a million workers spent 15 years in its construction. Materials came thousands of miles from all parts of the Middle Kingdom—precious woods from the sub-tropical south, bricks and silk from Jiangsu in the east.

The world's largest and best-preserved old palace lies within a rectangle 753 metres

(2 470 feet) east to west and 961 metres (3 153 feet) north to south. The complex is one huge monument to symbolism and poetic naming.

The Outer Court

To get into the palace compound you have to cross a southern causeway over a 6-metre (20 feet) deep, 52-metre (171 feet) wide moat. You then go through the Meridian Gate with its nine by nine array of golden nails—nine being a number that only the emperors could use, yellow being a colour that only the emperor could wear. The roof tiles on almost all the buildings in the compound are yellow glazed.

The Meridian Gate penetrates the surrounding rammed earth, tile faceted wall—7.9 metres (26 feet) high, 8.62 metres (28.28 feet) wide at the base and tapering to 6.66 metres (22 feet) wide at the top. Four towers sit at each corner of the wall.

As you walk north you're following the Imperial way—the stone-flagged path that forms the central axis of the Forbidden City and the central axis of the ancient city of Beijing itself. Only the emperor could walk the Imperial way at all times. The empress could use it on her wedding day and scholars could use it on their day of final examination. Everyone else had to walk on the edges.

Some scholars now believe that this path also aligned with Xanadu, Kublai Khan's summer palace 275 kilometres (171 miles) north of the centre of Beijing. Xanadu was about 40 per cent of the size of the Forbidden City. Marco Polo's accounts describe its opulence but nothing remains of it today except for the remnants of its earth wall and

the ground level outline of a circular brick platform.

Back in the centre of Beijing you cross a smaller bow-shaped moat called the Inner Golden Water River. You then proceed to the Gate of Supreme Harmony. Once through that gate, you're in the Hall of Supreme Harmony square with the eponymous 30-metre (100 feet) high hall ahead of you.

The hall is built on a triple-layered terrace and is the largest surviving wooden structure in China. It was within this hall that the emperors held court and it contained the largest of the thrones. If you're at the top of the hall's steps, looking south at the square, you're seeing the same point of view as the toddler Pu Yi did in Bernardo Bertolucci's film *The Last Emperor* when all those eunuchs were kowtowing to him. From this point, beyond the courtyard wall to the south east is the Hall of Military Eminence and to the east, the Hall of Literary Glory.

Continuing the journey north you reach in turn two further throne rooms, The Hall of Perfect Harmony, where the emperors prepared for state ceremonies, then the Hall of the Preservation of Harmony, which is at the centre of the Forbidden City, and therefore at the centre of the ancient plan of Beijing and by extension, the symbolic centre of the Middle Kingdom—the centre of the world.

It functioned as a rehearsal space for ceremonies but it was also where the government conducted the final stage of the Imperial Examinations, the selection system that the Chinese used for entry into the public service. The system lasted for 1300 years, right up until 1905.

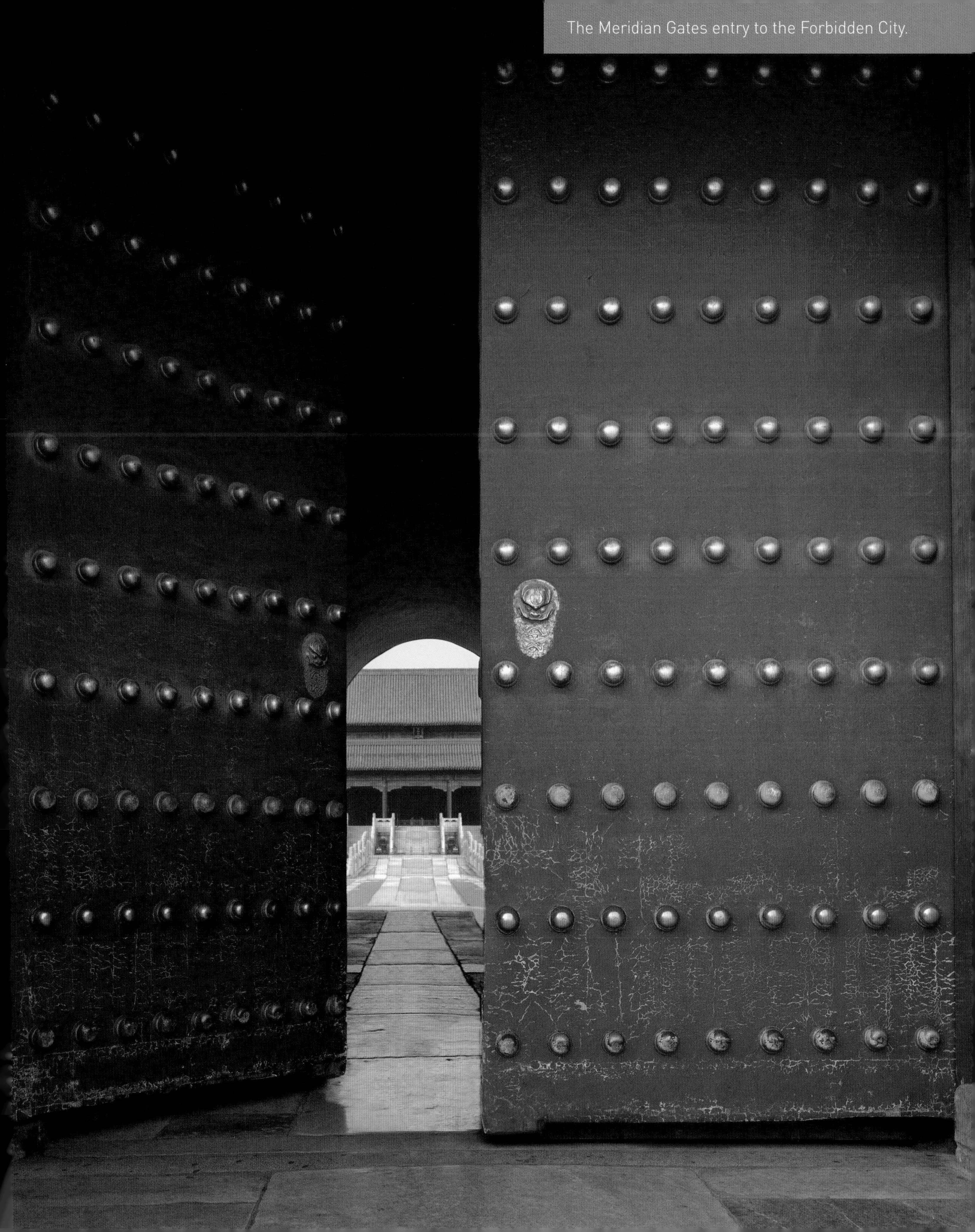

The Meridian Gates entry to the Forbidden City.

Behind Preservation of Harmony is the Northern Ramp, carved from a single piece of stone, 16.57 metres long, 3.07 metres wide and 1.7 metres thick (5436 x 10.07 x 5.57 feet). It weighs 200 tonnes and is the largest carved monolith in China. Two slightly smaller stones make up the ramp on the southern front of Supreme Harmony.

As you pass Preservation you leave the Outer Court and you're now in the Inner Court.

The Inner Court

Passing the inner wall through the gate of Heavenly Purity you're in a walled enclosure containing three palaces in line from south to north. Since in Feng Shui south is the preferred direction, the first palace is the Palace of Heavenly Purity. The Palace represented the male, Yang, 'heavenly' principle and during the Ming Dynasty this is where the emperor actually lived. During the Qing Dynasty the emperors moved to the Palace of the Culture of the Mind to the west. North of Heavenly Purity is the ceremonial Hall of Union and beyond that there's the Palace of Earthly Tranquillity.

This palace represents the feminine, Yin, 'earthly' principle and is where the empress lived. Given the history of unhappy imperial marriages, one wonders just how much tranquillity there was to go around, but perhaps it wasn't so bad, since the emperor seldom visited this palace except on his wedding night or other times that he needed to sire an heir. Under the later Ch'ing Dynasty (1644 –1912) Earthly Tranquillity became the venue for all sorts of shamanistic practices that the Manchu imported from the northern steppes from which they had originally come.

As you pass through the Gate of Earthly Tranquillity and out of the inner palace compound you find yourself in the Imperial Garden with the Northern Gate of Divine Pride exiting the Forbidden City just beyond the Pavilion of Imperial Peace.

The Forbidden City Today

When you add up all the buildings within the compound, the palaces where the concubines and their children lived, the bureaucrats' offices and other residences for the eunuchs and guards there's a total of 980 surviving buildings with 8 707 rooms.

Within these rooms were art objects collected over the centuries. The Manchu Dynasty fell in 1912 and there followed years of political instability. In 1933, when the Nationalist government feared the extent of the Japanese invasion of China they evacuated 13 427 boxes of objects. Of the 10 455 that were later returned to China, 2 221 are now in Nanjing and 8 234 are in Beijing. The remaining 2 972 are in the National Palace Museum in Taipei.

The Forbidden City Palace Museum holds 340 000 pieces of ceramics and porcelain, 50 000 paintings, almost 30 000 pieces of jade carving, 10 000 pieces of bronze ware and more than 1 000 timepieces.

The Forbidden City is no longer forbidden. In 2007, 7.2 million Chinese visited it, along with a further 1.5 million foreigners.

The Forbidden City in Beijing is said to attract about 25 000 tourists per day. In 2000, a Starbucks coffee shop opened inside the gates, but closed its doors in July 2007.

Chan Chan

Prior to the Inca conquest in the late 1400s the Chimu Culture established the Kingdom of Chimor. Beginning around 850 Chimor would, at its maximum, take up the northern half of the Peruvian coastline and a small portion of what is now south Ecuador. This area stretches for 1 000 kilometres (621 miles) accomodating two-thirds of the Andean population at the time.

Their capital city, Chan Chan, took up an area of 20 square kilometres (7.7 square miles) of which 6 square kilometres (2.3 square miles or 1 483 acres), or 30 per cent of the city, were devoted entirely to 9 or 10 palaces for the nobility.

The Peruvian coast is a desert, the Andes provide a rain shield that drenches the eastern part of northern South America and creates the Amazon and its rainforest, but the west is some of the driest land on earth. How

Brasilia

The legend goes that the Italian founder of the Catholic Silesian Order, Saint Don Bosco, had a prophetic dream in which he described a city in the midst of the Amazonian jungle which closely matched the current reality of Brasilia. Wherever the idea came from, it stuck, but it wasn't defined until 1922.

The driving force for Brasilia was President Juscelino Kubitschek de Olivera. Architect Lucio Costa won the design competition in 1957. Costa's vision was that the city be built in the dominant shape of a cross, a sort of 'X marks the spot'. Others see it as a plane, or even as a bird. In any event it was built at lightning pace—41 months—between 1956 and its official inauguration on 21 April 1960.

Many of Brasilia's landmark buildings are justly lauded—especially those of Oscar Niemeyer's design—but there are many critics of Brasilia's ground plan. It's a city both famous for being unfriendly to pedestrians and infamous for being the only 20th century-built city in the world so far to be declared a World Heritage site (1987)—a move that effectively makes it impossible to correct its problems. But at least the weather is good—far nicer than Washington or Canberra—although you should avoid spending the summer there if you don't like the humidity that steeps the Amazonian rainforest.

then did Chan Chan support a population of 20 000? The answer lies in an extensive irrigation system in which water was kept in holding tanks with high walls, and judicious planting to reduce evaporation. The Chimu grew food in small, intensive plots and they also had an elaborate aquaculture industry going, supplemented by ocean fishing.

Chan Chan's regular grid and arrangement of buildings demonstrate intelligent planning but most impressive of all was that the entire city was built out of adobe. In other words, the city of Chan Chan is the largest mud-built structure ever.

The Capitol dome in Washington DC, inspired by the classical ideas of the enlightenment, like the city itself.

Washington
DC

From the date of the United States of America's Independence, Congress has sat in ten cities over various times, so these cities can all claim to have once been the capital.

Of these ten, the most important have been: Philadelphia (on four occasions between 1776 and 1800), New York (twice between 1785 and 1790) and, of course Washington, since 17 November 1800.

Washington was always conceived as a planned city. George Washington himself picked the site on the Potomac River. The District of Columbia—a 10 x 10 mile (16 x 16 kilometre) diamond of mostly swampland taken from Maryland and Virginia was defined to contain it, leading people ever since to observe that the city is still a swamp.

The area is smaller now than it used to be, presently covering only 68.3 square miles (177 square kilometres) because Virginia took its land back in 1846.

The United States has had a long and friendly relationship with its fellow revolutionary country, France, and Washington's planning was initially the work of Pierre Charles

L'Enfant. Pierre's grid for the city is in a typical classical style that reminds one a little of the overview of Versailles, and it was he who decided that the main diagonal avenues of the city be named after the original 13 states.

Washington fired L'Enfant in 1792, possibly because of endless arguments between the Frenchman and Washington's supervising committee. There's a juicy legend that tells that when L'Enfant wanted to remove a house that was in his way he persuaded the owner to leave and then blew it up without asking permission.

With L'Enfant gone, Washington appointed the original surveyor of what would become the District of Columbia, Andrew Ellicott, to finish the design.

Ellicott revised the plan somewhat so it was Ellicott who set the basis for Washington's eventual development. L'Enfant didn't like the changes, but there was nothing he could do about it.

George Washington lived long enough to have the nation's capital named after him, but not long enough to see the city as official capital. He died in 1797.

L'Enfant was never paid for his work and in spite of his efforts to get compensation Congress ignored him to the end of his days. In 1812, West Point Military Academy offered him a job as Professor of Engineering but he declined. He died in poverty at the age of 70 in 1825. It wasn't until 1909 that his remains were reinterred at Arlington National Cemetery. Modern Washington now has a L'Enfant Plaza with an underground Metro stop.

Freemason designs

Few people know that both L'Enfant and Washington were Freemasons. There is an intriguing theory that the grid and the placement of the main buildings is replete with Masonic imagery and symbolism. The White House, for example, is at the apex of a pentagram (although the pentagram is incomplete, perhaps because of Andrew Ellicott's revisions. If the hidden Freemason architectural agenda is true, it might explain that there were reasons that L'Enfant objected to Ellicott's changes that went beyond ego.

This may not be as far fetched as it sounds. Nine of the 55 men who signed the Declaration of Independence were Freemasons, 13 of the 39 signatories of the Constitution were or would become Masons as have been 15 US presidents to date, including most recently, Gerald Ford. And the all-seeing eye on top of the pyramid—the Great Seal of the United States—and on the back of dollar bills is a classic (but not exclusive) Masonic symbol.

Canberra

When Australia became independent on 1 January 1901 the Federal Parliament sat in Melbourne. This, of course, was intolerable to Sydneysiders. The two cities have a rivalry that is incomprehensible to outsiders. Nevertheless the rivalry is, or was, real, and even section 125 of the Australian Constitution explicitly stated that the new capital should be at least 100 miles from Sydney.

Archaeological investigation shows that Aborigines had lived in the area upon which Canberra would be founded for at least the last 21 000 years. It's a flat, largely featureless plain, leading to current witticisms that it's still a large, featureless plain.

Government Surveyor Charles Scrivener finally chose the site in 1908, and the New South Wales Government ceded the 2 358 square kilometre (910 square mile) Australian Capital Territory (ACT) on 1 January 1910.

The government then held an international competition for the design of the new city. The committee chose from 137 entries, announcing the winner on 23 May 1912. The winning design for the capital was won by an American, Walter Burley Griffin, an ex-employee of Frank Lloyd Wright.

Griffin had never designed a city before in his life. Even then his plans were a joint creative vision of both Griffin and his wife Marion (another ex-FLW employee), who was one of the world's first licensed female architects. They worked on the plans during their honeymoon. Canberra was conceived in an atmosphere of romance. Many believe that it was Marion's watercolour perspectives of the proposed city that were crucial in the competition win.

The Naming of a City

Proposed names for the city included such bizarre suggestions as Captain Cook, Shakespeare, Kangaremu, Eucalypta and Myola. Lady Denman, wife of the Governor General announced the winning name on 12 May 1913 in the groundbreaking ceremony on what was then Kurrajong (now Capital) Hill. She hadn't seen or heard the name before she opened the envelope. She mispronounced it and what should have been CanBErra is now almost universally CANberra.

Only Queenslanders pronounce the name 'properly'. There are many explanations for the name, the most common being that it comes from Ngunnawal word meaning 'meeting place'.

The city was flooded in 1968 to form the 6.64 square kilometre (2.56 square mile) body of water called Lake Burley Griffin.

The Capital Opens for Business

In July 1913 the Australian Government invited Griffin to inspect the site. The government offered him a job as Federal Capital Director of Design and Construction. He accepted, possibly because he felt that the design was being compromised, but he had to tolerate further compromise when World War One began and funds originally allocated for the city went instead to the war effort.

Griffin argued constantly with Australian Bureaucracy and faced continual attacks from the press.

In December 1920 he resigned and declined further involvement in the project.

The aerial view of Australia's capital shows nothing like Walter Burley-Griffith's grand vision. None of the buildings he and his wife Marion designed for the city were ever built and all we really have of theirs is a street plan. New Parliament House (in the background), itself a grand vision was also designed by Americans and wasn't opened until 9 May, 1988—too late for the bicentennial of European settlement on 26 January.

None of the buildings he designed for Canberra were ever built.

The groundbreaking was as much of an opening as Canberra ever got. The third Monday in May is still Canberra Day, and 1913 still marks its foundation, but the first plots of land didn't come up for auction until 12 December 1924.

Federal Parliament moved in on 9 May 1927, thus making Canberra de facto and de jure capital of Australia.

One of Parliament's first acts in its new home was to repeal a 1 January 1910 statute forbidding the consumption of alcohol in the Australian Capital Territory, demonstrating the Australian Parliament's priorities. Incidentally, the ACT is also one of the few places where the sale of X-rated pornography is legal.

0155

Today, with a population of 330 000, Canberra is Australia's largest inland city.

The Griffins remained in Australia and worked in Melbourne for over a decade. Griffin later designed the cities of Leeton and Griffith in New South Wales and the suburb of Pyrmont in Sydney.

In 1935 he left Australia to work on several projects in India, where he died, two years later, of peritonitis at the age of 60 amd ending a personal and creative collaboration with his wife that had lasted 28 years. Marion Mahoney Griffin closed the businesses in Australia and returned to Chicago. She died in 1961 at the age of 90.

Part 07
Castles &
Palaces

Castles are multi-function buildings. Part residence of the local lord, part foodstore, part bank, but mostly they were military barracks and safe houses. The one place where the peasants could retreat to behind safe, thick, stone walls when the rampaging hordes would come to pillage and plunder. Like everything else, castles could be a double-edged sword, concentrating the population in one place so that you could lay siege and wait until the inhabitants starved to death or died of disease.

From castles evolved palaces—think of them as castles on steroids.

The top priority of most palaces is that they were meant to impress both the locals and foreigners and to reflect directly the grand visions that those in power had of themselves and of the people they squeezed for taxes. Secondly, they were seats of government, and the design of palace buildings or complexes could tell you a lot about the political nature of the nations they serviced. In highly centralised administrations, sometimes the distinction between palace and city became quite blurred, as in the case of places such as Persepolis, Chan Chan and The Forbidden City, which were virtually cities within cities.

Typically, more is better. The larger the palace, the more room there is to house nobles and entourages. Not only does this make communication of policies and edicts easier, having the nobility close to hand is an excellent way of distracting them with games of courtly intrigue so that the high-born can waste their energies on petty rivalries and courting the king's favour instead of planning real coups in their country estates, far from the prying eyes of his majesty's spies.

Palaces then, had a lot of baggage. The peasants of the past, and many of the peasants of the present, would have been surprised to learn that for all the glitter and gold, palaces were often not particularly great places to live.

Imperial Roman
Palaces

Roman history is complicated when you get to the details. At its height in 117 under Trajan—who wisely decided that the dominion of Rome could only get so big before it became completely unmanageable—the Roman Empire covered an area of 5 million square kilometres (1.93 million square miles) and embraced 88 million people and hundreds of cultures. This may not seem like much by today's standards. The United States, for example, covers an area over 9.8 million square kilometres (almost 3.8 million square miles) and has a population of over 300 million. But in the days before modern methods of communication and travel, it would take weeks to send messages. Administration has its limits.

Nevertheless, as far as the emperors were concerned, Rome was effectively the known world and they often built palaces for themselves as befitted their station. Even our word 'palace' comes from the Palatine Hill upon which many of them built their houses. But war, insurrection and the continual occupation of Rome for over 3000 years means that there isn't necessarily much left of the imperial palaces, and the rather humid climate of Rome hasn't helped much either.

Augustus' Palace

When Gaius Julius Caesar Octavianus became imperator of the Romans in 27 BCE he had to walk a fine line between many competing political factions. Although history records him as the first Roman Emperor in his lifetime, he had to keep up the pretence that he was really just a consul. The fact that he was continually re-elected to that position was simply a reflection of how much his country needed him. This sort of thing is a game that many despots like to play. Mao Tse Tung was, effectively, Emperor of China and 'Premier' in the same sense as Augustus was 'Consul'.

Still, Augustus knew that the Romans appreciated a certain level of modesty and in his residence he chose to embody what we'd now call middle-class values. Augustus had already lived in this house before becoming one of the most powerful people in antiquity and he wasn't going to let a little thing like becoming emperor make him move.

Built around 40 BCE, the 'palace' was constructed on Rome's Palatine Hill above a grotto that may once have been dedicated to Romulus, Rome's legendary founder. What survives of the building shows that it really wasn't much more than a typical residence of a well-to-do contemporary Imperial Roman. It was by no means the richest and most ostentatious house in Rome at the time, and it was nothing like the grand, treasury-bankrupting edifices of his successors, but it did have the frescoes and painted walls that were typical of the time.

There isn't much left of Augustus' Palace today. It was only opened to the public in March 2008 after over 20 years of restoration work. It took $18 million just to restore the garden and its frescoes. But the lasting impression of Augustus is his frugality and his palace sets an example of Roman stoicism and sobriety rather than opulence.

See what's left of it for yourself at: www.guardian.co.uk/world and search for 'Inside the palace of Augustus'.

Nero's Golden House

Nero's Palace that covered the slopes of the Caelian, Esquiline and Palatine Hills was a much grander vision than Augustus'. Taking advantage of the real estate that became available after the fire of 64 gutted a few aristocratic houses, Nero built a concrete and brick villa for himself.

The Domus Aurea, or Golden House, took its name from the mansion's extensive use of gold leaf. Each room had its own theme. Frescoes adorned the walls, semi-precious stones and ivory veneers adorned the ceilings. Scholars can't agree on the extent of the property and estimates range from 100 acres to 300 because a lot of it remains unexcavated, but Suetonius, who was always good for describing the dirt on the early Roman emperors, called Nero's efforts to create a rural pastiche in the middle of a city 'ruinously prodigal'. What could have upset Suetonius so much?

Maybe it was the 300 rooms, many sheathed in polished white marble, that was too much. Or the 30-metre (100 feet) high bronze statue of the emperor himself, the Colossus Neronis, that stood at the entrance to the grounds at the end point of the Appian Way. Maybe it was the fountains in the corridors and the pools in the floors. Maybe it was the mosaic-studded feature dome which had a mechanism that allowed it to turn like the night sky.

In any case, Nero didn't live long enough to enjoy it. The revolution came and he had to commit suicide in 68 CE at the age of only 33. After his death, his successors stripped the place of valuables. Within 40 years, the villa was virtually gone.

Nero had built an artificial lake in an area of the garden because the site was so marshy. So around 70 CE, Vespasian built the 50 000 seat Colosseum in the same place because it was easy to bring water to flood the arena for mock sea battles. Between 104 and 109 Trajan built a 330 x 215 metre (1 082 x 705 feet) bathhouse complex on a portion where the Domus Aurea once stood, and between 135 and 141 Hadrian and Antoninus Pius built the Temple of Venus and Roma, also on the grounds of Nero's ex-Palace.

So it is outside of Rome that we need to look for more evidence of how Roman emperors lived.

Hadrian's Villa

Putting Nero's Golden House to shame, Hadrian's Villa in Tivoli was a palace on a grand scale. The builder of the Pantheon set his retreat on 120 hectares (300 acres) of grounds, making it twice the size of the city of Pompeii. Located 28 kilometres (17 miles) from Rome, the villa was meant to reflect the rich variety of cultures that made up the empire.

The complex included a 121.4 x 18.65-metre (398 x 61 feet) canal, a 59 x 88 metre (194 x 289 feet) piazza (open square) and an artificial lake with an artificial island and a villa built upon it. The site had over 100 water features that modern archaeologists have been able to identify including its own aqueduct—to divert water from other aqueducts—30 fountains, 6 grottoes, 19 pools, 6 bath complexes and 35 lavatories. Although the site is now a ruin, it's not in bad shape and it gives visitors a good sense of grandeur past.

Diocletian's Palace

Perhaps the most impressive imperial villa wasn't even in Italy. On 1 May 305, to relax after a career spent persecuting Christians, Emperor Diocletian did the unprecedented and retired

The ruins of Hadrian's villa in Tivoli are but a shadow of a sumptuous, luxurious complex of palaces and gardens of earthly delights twice the size of the city of Pompeii. Hadrian was one of the great visionary builders—his Pantheon, which features the largest dome in antiquity—is still standing virtually intact today.

rather than wait to be assassinated. He chose a nice spot on the Adriatic, near Salona in his homeland of Dalmatia—now modern Croatia. There he built a singular white limestone and marble palace.

It was one integrated building, built in quadrangular form within a rectangle 180 x 213 metres (592 x 698 feet) covering an area of nearly 15.5 hectares (9.5 acres). It contained not only apartments for the retired emperor, but accommodation and training facilities for a cohort of Praetorian guards, as well as two temples. By all accounts the building was sumptuous and it was large enough to accommodate 9 000 people. But he wasn't happy there. He'd left behind an empire still

racked with internal squabbles. He lived long enough to hear that his successors were tearing each other apart and he died, possibly by suicide in December 311.

But the building was so dominating that the town of Split formed around it and much of the palace survives to this day.

The Potala
Palace

I t's big and it's in a spectacular setting. The Potala Palace in the Tibetan capital of Lhasa was built by Lozang Gyatso, the Fifth Dalai Lama, to house him and no doubt his future incarnations. Begun in 1645, it wasn't finished until 1694. By that time his old body had worn out and he had to be reborn before he took up residence again. From then, until the Chinese took over Tibet in 1959, it was his winter palace and the living, working, praying and meditating residence of the Tibetan government, housed in its thousand rooms.

The main building array is 13 storeys, 117 metres (384 feet) high. Its sloping stone walls are 3 to 5 metres (10 to 16.5 feet) thick. It's built on top of Marpo Ri ('Red Hill'), which is itself 300 metres (984 feet) above the floor of Lhasa Valley, but because this is Tibet, the building is at an altitude of 3 700 metres (12 139 feet).

Potala Palace in Lhasa, Tibet. The final resting place of the Dalai Lamas' mortal bodies, if not their immortal soul.

The White Palace was the residence of the Dalai Lama and was the first part of the complex to be finished. The Fifth Dalai Lama took up residency in 1649. Aside from living quarters, it contains a seminary, a monks assembly hall, two libraries and eight gold stupas—tombs for the Dalai Lama's old bodies.

The central portion of the structure is the Red Palace, so named because of the colour of its stucco facing. The building's use is entirely religious. Its main features are the Great West Hall, the First, Second and Third Galleries and the North, South, East and West Chapels. The West Chapel contains five golden stupas, of which the Central Stupa is the largest. It's built of sandalwood, rises to a height of 14.85 metres (49 feet) and is coated with 3 727 kilograms (8 200 pounds) of solid gold studded with 18 680 pearls and semi-precious stones. Within

it is the mummified body of the Fifth Dalai Lama.

West of the Great West Hall is the tomb containing the body of the current Dalai Lama's immediate previous incarnation. This stupa, built in 1933, is 14 metres (46 feet) high and contains 1 000 kilograms (2 200 pounds) of gold. Among the other devotional offerings within the tomb is a pagoda made from over 200 000 pearls.

On the north side of the Great West Hall is the Saint's Chapel. It houses a small, bejewelled statue of Avalokitesvara (Sanskrit 'The Lord Who Looks Down'), the Bodhisattva who 'embodies the compassion of all Buddhas' and who is incarnated in the Dalai Lama(s). The faithful consider the Chapel to be the holiest shrine in the Potala.

Together, the buildings contain some 10 000 shrines and 200 000 statues.

It's amazing that this much has survived. The Chinese takeover in 1959 was a cultural disaster. Possessed by communist fervour the Red Army destroyed over 100 000 documents, scriptures and works of art. Although still somewhat damaged, the Potala has undergone $30 million worth of restoration. In spite of its remote location, it's getting less remote every day and the authorities have been forced to enforce quotas of 6 000 visitors per day during the peak months of July to September.

The Palace of Versailles

Louis the XIV had had his eye on the sleepy little village of Versailles (population 60) for some time. His father, Louis XIII had built a hunting lodge there in 1624.

Louis XIII died in 1634, leaving his kingdom to a six-year-old. By the time he reached his majority and was crowned at the age of 15 in 1654, Louis XIV had observed enough aristocratic intrigue to last a lifetime.

The endless squabbles of the feudalistic nobility threatened to keep France in a state of perpetual high-level dissent in which nothing could really be done, and Louis realised over time that what France needed was a strong, centralised absolute monarchy.

To give expression to that vision, and as a practical measure to keep the nobility under constant observation and to some measure under control, Louis needed something more than his current residence at the Palais de Tuileries in Paris.

So Louis decided on an expansion of the Versailles hunting lodge. The first stage, from 1664 to 1668 created additions to the château that began as a pretext to accommodate 600 guests at a party called the *Fête de plaisirs de l'Ile enchantée.*

The commencement of the further additions tended to coincide with the signing of peace treaties. After the signing of the Treaty of Aix-la-Chappelle that ended France's war with Spain, the second stage, between 1669 and 1672, created the Château Neuf that enveloped the hunting lodge on the north, south and west.

Designed by Louis le Vau, this was to be the private residence of the King. Louis' apartments were in the upper north wing. His wife and family were in the south wing. The king's beloved, transvestite, homosexual brother, Philippe I, the Duc d'Orleans, known universally and affectionately simply as 'Monsieur', occupied the ground floor with his wife, Princess Henrietta Anne ('Minette'), daughter of the beheaded Charles I of England, and their family.

Stage three began with the signing of the Treaty of Nijmengen that ended France's war with the Dutch. Between 1678 and 1684 the western terrace of the Château Neuf was demolished in order to build the famous Hall of Mirrors.

Designed by Jules Hardouin Mansart, the 73 metre long, 10.5 metre wide and 12.3 metre high (239 x 34.5 x 40.3 feet) Galerie des Glaces' formal function was simply to

The Palace of Versailles—the grand vision of King Louis XIV, who ascended to the throne at the tender age of six.

connect the king's apartments to the chapel and queen's residence in the south wing, but the room was so grand, and life at Versailles so regimented that Louis' daily procession through the Galerie was an opportunity for the nobility to present themselves and ask for favours or private meetings, which was exactly the way Louis wanted it.

The hall also served as a venue for state occasions, such as the Siamese Embassy of 1685–6. The necessity that the hall be decorated with 357 expensive mirrors that could only be French-made, required that

Finance Minister Jean-Baptiste Colbert establish an entire industry to manufacture them.

Two years after the end of France's defeat in the War of the League of Augsburg in 1697, Louis commenced the final stage of the building of Versailles that was to occur during his lifetime. The years from 1699 to 1710 concentrated on the building of the Royal Chapel.

In all, the building of Versailles took 46 years, a considerable chunk of Louis' 72-year reign. The total cost of the building is difficult to calculate, but if you consider that just one feature, the silver balustrade, cost the modern equivalent of $2 million in materials alone, it's easy to imagine the building costing billions. That's how much the modern French government has spent to date in restoration and upkeep.

Uncomfortable Living

But for all the expense, the building was virtually uninhabitable by modern standards. It wasn't meant to be comfortable, it was meant to be grand, a showcase of French power and artistry. It was a place where the nobles could gather and Louis could pull strings, rather than let the aristocracy get annoying ideas of independence in their own chateaus.

Internal plumbing at Versailles was virtually non-existent. The building only had one bath and it had no internal toilets, meaning that the nobility had to urinate in corners of the sumptuous halls. To add to the discomfort, the rooms were so high and large that the building was impossible to heat.

Gardens Fit for a King

A huge pumping station, the Machine de Marly, was built in 1684 to provide water, not so much for the palace itself, but for the fountains in what would ultimately be an incredible 11 000 hectares (27 182 acres) of gardens

and grounds—the border of which was 43 kilometres (26.7 miles) long with 24 monumental gates to allow access. The inner park, to the west of the palace was called the 'Little Park', yet it alone covered 2 600 hectares (6 425 acres).

Versailles gardens needed almost as much water as the whole city of Paris did at the time. The Marly machine had 14 huge water wheels, each of which had a diameter of about 11 metres (36 feet) to drive 221 pumps that carried water 162 metres (177 yards) from the River Seine.

But the machine was so complicated that it was constantly breaking down and needed a permanent staff of 60 to keep it running. Later, after the completion of an aqueduct, it fell into disuse and no trace remains of it now.

The grounds also included botanic gardens, grottoes, a zoo, artificial lakes and canals. There was a large market garden for the huge kitchens catering for the exclusive needs of the royal table—Le Potager du Roi.

A stable and gate houses—Les Ecuries— could park and service more than a hundred carriages and the horses to pull them.

Several other smaller and more intimate palaces were built in the grounds, including Le Château de Marly and Le Grand Trianon to the north and northwest. There were also numerous buildings to the east of the palace for the aristocracy and government—les Hôtels Particuliers.

An Unhealthy Home

Today, Versailles has become a suburb of Paris. The chateau is still one of the great buildings of the world, but it was not a happy place even in Louis' lifetime. Neither the king nor his brother had happy marriages.

Almost all of Louis' legitimate children died in their childhood. Louis lived long enough to see the deaths of his brother's only surviving son (1683) from his first marriage, and then Monsieur himself in 1701.

In 1711 Louis lost his eldest and only surviving son Louis, Le Grand Dauphin, when the younger Louis was 49. Then Le Grand Dauphin's firstborn died of measles in 1712 and his five-year-old eldest surviving son a month later of the same disease.

Le Grand Dauphin's 28-year-old third born son Charles, Duc de Berry, died in 1714 from internal injuries resulting from a hunting accident. Since the second-born son, Philippe, had renounced his claim to the French throne to take the throne of Spain, the only surviving heir was Louis XIV's great-grandson.

The Sun King hurriedly legitimised two of his illegitimate sons just in case, but the five-year-old great-grandson would shortly become Louis XV and reign for 59 years, the first eight of which were under the regency of his uncle, Philippe II, the only surviving son of Monsieur's second marriage and after whom the city of New Orleans is named.

Louis XIV himself died of gangrene, a

few days before his 77th birthday. Perhaps many of these deaths could have been avoided if Versailles had had better plumbing and heating.

King Ludwig's Castles

While the Potala Palace in Tibet is serious and religious, and Versailles is magnificent and sumptuous, the visions of 'Mad King' Ludwig II were pure romance. Schloss Neuschwanstein—the New Swan Stone Castle—a confection in stone built on a promontory enjoying magnificent views, is the most photographed building in Germany. Since it opened in 1886 over 50 million people have visited it. It was expensive to build and remains expensive to restore, run and maintain, costing the German government about a million euros a year ($1.5 million). But it's one of the most incredible buildings ever built—the inspiration for Sleeping Beauty's Castle at both Walt Disney World and Tokyo Disneyland.

Was Ludwig mad as his nickname suggests, or was he just eccentric? A completely incurable romantic, Ludwig Friedrich Wilhelm II, King of Bavaria, was one of the few people with not only the money and power but also the imagination, to turn his architectural fantasies into stone and mortar realities. He wasn't close to his parents and far preferred the company of his deposed grandfather. He seems always to have been independently minded. An 1864 photograph of the 18-year-old Ludwig taken just after his accession, shows him with his arms crossed and his gaze turned up and sideways as if he's already jack of it all.

He was probably in a hurry to get on with his friendship with Richard Wagner, whom Ludwig had admired ever since he first heard Wagner's 1848 opera *Lohengrin*. Wagner may have been a crabby, anti-Semitic sex maniac and a bad credit risk, but Ludwig thought of him as a fellow visionary, and the young king found in Wagner a minstrel who could provide the musical score for his imagination.

Ludwig commissioned *Tristan and Isolde* from Wagner, got him out of debt and salvaged his career. But Wagner was his own worst enemy and his affair with Franz Liszt's daughter, who was 24 years his junior and the wife of his friend Hans von Bulow, didn't go down well with the bourgeoisie of Munich, and Ludwig distanced himself from the composer for a while. But the king was faithful to his muse and continued to fund Wagner's career while building his castles in the air, replete with Teutonic romance.

In 1870, Ludwig endorsed the creation of the German Empire, effectively demoting himself from an independent king to a vassal of the Prussian Kaiser. But this didn't affect his income and he didn't really care about ruling. He just wanted to build his castles. His ministers didn't like the way he spent his time, but the people loved him for them and for the employment they provided.

King Ludwig's most famous architectural confection and the model for the Sleeping Beauty Castle at Disneyland.

He was a champion of electrical power and his castles, including Neuschwanstein, were among the first buildings ever conceived with integral electricity. At the same time, his buildings required artisan skills that might have vanished if he hadn't provided jobs to men whose trades were dying out.

Swan Knight

New Schloss Hohenschwangau, ('Castle of the High Stone County') was Ludwig's first castle, named in homage to Ludwig's childhood home the old Hohenschwangau. It wouldn't be called Schloss Neuschwanstein, or 'New Swan Stone' until after Ludwig's death. Construction began on 5 September 1859. The architect was a theatrical set designer, Christian Jank, but the real architectural and engineering expertise came from Eduard Riedel and Georg Dollman.

The main sections are a gatehouse, a bower, a square-towered Knight's House and a citadel, the Palas, with two asymmetrical towers on its western end. Ludwig oversaw even the finest details as everything about the castle had to reflect the character of Lohengrin—the Swan Knight.

The castle isn't very big as palaces go, but its interior decoration is complex and detailed, and only 14 rooms were finished at the time of Ludwig's death. The castle remains unfinished, even today. It still features the foundations for a keep that was never built. The building was meant to look medieval, but the middle ages that it suggests bear no more resemblance to the real middle ages than the romanticised pastiche images in

Sir Walter Scott's novels or depictions in old Hollywood movies. Less 'authentic' still, the building even has modern venting and steam radiator heating.

Better than Versailles

While Neuschwanstein was under construction, Ludwig commissioned Jank, Dollman and Franz Seitz to build Herrenchiemsee. Unlike Neuschwanstein, Herrenchiemsee isn't a Romanesque medieval fantasy, but an homage to Versailles. Built between 1863 and 1886 for the comparatively modest modern equivalent of around $150 million, it too remains unfinished. Workers only completed 20 out of its 70 planned rooms but it, at least, has toilets.

Its Hall of Mirrors is even bigger than the original and its dining room has the largest porcelain chandelier in the world.

Built on an island in the Chiemsee Lake, you can only visit the castle by ferry, so it doesn't get as much attention as Neuschwanstein, but it's nevertheless an impressive building and the garden has stone dragons unlike anything that Versailles ever had. Tourists from France come to see the replica of The Ambassador's staircase, as the real one was demolished in 1752. Ludwig himself spent only 10 days at Herrenchiemsee in his entire life.

Linderhof

In contrast to the other two, Ludwig's Linderhof Palace is small and intimate but demonstrates the same richly ornate,

Herrenchiemsee Palace, Mad King Ludwig's homage to Versailles, in many ways improves on the original.

romantic interior design that Ludwig favoured. Perhaps because of its size, the Linderhof was the only castle that Ludwig lived to see completed, but what most people admire today is not so much the palace, but its gardens.

The gardens feature structures such as the Venus Grotto, Hunding's Hut and the Gurnemanz Hermitage. All look as they were intended to look, like baroque sets from Wagner's operas. There is also a Moorish Kiosk and a Moroccan House that Ludwig bought, transported to the Linderhof and redecorated. They offer a hint of what might have happened if Ludwig had lived longer and continued to indulge a taste for faux Orientalism.

An End to His Madness

Unfortunately, Ludwig didn't live long at all. In building his visions Ludwig spent all of his personal fortune and was a further 14 million marks in debt. Rather than curtail his spending and live in the real world, Ludwig wanted to borrow more money. His ministers conspired to put an end to this and in early 1886 commissioned a report on Ludwig's fitness to rule.

The report documented all sorts of bizarre behaviour—conversations with imaginary people, expensive tours to research architectural details and moonlight picnics with his groomsmen. And of course, the building projects. By June, four psychiatrists who had never met or examined the king, including the Chief of Munich Asylum, Bernhard von Gudden, signed the report diagnosing paranoia. This is a little rich since it's obvious that the king's feelings of persecution were by no means delusional. His political enemies moved in for the kill, and Ludwig ended up a prisoner at Neuschwanstein. On 12 June he was arrested and taken into forcible retirement to Castle Berg on the shore of Lake Starnberg, south of Munich.

With true irony, the kingship passed to his younger brother Otto, who wasn't eccentric at all but really mentally ill, so the real power went into the hands of Ludwig's uncle Luitpold, who had been behind the conspiracy to oust Ludwig in the first place.

The next day, 13 June at around 6pm, Ludwig suggested to Herr Doktor von Gudden that they take a stroll by the lake, alone. At 11.30pm searchers found the bodies of both men, drowned and floating near the shore. Ludwig was 40.

Years later, among the posthumous notes of the king's personal fisherman, Jakob Lidl, was a confession that Lidl had been hiding in a boat, waiting to help the king escape when a shot rang out and the king fell down dead. Lidl had kept his mouth shut because certain people promised that he and his family would be 'looked after'.

Luitpold served as regent and had Otto declared insane in 1875. Luitpold died in 1912 at the age of 91. His son Ludwig III then took over as regent until November 1913 then declared the regency at an end, but his reign as king ended in turn at the end of World War One. Otto died in 1916, Ludwig III in 1921.

Ludwig had his selfish side, and had stated that in the event of his death he wanted Neuschwanstein demolished. Luitpold refused to do it and within weeks of Ludwig's death visitors were taking tours through the palace. As a final irony, the castles whose expense had provided Luitpold with a pretext for deposing his nephew are now serious money earners that have repaid their investment many times over.

Ludwig left behind numerous plans for additions and new castles that were never built. The plans are now at the King Ludwig II Museum in Herrenchiemsee—a poignant reminder of what else might have been.

Hearst Castle

Before the Americans reinvented income tax in 1913, individuals were able to amass huge personal fortunes. One such fortune belonged to mining magnate George Hearst, and in 1865 he bought 40 000 acres of land near San Simeon, about halfway between Los Angeles and San Francisco. This holding later increased to 250 000 acres (101 171.4 hectares), making the land over nine times bigger than the grounds of Versailles at its greatest extent.

George's eldest son, William Randolf Hearst, was more interested in newspapers than in mines and managed to make a lot more money than his father. He liked the San Simeon Estate a lot and called it La Cuesta Encantada—The Enchanted Hill. In 1919 he started working on a huge house, the Casa Grande, a project that would end up having 165 rooms and a floor area of 5 634 square metres (60 645 square feet). Later he built other, smaller houses on the property, including the Casa del Mar, the Casa del Monte and the Casa del Sol, bringing the total combined floor area of the houses to 90 000 square feet (or just over 2 acres).

Designed by 47-year-old Julia Morgan, the building now called Hearst's Castle was an extraordinary exercise in conspicuous consumption. His endless tinkering meant that the building wouldn't be finished in his lifetime.

The Casa Grande was virtually a small, self-contained town—56 bedrooms, 61 bathrooms, 19 sitting rooms, one movie theatre and a library of 4 000 books. Landscaped gardens totalling 127 acres included indoor and outdoor swimming pools, tennis courts and an airfield as well as the world's largest private zoo. Julia Morgan also used her civil engineering skills to design a gravity-fed water system.

The castle housed a vast private collection of art. There are whole ceilings that Hearst imported in their entirety from Egypt and Europe to be reassembled and installed, and the facade resembles a Spanish Colonial cathedral.

In contrast to Orson Welles' send-up of Hearst in the movie *Citizen Kane*, the real Hearst Castle was no Xanadu. Hearst's mistress, Marion Davies, liked to party and the castle was THE place to be invited to in the 1920s and 30s, with guests such as Winston Churchill, the Marx Brothers, Charles Lindbergh and Calvin Coolidge.

When 88-year-old William Randolf Hearst died in 1951 he left the estate to the State of California on the condition that members of the Hearst family could use it whenever they liked, but since his granddaughter Patty's stint with the Simbionese Liberation Army in the 1970s, no Hearst has ever lived there.

Part 08

Attack &

Defence

From what we can tell, the earliest human settlements show no sign of any defensive fortifications at all. This may just be because our ancestors' earliest building materials were wood and mud and whatever they might have built hasn't survived, but equally likely is that they just didn't need them.

However, as time went on people grew more numerous while the area of available land stayed the same. Settled people would have started thinking that the other tribe's grass was greener than theirs and nomadic people would have started feeling that strangers were building villages on the sites of their ancestral hunting grounds. The result would have been fights for resources.

Attacks imply defence. One early defence strategy was to build an enclosure where everyone could run to if there was a raid. If you have a hill or other raised land you can build a citadel and exploit the advantages that height gives you—especially as being higher up allows you to see trouble coming from farther away.

If you're on a plain and you have the resources you can build a wall around the entire town—a very effective defence that was used for thousands of years. You supplement this with lookout towers and sentries watching the distances for danger.

Human beings don't just have to worry about attacks from other human beings. Nature itself often seems to have it in for people too. Even though nature is probably just doing her own thing with little regard to what people are up to, it nevertheless helps to treat nature as something that you need to defend yourself from, especially when you're dealing with the awesome power of the sea.

The great dangers to shipping include storms and currents. Of particular concern are hidden and submerged rocks and reefs that can wreck ships before crews even know that they're there. But even land isn't safe, rivers aren't the only source of floods, storm tides can wreak their own havoc. Here too the answer seems to be walls and towers and the more that you have to defend, the grander the vision you have to have.

Ancient Walls and Towers

The earliest walled city so far discovered is Jericho. Some archaeologists believe that people have continuously inhabited the town since around 9 000 BCE and they've found evidence of over 20 successive settlements on the sight. The walls of the town are famous for having fallen to Joshua and his people in around 1550 BCE.

The Walls of Babylon

Babylon was one of the great cities of the world. Built by Nebuchadnezzar around 600 BCE, the city's outer wall was actually comprised of several layered walls, 25 metres (82 feet) high with a combined thickness of 25 metres (82 feet) and 12 kilometres (7.5 miles) long. This supplemented a similarly constructed and equally thick 8.5 kilometres (5.3 mile) inner wall surrounded by an 80 metre (262 feet) wide moat constructed by Nebuchadnezzar's father, Nabopolassar. Together, the two walls would have enclosed an area close to the size of Manhattan.

Thirteen main gates pierced the wall, of which the most famous was the inner wall's eighth gate, the Ishtar Gate, glazed in brilliant blue tiles and decorated with shallow relief sculpture tiles of lions, dragons and bulls of extinct ancestral cattle—aurochs. Although long gone, enough of the ancient gate survived to reconstruct it in the Pergamon Museum in Berlin. The gate was actually divided into two sections. Only the smaller outer gate could fit into the museum and there are portions of the original further scattered around the world.

The Walls of Babylon were made of millions of baked earth bricks and were rightly thought to be impregnable. The Babylonians also felt that the Euphrates River was enough of a barrier for that part of the city that the wall didn't protect. Then in 539 BCE, Cyrus the Great, founder of the Persian Empire, finally took the city, but he had to divert the Euphrates River to do so. His army marched across the dry river bed.

Troy's Defences

Troy's walls, however, are famous for never having fallen and it took Odysseus' soldier-filled wooden horse to bring down the city. Some scholars, though, believe that the horse, as a symbol of the sea god Poseidon, was actually a metaphor for an earthquake, for which the Greeks also held Poseidon

Maiden Castle in Dorset, England. Not really a castle at all but an iron-age hill fort.

responsible. The evidence on the ground also supports this idea.

Archaeologists believe that one version of Troy—Troy VI—suffered such a devastation around 1300 BCE. But Troy VI is about a hundred years before Homer's Troy—Troy VII—so the two stories may have been confused.

Maiden Castle

The world of southern Britain in the 1st millennium BCE must have been a dangerous place. Archaeologists have found over a thousand iron-age hill forts in the region. This tells us that there were a lot of tribes fighting over bogs. The biggest of these forts is the one we call Maiden Castle, although it's not really a castle. It may have got its name from crusaders in the 1100s whose heads were still full of romantic legends from Muslim poets.

Maiden Castle is actually a hill fort comprising just over 17 hectares (42 acres) of hilltop surrounded by two or three deep trenches around its entire perimeter.

The trenches extend this border perimeter to up to 190 metres (623 feet), bringing the total area of the castle to over 45 hectares (111 acres). Whoever; these people were, they moved a lot of dirt—the rampart of earth around the inner perimeter was 14 metres (46 feet) high.

Maiden Castle was at its peak around 400 BCE and it may have protected as many as 150 families. It's difficult to gauge how effective this huge amount of work was at protecting them, but like anything else it wasn't foolproof. Human remains uncovered there show signs of considerable trauma and painful, bloody deaths.

The Pharos of
Alexandria

We don't know who first came up with the idea of lighthouses to serve as beacons to guide ships to safe passage, but the most renowned early example was the Pharos of Alexandria—one of the seven wonders or theamata ('must sees') of the ancient world, according to writers such as Herodotus, Callimachus of Cyrene and Antipater of Sidon.

After Alexander the Great conquered Egypt he rather inconveniently died young, so his ex-general, Ptolemy Sote,r became Satrap, or Governor, of the country in 323 BCE. But to all intents and purposes Ptolemy became ruler of Egypt, formally took the title of king in 305 BCE and started a dynasty that was to last until Cleopatra decided to end it all with an Egyptian cobra 12 or so generations later.

Ptolemy was the visionary behind the Pharos. The king simply wanted a landmark to tell sailors 'Alexandria is here', a necessity in a country that's basically flat and featureless, so ironically, the most famous of early lighthouses wasn't conceived as a lighthouse at all.

The actual work came down to a Greek architect and engineer, Sostratus of Cnidus. The island of Pharos is small and connected to the mainland by a causeway, the Heptastadion, which, as the Greek name implies, is seven stades long (1 470 metres or 0.9 miles).

The tower was built in three sections. The square base incorporated granite stones, some weighing as much as 75 tonnes. Rising as high as seven storeys, the tower mostly comprised white limestone in its main structure. The middle section was octagonal, and the upper section was round.

The Romans eventually placed a statue of Poseidon at the very top. Scholars disagree as to the final height. 135 metres (443 feet) seems a common estimate, but it could have been as high as 180 metres (590.5 feet). If it had been as high as that, it was taller than the Great Pyramid and therefore the tallest building in the world for over a thousand years. At the very least, it was the second tallest.

It finally became a lighthouse proper after the conclusive Roman conquest of Egypt in 30 BCE. People could see its light up to 56 kilometres (35 miles) away. In the Muslim era it became the model for the minarets from which muezzins call the faithful to prayer.

Construction of the tower began in 297 BCE and was completed in 283 BCE, shortly after the death of Ptolemy I in the first year of the reign of his son, Ptolemy Philadelphus. It had cost the state 800 talents. It's hard to estimate what this means in modern terms, but if you figure money on the basis of what kings paid

An early impression of the Pharos of Alexandria bears little resemblance to the reality revealed by scholarly research.

soldiers in those days then 800 talents represents either $240 million in silver or $2.4 billion in gold.

But it was money well spent. Molten lead helped to keep the masonry together and the tower was so well built that it was still standing in the 12th century. Severe earthquakes damaged it in the 1100s, irreparably in 1303 and it toppled altogether in 1323. In 1480, Sultan Qait Bey used the leftover stones in the building of Fort Qaitbey, which now stands on the site of Pharos.

If you dive around the island of Pharos you can still see the ruins of the building whose name still literally means 'lighthouse' in many languages.

A story states that Ptolemy didn't want Sostratus to put his own name on the building, but Sostratus cheated. First he carved an inscription in the stone of the base of the tower—'Sostratus [son] of Dexiphanes the Cnidian to saviour gods for the seafarers'. Then he covered the inscription with a layer of plaster in which he carved another inscription crediting Ptolemy with the work.

After some centuries the plaster wore away, revealing his original writing. Sostratus had the last laugh.

The Great Wall of China

The Wanli Changcheng ('long wall of 10 000 li') is frequently cited as being the only human-built structure so large that it can be seen from the moon. Unfortunately, this isn't even remotely true. Even from low earth orbit it's hard to see the wall because it's virtually the same colour as the surrounding earth and rocks from which it was built.

Nevertheless, the wall is big, or at least long. Even though the length of a 'li' changed somewhat over time, the current standard length at 500 metres makes the Great Wall actually about 13 000 li long, or to be a little more exact, roughly 6 700 kilometres (4 160 miles) or end to end around 6 400 kilometres (4 000 miles) if you allow for its kinks and curves.

The Great Wall predates the foundation of China as a single political unit. During the Warring States Period (c.450 BCE–221 BCE) the states of Qi, Yan and Zhao built extensive gravel and earth fortifications to protect their borders.

But when Qin Shi Huang Di unified the country and became the first legitimate historical emperor of the state of Qin (pronounced 'Chin' and from which we derive 'China'), he ordered the destruction of the state border defences, with the exception of those to the north. Then he ordered that the northern fortifications be connected up with new walls.

Using local materials, thousands of labourers worked for years to consolidate the Qin wall. We don't really know just how many people were involved and the true extent of the Qin wall because to date we haven't found any historical records. Large sections of the wall were made from rammed earth, which hasn't survived the centuries.

Later dynasties, with varying degrees of enthusiasm, rebuilt sections of the wall with varying degrees of success.

The Ming Wall

It wasn't until the Ming (or Dai Ming—'Great Bright') Dynasty came along in 1368 that things got really serious.

The Ming were native Han Chinese and had wrested power from the hands of the previous Mongol Yuan Dynasty, the descendants of Genghis Khan, so the Ming well knew the potential danger of the northern barbarians.

Consolidation of power took a long time for the Ming, and when another Mongol Tribe, the Oriats, defeated the Ming at the Battle of Tumu in 1449, the Ming decided that the situation was getting out of hand.

Continual warfare with the north was taking its toll on the empire, so the Jintai Emperor Zhu Qiyu decided to look at the feasibility of using walls as a defence again so that he could protect his 75 million subjects and get on with the serious business of making priceless porcelain for the delectation of future generations.

There was also something personal in it for Zhu, since after the Battle of Tumu, his brother Zhentong, the previous emperor, was being held captive by the Oriats and he didn't want the same thing to happen to him.

Facing the fact that the Mongols controlled Ordos Desert, and not feeling the loss of that territory too keenly, Zhu Qiyu ordered a massive rebuilding scheme creating a virtually continuous wall between the Jiayuguan Pass in the far west to the Shanhai Pass in the far east on the coast of the Bo Hai Sea.

At one point the wall is only about 200 kilometres north of Beijing and, not surprisingly, it was rebuilt to be especially strong around there. Instead of rammed earth, the Ming wall was constructed out of bricks and stone and the Great Wall that tourists flock to see today is the work of the Ming.

During the highpoint of the Ming Dynasty, over one million men guarded the wall. Add this to the 2 to 3 million men who are estimated to have died during the building and rebuilding of the wall over the centuries and it becomes obvious that the Great Wall was an expensive undertaking.

And it seemed to work, for a time.

Defence

Then, around the year 1600, those pesky northern barbarians were at it again, this time in the form of Manchu. In 1616 a Manchu leader called Nurhaci could see the writing on the wall for the decadent Ming and consolidated his position in his homeland in Manchuria, unifying the Manchu tribes under the short-lived Jin Dynasty. Nurhaci's son Huang Taiji then did a little more politicking, uniting even more northern tribes, including the Mongols, and established the Qing Dynasty in 1636 upon the conquest of the city of Shenyang, then called Mukden.

It's said that Huang Taiji was able to penetrate the Great Wall and its defences not because of a massive army, but because he bribed the guards. In effect, all the expense of building the Great Wall counted for nothing, once the gatekeepers had lost faith in the government and saw a good thing when it was coming. Huang Taiji died a few months short of Li Zhicheng's peasant revolt and capture of Beijing in 1644, but his five-year-old son, the Shunzhi Emperor, became the second Emperor of the Qing, and later the first true ruler of China under that Dynasty.

Shunzhi reigned only a short time but his son, the Kangxi Emperor, had the longest reign in Chinese history. The Ching held onto power until they too became too decadent and out of touch, or to put it in Chinese terms, lost the 'Mandate of Heaven', and the Kuomintang took over in 1912.

So while the Great Wall was historically, culturally and even psychologically significant, in the final analysis as an exercise in military

Only a small section of the Great Wall of China looks like the postcards. For the most part, little remains but a line of raised, rammed earth that continues for hundreds of kilometres.

defence, it was a spectacular failure. More than 25 million people died as a result of the Manchu invasion of China—by some estimates 10 per cent of the population of the country at the time.

A more effective defence were the Chinese people themselves. In the centuries before their fall, the non-royal Manchu population intermingled and interbred with the native Chinese so thoroughly that the Manchu culture is all but assimilated into the mainstream Han culture and the Manchu languages are all but extinct.

The Wall Today

As for the wall itself, much of it again lies in ruins, its structure either eroded or cannibalised by locals for the construction of houses. The Qing had no use for the wall, since they were the very barbarians the Ming had tried to keep out, although they did build walled fortifications at the other end of China to keep out the barbarians from the south.

Ironically, what finally did the Manchus in was their own insularity, and barbarians from the west, as the European nations successfully destabilised China with gunboat diplomacy and aggressive trading in opium.

The parts of the wall that tourists visit today are heavily restored sections close to Beijing that give people an idea of how the wall looked at its best, dotted at regular intervals with guard towers and barracks and signal towers at the crest of hills to afford maximum visibility. There were once thousands of such structures along its length.

There's no comprehensive survey of just how much of the wall still exists or what state it's in. Some sections are covered in graffiti, other parts vandalised, other parts are broken up and sold to tourists as souvenirs. Large sections, especially those made of mud or rammed earth, are disappearing very quickly under the ever-present pummelling of sandstorms.

Bell Rock
Lighthouse

The hidden rock reef of Inchcape lies in the North Sea just over 11 miles (18 kilometres) off the coast of the county of Angus (prior to 1928, known as Forfarshire) in Scotland. Its highest point was only above the waterline for a few hours at low tide each day. At high tide up to 6 metres of water covered it, so the reef was easy to miss and very easy to run aground on. Its danger to shipping was well known to anyone in the area for centuries.

In the 1300s an abbott from Forfarshire's largest town, Arbroath, felt moved to install a warning bell on it that would sound with the wind. One story tells that a Dutch pirate removed the bell, all the better to profit from wrecks, but it's more likely that the same very vicious North Sea storms that brought ships to their doom on the rock also made short work of the bell.

It only lasted one year, but the name endured, and Bell Rock continued to be the cause of numerous accidents—at least six every winter when the weather was at its worse.

The authorities in the form of the Northern Lighthouse Board didn't do much about it, even after one particularly nasty storm in 1799, when 70 ships were lost to Bell Rock. But the following year a 28-year-old Scottish civil engineer named Robert Stevenson presented the Board with a plan to build a lighthouse.

But when the Board saw his estimated cost of £42 000 (roughly $50 million) to build the lighthouse, they baulked. They said it couldn't be done, the tides were a killer and how much work could you do when you only had a couple of hours a day to do it in anyway?

So they shelved Stevenson's idea and concentrated on building lighthouses in less challenging locations.

Then on 26 December the *HMS York*, a 64-gun third-rate ship of the Royal Navy under the command of Captain Henry Mitford, began a routine patrol of the North Sea. In January the *York* struck Bell Rock during a storm and sank. All 491 men and boys aboard were lost. The public demanded that the authorities do something. It took eighteen months before Parliament passed an act authorising and funding the Bell Rock Lighthouse in July 1806.

The Board didn't trust the project to a man who was still only 34, so the Board appointed the respected canal builder John Rennie as Chief Engineer and gave Stevenson the title of Assistant Engineer. But Rennie's role was to remain marginal. Bell Lighthouse would be the achievement of Robert Stevenson, and the men working under him.

Building a Beacon

Stevenson hired 60 workers at the rate of £1 per week ($1 500). It was great money, but required skilled or dangerous work, or both.

Most of the construction was on land. Stevenson planned the precision cut of every stone, each weighing one tonne of Aberdeen granite. Each stone took months to cut.

On 17 August 1807, when the weather was clement enough to make on-site work on the lighthouse possible, Stevenson and his work crew set out. They moored their ship one mile away from the rock and began work on the foundations of the lighthouse and on a temporary beacon house that would shelter the workers and protect them if they couldn't get to the ship—which is just what happened.

On 2 September the work crew lost a boat and since swimming was out of the question and the only boat they had would have floundered from overload, the crew were in danger of their lives. They would have drowned if an early supply boat hadn't shown up in time. Needless to say, this didn't inspire confidence in Stevenson's leadership, but the work recommenced anyway, and by 6 October the crew had only partially completed the lighthouse foundation pit and the leg array of the beacon house.

Two things made the work even slower. The first was physical. Stevenson couldn't use gunpowder to blast away extraneous rock for fear of damaging the foundation structure. The second was religious. Stevenson's men refused to work on the Sabbath; a decision that Stevenson, a self-taught and very religious man, struggled with himself.

In the off season on the mainland, Stevenson continued to supervise the stonecutting and refining the rotating array of six reflectors of 24 oil powered lanterns. When finished, the beacon would flash in alternating red/white flashes and be seen for miles.

The 1808 season saw only 80 work hours actually done on the rock, but in that time the work crew laid the first three stone courses of the lighthouse and completed the beacon house, providing enough accommodation for 15 men.

The 1809 season had an early and particularly bad winter, further complicated by a visit from John Rennie. To keep control of the project Stevenson embarked on an exhaustive program of misdirection. He wrote letter after letter to Rennie asking his advice on every aspect of the project. Rennie dutifully replied with comprehensive answers, all of which

Stevenson ignored. This tactic seems to have worked as Rennie continued to feel in charge, while Stevenson got his own way and avoided any further visits.

During this season, worker Michael Wishardt broke his leg. This effectively made Wishardt virtually unemployable in an age when most men who worked with their hands were illiterate, and when there was no such thing as workers compensation, comprehensive pensions or social security. Stevenson, nevertheless, promised to do what he could for him. And even though the third season ended early on 22 August, by now half of the lighthouse was complete.

In January 1810 three of Stevenson's children died of whooping cough. Even in his grief, the lighthouse builder continued with his project.

Even before the start of the fourth and last season the lighthouse was becoming a tourist attraction. Work recommenced on 7 May with the work crew now labouring on the Sabbath to complete the project.

But tragedy struck again when worker Charles Henderson was swept out to sea during a violent, seven-hour storm. His body would never be recovered, and the work crew considered that maybe this was God's punishment to them for not keeping His Holy Day. And yet the work went on.

Now that the lighthouse was almost finished, it provided enough protection to allow a longer work day and with the 90th and last course laid, the inner structure of the lighthouse and the lighting array could be installed. By 27 December nearly everything was in place. It comprised 2 500 stones, all of them carted to the docks by the same horse.

The Lamp is Lit

On 1 February the lanterns were finally lit. Stevenson would quote the following words from Exodus:

'And the Lord went before them by day in a pillar of cloud to lead them the way, and by night in a pillar of fire, to give them light'

Being a man of his word, Stevenson kept his promise to Michael Wishardt and made him one of the first keepers of the Bell Rock Lighthouse.

Stevenson went to build another 14 lighthouses. Three of his sons, Alan, David and Thomas; two grandsons, David Alan and Charles Alexander; and one great-grandson, Alan, son of Charles, would continue the family business. Between them they would design and build well over a hundred lighthouses. The dynasty of Lighthouse Stevensons ended with the death of Alan in 1971.

Of them all, Thomas was the most brilliant and talented. The writer Robert Louis Stevenson, author of *Treasure Island* and *The Strange Case of Dr Jekyll and Mr Hyde* was Thomas' son. In 1880, Robert Louis wrote that 'Whenever I smell salt water, I know that I am not far from one of the works of my ancestors...When the lights come out at sundown along the shores of Scotland, I am proud to think they burn more brightly for the genius of my father!'

Today, the 33 metre (100 feet) Bell Rock Lighthouse is the world's oldest offshore lighthouse and continues to save lives in the North Sea.

North Sea Protection
Works

Although the lowest city in the Netherlands lies only 7 metres (23 feet) below sea level, it's still below sea level. Half the country is only 1 metre above sea level and one eighth lies below sea level.

The Dutch have been fighting back the sea for centuries and since the 13th century, have used a combination of dykes—water-retaining walls—and windmills to pump water away. These methods have resulted in the creation of polders, isolated self-contained units of land. Some polders are quite extensive; the Noordoostpolder covers an area of 595.41 square kilometres (300 square miles).

On the night of 31 January/1 February 1953, a combination of high spring tide and windstorm caused a huge storm tide that raised the level of the North Sea to 5.6 metres (18.4 feet) above normal. The resulting flood covered 1 365 square kilometres (527 square miles) of the Netherlands, including 9 per cent of all Dutch farmland, and forced the emergency evacuation of 70 000. It killed 1 835 people, 30 000 farm animals and damaged 47 300 buildings—10 000 totally destroyed.

Measures to protect

In response to the flood, the Dutch began a decades-long project to protect their country with more comprehensive measures. The Deltaworks involved blocking or flood-protecting three major estuaries—the Grevelingen, the Haringvliet and the Oosterschelde. Between 1953 and 1997 the Dutch also built or reinforced 300 structures integrated into 16 500 kilometres (10 500 miles) of dykes. Arguably the most impressive single construction is the 9 kilometre (5.6 mile) long Oosterscheldekering (Eastern Schelde Barrier). Four ships had to be designed and built especially to create this barrier, which took 10 years to build.

For over half its length it's a closed dam but a 4 kilometre (2.5 mile) stretch comprises 65 concrete pillars, each between 35 and 37.5 metres (115 and 123 feet) high and weighing 18 000 tonnes a piece. These pillars frame huge, 42-metre (138-feet) wide steel doors designed to shut in the event of a predicted storm surge, every time water levels are predicted to rise over 3 metres (10 feet).

Since the barrier's official opening on 4 October 1986 the Dutch have closed the doors 24 times. Early warnings are vital as the doors take an hour to reach their fully closed position.

The barrier costs $26.66 million a year to operate—cheap, when you consider the cost to the Dutch of not operating it. Engineers estimate that the dam will last 200 years.

The Pentagon

In an era of aerial warfare, walls and towers have become obsolete, so the United States constructed a unique building to house their Department of Defense headquarters. 'The Pentagon' refers to the building itself, and the institution it houses.

Located in Arlington, Virginia, the Pentagon's gross floor area of 616 540 square metres (152.35 acres) and volume of 2.2 million cubic metres (2.8 million cubic yards) makes it one of the world's largest office buildings. The central plaza alone comprises 2 hectares (5 acres), while the entire building has a footprint of 12 hectares (29 acres).

Brehon's brainchild

The Pentagon was General Brehon Somervell's grand vision, while Colonel Leslie Groves and Major Clarence Renshaw oversaw the building project and the Pentagon was built in response to what seemed to be an unavoidable increase in militarisation.

Groundbreaking began on 11 September 1941 and the dedication ceremony was 16 months later on 15 January 1943.

George Bergstrom made the design a pentagon to best use the original intended site. President Roosevelt wanted to relocate the building but he liked the shape so much that he kept it even after the new location was chosen.

Some 680 000 tonnes of sand was dredged from the Potomac to build the Pentagon. Forty-eight kilometres (30 miles) of access highways and 35 bridges and overpasses were built to service it. The final price tag was $83 million (which at a modern value of around $3 billion is quite reasonable for what the Defence Department got).

The Pentagon's features

• Five above-ground floors reaching a height of 24 metres (77 feet) and 2 basement levels serviced by 131 stairways, 19 escalators, 13 elevators.

• Five co-centric main corridors per floor named 'A' to 'E' from the centre out. The basement also has 'F' and 'G' corridors for a total of 28.2 kilometres (17 miles) of corridors.

• Outer walls of buildings are 281 metres (921 feet) long.

• Employs 26 000 people—23 000 of them military or civilian support. They work under 16 250 light fixtures and they have the use of 691 drinking fountains but only 284 rest rooms. They make 200 000 telephone calls every day that travel along 160 000 kilometres (100 000 miles of cable)

• A shopping mall—you can arrive there at its own train station if you don't want to park in the 107 hectares (264 acres) of parking lots servicing 8 700 vehicles.

• The Defense Post Office handles 1.2 million articles sent to the Pentagon's six zip codes every month.

Part 09

Worship & Entertainment

T he human imagination does not live by the practical alone. Securing a food supply, government, trade and military protection only keeps the body together, but the human soul cries out for more, it always longs to play and to achieve something greater than mere survival and just because you've reached for heaven, doesn't mean that you can stop giving the gods their due. If there's one thing the gods don't like, it's a 'What have you done for me lately?' attitude.

In the modern world, games and sports are secular affairs. The worlds of gaming fields, the theatre and of the church are quite separate. But for much of human history, sports, games and artistic endeavours were dedicated to the glory of the gods, and later, to God. Religion has inspired some of the grandest sporting and cultural visions of all and many observe that even today there's something religious about the dedication that people give to sports and the arts even when their practitioners and spectators aren't consciously or overtly dedicating their activities to the glory of a deity. Nevertheless, the visions that the mixture of religion, art and games create are some of the grandest of all. Why else would people invest so much in something that is fundamentally a feeling?

0193

Ancient Greek Dedications

After the Persian burning of Athens in 480 BCE that Alexander the Great would later avenge with the burning of Persepolis, it took the Athenians and their economy about 30 years to recover. When they did, the Athenian statesman Pericles decided that Athens really needed something to express her glory, so he initiated a building program.

The Parthenon

The highpoint of Pericles' passion was the Parthenon, a combination of temple and treasury dedicated to the goddess Athena. Building the Parthenon was a tremendous commitment for the Athenians.

The design, by the architects Callicrates and Ictinos, required a virtually all-marble building 30.88 x 69.5 metres (101 x 228 feet) at its base. The foundation alone would need 8 000 x 2 tonne paving stones, a further 130 x 5 tonne building stones and 4 corner stones each weighing 7 tonnes.

Above the three-tiered foundation would rise an external border of 46 columns (8 x 17) to support a closed roof. Each column was 10.43 metres (34.22 feet) high and consisted of 11 precision-cut drums each weighing 5 to 10 tonnes, crowned with an 8- to 9-tonne Doric capital. The roof would require 8 480 marble tiles, each weighing 20 to 50 kilograms (44 to 110 pounds) a piece.

The Parthenon was designed to curve subtly to compensate for distortions of perspective, giving the illusion of straightness while not in fact being straight at all. The result was that there was practically nothing mass-produced about the Parthenon. Each piece of the upper building had to be individually created to fit a predetermined position within the edifice after workers had carried the stone all the way up to the top of the Acropolis from Mount Pentelicon, 13 kilometres (8 miles) away.

To carry an average-sized column drum would have taken a full day and required a team of 33 mules to pull a specially built strong wagon and a team of a minimum of 28 men to put just one into position. The project in total used over 230 000 tonnes of stone and took nine years (447–438 BCE) to build. Allowing for religious holidays and other downtime this meant that almost 100 tonnes of stone were quarried, transported, finished and positioned every day.

The external sculptures, including the famous Parthenon marbles (previously known as the Elgin marbles), and the 10 metre high ivory statue of Athena within the Parthenon, took master sculpture Pheidias and his artists six years to carve and colour.

In the end the Parthenon was a masterpiece, but it virtually bankrupted the state. Athens

Sitting atop the Acropolis, even in ruin, the Parthenon still commands attention.

soon fell into the mire of the disastrous Peloponnesian war against Sparta. Then in a particularly bad move in 430 BCE Pericles ordered the citizenry from the surrounding countryside within the walls of Athens for their own protection. The result was a concentration of people so dense that plague soon spread, decimating the population. Pericles was himself a victim.

The Parthenon remained in reasonably good condition as a temple to Athena for almost a thousand years. At some point in the 400s Pheidias' looters took the statue of the goddess to Constantinople where it was eventually destroyed, possibly during the sacking of the city in 1204.

The Parthenon was later a Christian Church dedicated to Mary—the Church of the Parthenos Maria—for about 250 years before Athens itself fell to the Ottoman Turks in 1456. Then it became a mosque. When the Venetians attacked Athens in 1687, the Turks decided to use the Parthenon as a gunpowder magazine. On 26 September Venetian soldiers fired a mortar from the nearby Hill of Philopappus and it hit the Parthenon, exploding the gunpowder magazine inside. A building that had remained in good condition for almost two thousand years narrowly escaped complete destruction. But the damage was still extensive and the Parthenon today is but a shadow of what it once was. It's now undergoing extensive restoration, but pollution in the modern city of Athens continues to eat away at the structure and its long-term survival is uncertain.

If you want an idea of what the Parthenon was like in its prime, you have to go to Nashville, Tennessee. A full-size, full-colour replica of

the Parthenon was built there as part of the Tennessee Centennial Exposition of 1897. It even houses a full-size, full-colour replica of Pheidias' statue of Athena.

The Statue of Zeus

While Pericles and his fellow Athenians were dying, Pheidias and his team had moved to Olympia in the north. The town had hosted the religious dedication of the Olympic Games since 776 BCE. The Games were so sacred that the Greeks even stopped their wars to hold them, in stark contrast to the modern world where the games stop on account of war.

Pheidias and his craftsmen had been commissioned to build another ivory-clad statue. The project took two years, but the result was a wonder of the world—a 13 metre (43 foot) high seated figure of Zeus.

Artisans made ivory sheathes by softening elephant tusks by boiling them in water or soaking them in vinegar, before carefully peeling away the ivory veneer. Pheidias then sheathed, shaped and carved the ivory around a core of 780 cubic metres (27,545 cubic feet) of wood. Pheidias used gold for Zeus' hair, laurel wreath, robes and sandals. Before the statue a pool of olive oil reflected the image to add to the effect of wonder and splendour.

The statue of Zeus lasted for centuries at its site. Emperor Caligula wanted it so much that he even tried to have it moved to Rome, but failed. In 391 CE the statue was moved to Constantinople, only to perish in a fire in 462. No-one ever made a copy of the statue and all we have are descriptions.

The Greek Government
continues to spend millions
restoring the Parthenon but
Athens' polluted air continues
to eat away at the limestone
from which it is made.

Ancient Roman Sports
Arenas

The Romans, whatever their faults, were good at two things: feeding their people and entertaining them. The expression 'bread and circuses' as a shorthand way of saying 'keep the folk happy' came directly from the Roman model of dealing with the reality that military dictatorships need more than just the military to hold together a civilisation for over a thousand years.

The Romans knew how to put on a good show, and in the ancient world the very best shows involved a lot of killing, or at the very least a lot of blood.

When you think of Roman mass entertainment, you think gladiators fighting to the death and slaughtering prisoners or political dissidents like Christians.

But in terms of sheer numbers, the most long-suffering victims of the Roman need for blood were animals. Vast numbers of exotic animals from the farthest reaches of the empire and beyond died in Roman arenas.

Two thousand years after the events it's impossible to calculate the true cost of this ravenous consumption, but it's clear that the industry created to satisfy the bloodlust of the Roman citizenry would have decimated wildlife populations and destroyed ecosystems. Some historians even argue that this endless desire to finance these expensive

undertakings was a contributing factor in the final collapse of the empire.

Nevertheless, the people of the time must have thought spilling blood was great fun and they didn't mind creating suitable buildings for it. Two such grand visions were built within easy walking distance of each other in Rome.

Circus Maximus

The site of the Circus Maximus had been in use as a sporting field since the days of the Etruscans. But it was the inheritors of Etruscan culture, the Romans, who really liked to party and Julius Caesar constructed what was arguably the world's most spectacular racing track there around 50 BCE.

At 621 metres (2 037 feet) long and 118 metres (387 feet) wide, the Circus could accommodate around 270 000 seated spectators and possibly an equal number standing. The Melbourne Cup could be run there with the horses only having to make just over one and a half laps. The Kentucky Derby would take only a single lap. Roman chariot races, the bread and butter of the circus, typically went for 6.5 kilometres (4 miles). The best idea you're likely to get of these great races is by watching the brilliant and well researched 11-minute chariot racing scene in William Wyler's epic masterpiece *Ben Hur*

(1953). Compared to modern horse racing, chariot races were not very genteel. The risk of mutilation and death was very real.

Hardly anything of the Circus remains today.

The Colosseum

The Colosseum or the Flavian Ampitheatre, as it was originally known, is in much better condition than the Circus Maximus, but it's still a ruin. Emperor Vespasian constructed it between 70 and 72 on part of the grounds of Nero's old Domus Aurea.

The Colosseum was designed to entertain 50 000 spectators with gladiatorial spectacles, which were often held to celebrate a military victory and always dedicated to one Roman god or another. Religion, blood, sacrifice, entertainment; it was all one and the same in the ancient world.

Entry to these games was usually free, because you weren't really rich and important in Rome until you could afford to spend lavishly to fund a day of games or three and dedicate them to the glory of an ancestor, an emperor or a god, which was frequently the same thing. But inevitably it was the emperors themselves who had the power and access to public money or the spoils of war to provide the best shows.

In 107 CE Trajan held games there to celebrate his conquests in Dacia. Those games went on for 123 days and involved the participation of 10 000 gladiators and the slaughter of 11 000 animals.

Earlier amphitheatres were built into hillsides, but the Colosseum is an entirely artificial, freestanding structure. It's an ellipse, 189 metres (615 feet) long and 156 metres (510 feet) wide, with an outer wall 48 metres (157 feet) high. Most of the exterior wall is gone now, leaving us with a view of the interior wall the Romans would have never seen. The central arena is more of an oval, 87.5 metres (287 feet) x 55 metres (180 feet). Surrounded by a 4.6 metre high (15 feet) wall; this central arena could be flooded with water in order to provide a venue for holding mock sea battles. At the inaugural games in 80 CE, Titus held an exhibition of trained swimming horses and bulls.

The wooden floor of the arena has long since collapsed, and what we can see today are the chambers of the hypogeum—holding pens for animals and waiting areas for gladiators. Eighty shafts from the hypogeum provided instant access to arena.

In all, archaeologists currently estimate that the Romans used 100 000 cubic metres (131 000 cubic yards) of travertine sedimentary rock from—deposits in Tivoli—for the Flavian Amphitheatre.

In the centuries since its heyday, the Colosseum has suffered the effects of earthquakes and the predation of stone robbers to leave us with the remnant we see today. For an idea of how the building appeared in its prime, watch its digital recreation as seen in Ridley Scott's 2000 epic, *Gladiator*.

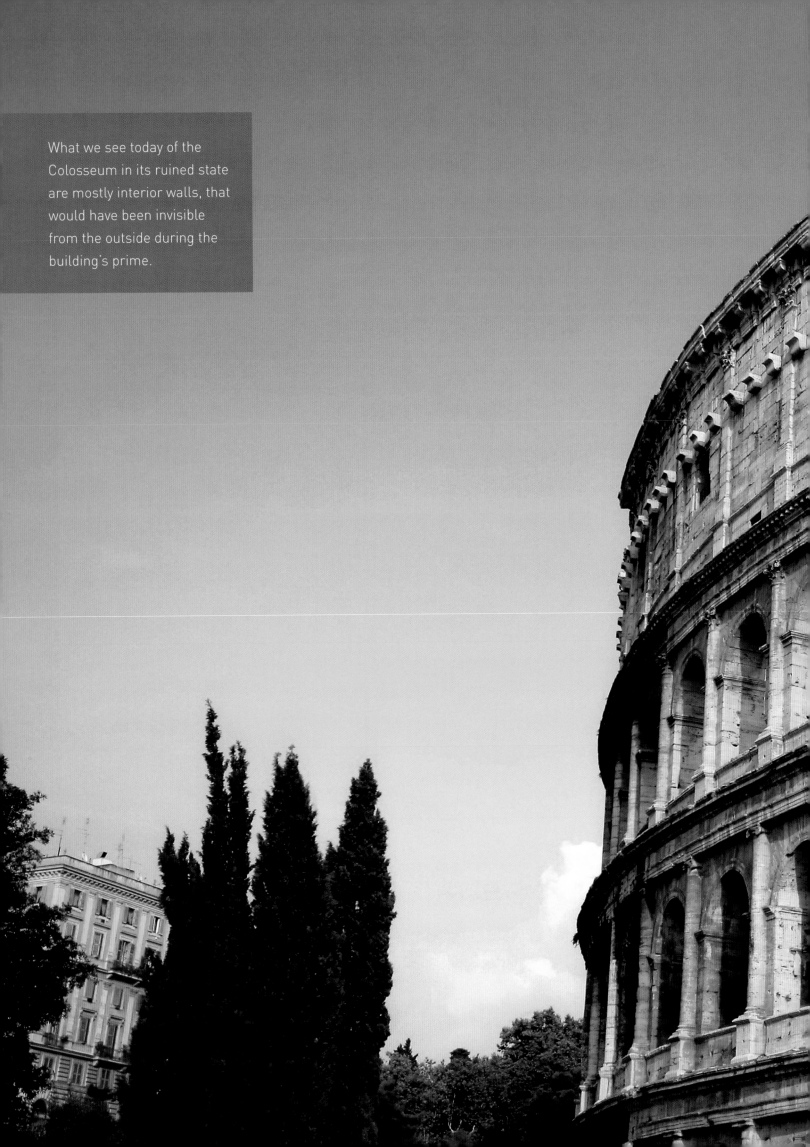

What we see today of the Colosseum in its ruined state are mostly interior walls, that would have been invisible from the outside during the building's prime.

The Moais of
Rapa Nui

They look as enigmatic as ever, but their gaze is inland, watching the inhabitants like stern parents, not looking outwards like guardians or sentinels. A fully restored Moai shows large eyes of white coral and a pukao topknot of red scoria, contributing to the eeriness. Theirs is a small realm, a triangular island called Rapa Nui, or Easter Island, only 22 kilometres (13.75 miles) at its longest and 16 kilometres (10 miles) at its broadest, with a surface area of only 163.6 square kilometres (63.1 square miles).

There are around a thousand massive statues on Rapa Nui. They were all carved from tuff, compacted volcanic ash, using basalt stone axes. Tuff starts out relatively soft and hardens on exposure to the elements, so it's a relatively easy material to work with.

The Moai all came from the same quarry in the crater of the extinct volcano that gave birth to the island. They come in a variety of shapes and sizes and range mostly from 2 to 10 metres tall (6.5—33 feet) although the most massive weighs 270 tonnes, and would have been 20 metres (66 feet) high if it had ever stood up. It and 395 others are still in the crater, surrounded by thousands of basalt axes, all of them incomplete, as are most of the other Moai, scattered at various points of the island.

At least this gives us an excellent idea of how they looked at various stages of carving, and of the 6 kilometres (3.75 miles) that teams of at least 25 men had to drag them to reach their final destination. But it's an unfinished project. In fact, only 125 of the statues were ever erected on their ahu, their ceremonial platforms, of which there are only 300.

Everything about Rapa Nui speaks of calamity. We don't even know the island's original name as it was only called Rapa Nui by its later inhabitants. When Dutch explorer Jacob Roggeveen and his crew first encountered Rapa Nui on Easter Sunday 1722 the statues that the islanders had put in place were all standing. Fifty years later, when Captain James Cook visited, many had been toppled. Those Moai that didn't land on their faces had their eyes obliterated, ritually murdering them.

It seems that whatever happened on Rapa Nui, the Moai project caused so much deforestation that every species of tree on the island became extinct. The islanders found that there was no more wood left to build fishing boats. Starvation followed and a cave on the island is still called Anai Kai Tengata— the place where men are eaten. Religious warfare seems to have occurred too, with the emergence of Makemake, the birdman god, supplanting the older gods.

In the absence of written records and with the almost complete annihilation of the native population and the destruction of their oral history, we know almost nothing about the Moais of Rapa Nui.

The islanders had painted themselves into a corner of unsustainability, and without the wood to build boats they couldn't even leave. They were prisoners on the most isolated inhabited island on earth, 3 747 kilometres (2 340 miles) from the coast of South America. You could practically fit the continent of Australia between the two.

Then, from December 1862, Peruvian slave traders kidnapped or killed half the population of the island. When a few made it back, they brought smallpox to the 1 500 who had stayed behind. Then in 1867, Christian missionary Eugene Eyraud brought tuberculosis, which killed 300 of the 1 200 islanders who were left. Further raids from slave trader Jean-Baptiste Dutrou-Bornier and missionary

evacuation of the islanders to Tahiti, had left only 111 people on Rapa Nui by 1876.

Today's 3 800 inhabitants are descended from people who lost practically all of their culture and we have only speculation and half remembered folklore to piece together the story of a grand vision that went disastrously wrong.

Cathedrals of
Europe

By any standard the cathedrals of Europe are monumental expressions of dedication to grand visions. Between 1050 and 1350 in France alone 500 large churches and 1 000 parish churches were built. There was a house of God for every 200 people, and during the 1200s and 1300s the French quarried more stone than had been used for all the buildings of Ancient Egypt put together.

Cathedrals weren't just houses of worship, they were the centre of the spiritual and the material lives of the community. They provided a livelihood for the priests and religious instruction in stone and glass for the illiterate as well as glimpses of the glories of heaven.

The entire economy of a city was centred on the cathedral and some became wealthy from donations from pilgrims flocking to the relics of saints in the hopes of a cure for their diseases, good marriages for their daughters or a 'get out of hell free' card if their lives were sinful.

The wealth of the cathedral would trickle up to the Church, sideways to the artisans who were employed in their construction and down to the innkeepers who would provide for the bodily needs of the pilgrims and souvenir sellers who would furnish them with proof that they'd actually been there.

With all this money and spirituality at stake, whole generations of artisans would dedicate their lives to the construction of these great churches.

Salisbury Cathedral

Cathedral building was a long and complicated process, even the fastest building times were far too long by modern standards. The main body of Salisbury Cathedral in south-west England, for example, was built between 1220 and 1258, a breakneck speed for 38 years, which nevertheless represented two generations of work. Its spire wasn't completed until 1320.

The cathedral was the project of Bishop Richard Poore who, in spite of his name, was very rich and donated the land upon which the building stands. There's a legend that the bishop shot an arrow into the air deciding that the faithful would build where the arrow fell. The arrow struck a deer, who wandered, and the cathedral was built on the spot where the deer died. All the canons and vicars of the south-west of England donated money to the project and artisans literally gave their entire working lives to it. The cathedral still has Britain's largest cloister and its 123-metre (404-feet) spire is still the tallest in the United Kingdom. It also houses the world's oldest working clock, dating from 1386.

The interior of Salisbury
Cathedral, England—
the grand vision of the
very rich Bishop
Richard Poore.

Notre Dame de Paris

Notre Dame Cathedral, built on the eastern half of the Ile de la Cité in Paris, represents another highpoint in Gothic architecture. Its twin, square, 63-metre high towers and thousands of carvings took almost 200 years to build (1160–1345). It was one of the first buildings to use the exterior arches, known as flying buttresses, to support the structure while reducing weight.

The legend of Notre Dame begins with the vision of Bishop Maurice de Sully, who sketched the image of the building in the dirt outside the original Church of Paris. The church, and several houses, were demolished to clear the site for the future cathedral. The building became one of the most important in France—the French kings were crowned there. Mary I of Scotland was married to François II there in 1558. Napoleon was crowned emperor there in 1804 and Joan of Arc was canonised there in 1920—489 years after her death. The cathedral wasn't really completed until the 1700s when the first organ worthy of the building was completed. Today's Grandes Orgues contains 7 800 pipes.

For all its historical importance, by the early 1800s the cathedral was in such a state of ruin that the city planners of Paris considered tearing it down. It was only after Victor Hugo penned *The Hunchback of Notre Dame*, especially to remind the world of cathedral, that public sentiment initiated a fund raiser that paid for the building's restoration in 1845.

Chatres Cathedral

Arguably the most beautiful cathedral in the world is Chartres, in the north-west of France. Begun in 1145, the unusual asymmetry of the 10 875-square metre (117 058-square foot) cathedral is the result of another long building effort. The main building was dedicated on 24 October 1260, but while the southern, 105-metre high south-west gothic tower dates to around this time, the 113-metre (377 feet) north-west tower wasn't finished until the 1500s.

The stonework is as intricate and detailed as you'd find in any great building of its type, and there's the famous inlaid labyrinth in the cathedral's floor. But it's the 2 500 square metres (26 900 square feet) of windows and the kaleidoscope of blue and red light that are Chatre's most famous feature.

Of the 176 stained glass windows in the building at present, 152 date from the medieval period. Three large rose windows dominate—The Last Judgement on the west front, The Glorification of the Virgin on the north transept and the Glorification of Christ on the south transept.

Notre Dame from the rear, arguably a more interesting perspective from an engineering point of view because from here observers can see the spectacular flying buttresses that help keep the walls up.

Cologne Cathedral

The prize for the longest building and perhaps the grandest vision of all goes to the Germans for Cologne Cathedral, whose towers are 157 metres (515 feet) tall. Rainald of Dassel, Archbishop of Cologne, first acquired the relics of the Three Kings in 1164, but workers wouldn't lay the foundation stone for the cathedral that would house them until 15 August 1248.

The Eastern arm was consecrated in 1322 but by 1473 the south tower had only been built up to the belfry level when workers installed the bell anyway. Work then stopped. After the Protestant Reformation began in 1517, people became distracted by centuries of warfare between the various sects of Christianity. Then in the middle of the 1800s a wave of nostalgia swept over what was now Prussia, and in an orgy of civic pride a movement started up and created the Zentral-Dombauvereinzu Koln von 1842—the Central Cathedral Building Society of 1842 or ZDV for short.

Together, the impassioned citizens of Cologne managed to raise two-thirds of the billion dollars necessary to complete the Cathedral, with the Prussian Government coughing up the other third. As if this wasn't enough, the ZDV then decided that everyone needed to get a clear view of the Cathedral, so they decided to raise another billion dollars to buy up all the buildings around the Cathedral expressly for the purpose of demolishing them. To do this, they created the Dombaulotterie, the Cathedral lottery that still provides a lot of the $3.5 million a year that the ZDV needs to keep the cathedral looking its best.

With all this money and enthusiasm the completion of the cathedral took less than 40 years and it was dedicated in 1880—632 years after the laying of the first stone. Protestants had finished what Catholics had started.

Even World War Two couldn't destroy the Cathedral. While allied bombs destroyed all the other buildings around it the great church stood immune. It made a convenient landmark from which pilots could calculate their position in order to bomb other German cities.

The Sistine Chapel

Michelangelo hadn't wanted to do it. He was more a sculptor than a painter (although Leonardo da Vinci wasn't very impressed with either of his skills) and the canvas was large, 40.5 metres x 14 metres (133 x 46 feet), irregular and in a really awkward position. But Pope Julius II liked his work and although Michelangelo was already working on his famous statue of Moses in the Pope's family tomb in San Pietro in Vincoli, the Pontiff nevertheless felt that the artist could spread himself a little thinner.

Contrary to popular belief, Michelangelo didn't spend four years (1508–1512) lying on his back to realise his visions from the Bible on the ceiling of the Sistine Chapel in Rome. But he stood on scaffolding trying to avoid paint getting into his eyes and getting a sore neck while painting as fast as he could, not only to avoid physiotherapy, but to apply the paint to plaster before it dried, so that it would last. Of course, drying plaster becomes hot, and gives off fumes—just to add to the discomfort.

Pope Julius lived just long enough to appreciate the ceiling, dying in 1513. Then he ended up in the Vatican, next to his uncle, Pope Sixtus IV in the floor in front of the monument to Pope Clement X.

Michelangelo wouldn't get around to finishing Moses until 1515 and it stayed in San Pietro. The tomb project, which was to have been so grand, was scaled down significantly.

Thirty years after the ceiling, Michelangelo began work on the Last Judgment that covers the entire eastern wall of the chapel, behind the altar. It took him from 1534 to 1541. It was controversial, because Michelangelo chose to depict the resurrected rising out of their graves, logically, in the nude. Cardinal Oliviero Carafa was incensed, and insisted something be done. Evidently the cardinal and the artist did not share the same vision. Carafa ordered Daniele da Volterra to paint robes over the offending genitalia.

In revenge, Michelangelo painted Carafa's likeness onto the face of Minos, the Judge of Hell. The story goes that when Carafa complained to Pope Paul III, the Pope replied that his jurisdiction did not extend to Hell, so the painting of Carafa would have to stay where it was and where it remains to this day, in the lower right corner.

The Last Judgement underwent extensive restoration in 1993.

By the late 20th century, hundreds of years of candle smoke had dulled the chapel ceiling's colours until they were practically sepia. The vibrant colors of the restored vision come from 20 years of work, from preliminary tests in 1979, to the restoration proper, which lasted from June 1980 to 11 December 1999.

Critics of Michaelangelo remark that the man was a better sculptor than painter, but his obsessive compulsions still created spectacular results.

Sydney Opera House

You've got to hand it to the Scandinavians. They know design. But when 39-year-old Danish architect Jørn Utzon won the 1957 design contest for Sydney's Opera House, many people throughout the world didn't know whether to laugh or cry or just feel impressed. Above all else, there was the question of how Utzon's vision could be built. In truth, it wasn't. The building that we see today is a compromise.

The story of what would become one of the world's iconic buildings began as far back as the late 1940s when the Director of the New South Wales State Conservatorium of Music, Eugene Goossens, argued for a venue for large productions. After gaining the support of Premier Joseph Cahill, the two men argued about the site. Cahill wanted it near Wynyard in the central business area, Goossens wanted the more remote (at the time) Bennelong Point, named after an aboriginal man who'd been conscripted as a sort of cultural attaché for the British in the 1790s.

The former Bennelong Island was once the site of the brick hut that was Bennelong's home, but by the 1950s it was the site for the Fort Macquarie Tram Depot. Goossens won the argument on the basis that it would be a more spectacular site.

Utzon Wins the Project

Cahill launched the design competition on 13 September 1955. It attracted 233 entries from 32 countries. The criteria specified two halls seating 3 000 and 12 000. The design was controversial, even among the judges. Eero Saarinen, designer of the Gateway Arch, who liked curves, loved the design so much he wouldn't endorse any other entry. Ludwig Miles van der Rohe, whose buildings are nearly all straight edges, hated it so much he wouldn't even speak to Utzon, who won in the end.

In 1957 he arrived in Australia to help oversee the project.

Construction of the building started in March 1959 after the demolition of the Tram Depot and would eventually proceed in three stages:

Stage I—5 December 1958 to 31 August 1963—Construction of the podium

Stage II—1963 to 1967—Construction of the outer shells

Stage III—1967 to 1975—Construction of the interiors.

Building the Opera House was to some extent a series of nightmares. Stage I started too early, before the site had been properly prepared and the original podium columns proved too weak to hold the roof and had to be rebuilt.

Between 1957 to 1963 Utzon, and engineers Ove Arup and Ronald Jenkins, went through over a dozen redesigns of the shells to find an economical way of building them. The investigation involved one of the first uses of a computer for structural analysis. The ultimate solution was to have all the shell components come from a singular sphere. This enabled the manufacturing of reusable moulds to create precast ribs (2 400 of them) and roof panels (4 000 of them) rather than individual and unique moulds for every component. Original completion dates for the shells were March 1965 at the latest. In the end the shells weren't completed until July 1967.

Opinions vary widely on Utzon's character, but Peter Murray, author of *The Saga of Sydney Opera House*, paints a picture of a deceptively quiet-spoken man, who nevertheless had an uncompromising stubborn streak and an inability to communicate the ideas he had in his head to the engineers on the ground.

Building Blow-out

In mid-1965, the people of NSW voted in Robert Askin as Premier and with him came a new Minister for Public Works, Davis Hughes. Although the building was still on budget, the cost overrun projections were beginning to get scary and Hughes began to micromanage Utzon's designs, schedules and cost estimates. Dissatisfied with the answers he was getting, Hughes stopped paying Utzon. The architect resigned in February 1966 and in April he left Australia.

With Utzon gone, any plans for realising his original interior designs were scrapped. The interiors we see today are largely the work of Peter Hall, who worked with David Littlemore and Lionel Todd to finish the project Utzon had felt forced to abandon in the flesh, if not in spirit.

In 1957 the original completion date of the Opera House was supposed to be 26 January 1963 at a cost of $7 million. With all the politicking and unforeseen problems and the necessary changes to the design the final completion date wasn't until 1973 at a cost of $102 million ($1.5 billion) of which $56.5 million went into building the shells alone.

Everything about the Opera House was complicated. Even the perspex architectural model of the Opera House that Bill Lambert made after Utzon's departure had required analysis of 8 000 detailed architectural drawings. The finished model was 4.5 metres long, 3 metres wide and 1.8 metres high (14.75 x 9.85 x 5.9 feet). It took two years to build. Then in 1974 the model was taken to the Washington World Expo. When the expo finished the model was returned, dismantled in crates. The crates were lost for 28 years until the Department of Public Works found them again in 2002. Porter Models then spent 2 000 man-hours over three months to reassemble it.

With hindsight we can argue that building Sydney Opera House required engineering solutions for problems that no one had ever encountered and the solutions were many and ingenious. The system designed to conditioning for the 600 000 cubic feet per minute of air that the complex requires utilises water taken directly out of Sydney Harbour. It's still working after almost 40 years.

Acknowledgement at last

Queen Elizabeth II opened the building on 20 October 1973. No-one had invited Jørn Utzon to the ceremony and the Queen's speech didn't even mention his name. It wouldn't be until the 1990s, until enough water had gone under Sydney Harbour Bridge, that the Sydney Opera House Trust would take steps at reconciliation. In the end, it worked.

In the years following, Utzon would receive an honorary doctorate from the University of Sydney, be made a Companion of the Order of Australia and be given the Keys to the City of Sydney. From Copenhagen he would be involved in the design of Opera House renovations for the Sydney Olympics. In 2003 he received the highest honour of architecture—the Pritiker Prize—and in 2004 the Trust completed and dedicated the first interior room based on Utzon's original designs and named it the Jørn Utzon Room in his honor. But the man himself never saw his completed masterpiece, as it were, in the flesh. He died in his sleep, of heart failure, in Copenhagen, aged 90, on 29 November 2008.

Few buildings in the world are instantly recognizable in silhouette, but Sydney Opera House's profile is absolutely unique and the image has sold a lot of postcards.

OPERA HOUSE FACTS

Building footprint—1.8 hectares (4.5 acres)

Length: 183 metres (605 feet)

Width at its broadest: 120 metres (388 feet)

Height: 67 metres (220 feet)

Support structures: 588 concrete pillars sunk to a depth of up to 25 metres (82 feet) below sea level. This was a necessity because the ground of Bennelong Point was never going to be strong enough to support the huge weight of the building.

Number of roof tiles: 1 056 million, imported from Sweden.

Window covering: 6 223 square metres (67 000 square feet)

The Opera House requires enough electricity to service a town of 25 000, fed through its 645 kilometres (400 miles) of cables.

Main Rooms and their seating capacities:

The Concert Hall (2 679)—containing the 10 000-pipe Sydney Opera House Grand Organ, the largest mechanical action tracker organ in the world.

Opera Theatre (1547)

Drama Theatre (544)

Playhouse (398)

Studio (400)

Utzon Room (210)

Part 10

Monuments to Memory

To the best of our knowledge, humans are the only animals who bury their dead or who observe anything that even remotely resembles funerary rites. This most human of characteristics isn't even confined to the sole surviving species of the genus homo, homo sapiens. In fact the earliest evidence that a human species was thinking about and ritualising death comes from the graves of sapiens' close cousins, homo neanderthalensis. There is some evidence of deliberate disposal of Neanderthal bodies in caves in Wales with remains dated to 225 000 years ago.

However, the earliest evidence of deliberate burial comes from homo sapiens in sites in modern Egypt and Israel dated to 100 000 years ago. Nevertheless there are also Neanderthal burials dating from 70 000 years ago. Given the fragmentary nature of paleoanthropology, and the reality that much evidence may have drowned when the seas rose at the end of the last ice age, we may never know whether sapiens taught Neanderthals the practice of burial, or the other way around, or if they were both so human they came up with the idea separately and independently.

Paleoanthropologists have discovered many cases where bodies were covered in layers of red ochre prior to burial. It's tempting to think of ochre as a sort of 'blood of the earth' and that covering a body in 'blood' and then putting them in a hole was an echo of the birth process. In the same sense that we are born covered in blood, by reproducing this ritually in death there might have been a hope for rebirth among our remote ancestors. We do know that people throughout history have invested considerable resources in death rituals because we have so many visions of death frozen in stone.

Newgrange

Around 3300 BCE, hundreds of years before the Egyptians were building pyramids and a thousand years before the Stonehenge now familiar to us, a group of Neolithic Irish were building a tomb complex in what is now County Meath.

The building we call Newgrange is just one of about 40 passage tombs in the 780 hectare (1927 acre) Brú na Bóinne complex and along with the similar tombs of Knowth and Dowth comprise the largest collection of megalithic art in Western Europe. All the tombs show signs of considerable astronomical sophistication. At the winter solstice on 21 December each year, the rising sun shines through holes in Newgrange's roof to illuminate the interior passages.

Newgrange itself is an artificial mound, a cairn, 12 metres (39 feet) high and approximately circular with a maximum diameter of 85.3 metres (280 feet). At the lowest level of its exterior wall 97 kerbstones, of which 31 are decorated, define the circumference. Within the mound is a chamber passage built from around 450 large stones that extends 18.95 metres (62.17 feet) into the mound. At the end of the passage there's an inner, cruciform chamber whose corbelled vault rises to 6 metres (19.7 feet). Newgrange was well built, the chamber is intact and has remained waterproof after over 5000 years.

The mound was unexplored for thousands of years until 'rediscovered' in the late 1600s, although Irish tradition told that it was one of the sidhe—the fairy mounds where the Tuatha De Danann lived—even though Newgrange had already existed for 2000 years before the Celts arrived in Ireland.

During extensive (and controversial) restorations between 1962 and 1975, scientists found the cremated remains of five people, placed in niches in the central chamber. Newgrange was almost certainly a tomb for some important people, but we have no idea who they were. We have precious little idea of how they lived, or what they believed, but they were important enough for a group of people living in stone age Ireland to transport 200 000 tonnes of material to make the mound. Some stones came from over 50 kilometres (31 miles) away.

We have no idea how many people were involved or how long it took, but there's no doubt that the builders were resourceful, organised and dedicated, and some might have devoted or might even have sacrificed their lives to it, in much the same way that their descendants would to the building of cathedrals millennia later.

Stonehenge

Whatever it might have been to later builders, and whatever it might have meant to their remote successors, archaeological evidence seems to suggest that the site we know as Stonehenge was originally a burial site.

Situated on a grassy plain that lies above a rich deposit of chalk 13 kilometres (8.1 miles) north of the modern city of Salisbury, Stonehenge is the most famous and largest one of about 400 different megalithic monuments in the general district that have survived until modern times.

The site was not the work of a single people. Somewhere between 3100 and 2950 BCE, when the grassy plain was a wooded grove, an unknown group of Neolithic people carved out a 110 metre (361 feet) circular, banked ditch using deer antlers. They left two 'entrances' to the circle, a large one in the northeast and a smaller one due south.

Just 5 metres (16.5 feet) deep inside the inner perimeter of the circle bank they dug a circle of 56 pits, on average about 1.06 metres (3.5 feet) in diameter and 0.76 metres (2.5 feet) deep. These are the Aubrey Holes, after John Aubrey, the gentleman antiquarian who in 1666 was the first modern person to identify them. 25 of the 35 holes excavated so far held the charred remains of human cremation, but only one has yielded useful carbon dating to around 2919 to 1519 BCE, although scholars favour the earlier date. Over succeeding centuries the holes may have been dug up and reused for cremains, but the original ditch and the holes now define what we call Stonehenge One.

We don't know if the holes had any other function. They may have been post holes for a wooden structure, they may not have, but other timber post holes and evidence of reuse of the Aubreys around the year 3000 BCE define Stonehenge Two.

Stonehenge Three

Four centuries were to pass before work began on Stonehenge Three—Phase 1. At this point either a new group, or descendants of the first, dug two new ditches starting at the north east entrance. The ditches defined a corridor, now known as 'The Avenue' that lead all the way to the Avon River, some 3 kilometres (2 miles) away. They also dug two new concentric rings of around 30 holes each within the area defined by the circular ditch. These holes may or may not have held stones at some time in the past.

If they did, they were the dolerite bluestones. Each standing around 2 metres (6.5 feet) high, between 1 and 1.5 metres (3.3–4.9 feet) wide and about 0.8metres (2.6 feet) thick, the bluestones weigh about 1.5 tonnes to 4 tonnes a piece. Archaeologists originally thought that they had come from Preseli Hills, some 250 kilometres (160 miles) away in what is now Wales. In teams of about 130 or so, the builders would have dragged the stones overland to Milford Haven, then floated them on timber rafts up Bristol Channel, then up the River Avon, then dragged them overland again down 'The Avenue' to the final site.

More recent thinking suggests that the bluestones may have come from a closer, and now exhausted, deposit closer at hand, and that most of the transportation had been done by a glacier that moved a monolith from the Preseli Hills, thousands of years earlier, to a more convenient location for the future builders of Stonehenge.

The builders placed several other important stones at about this time. The 'Altar Stone' in the centre of all these circles is still in place, but fallen. Made of sandstone speckled with purple-green mica, the six tonne monolith originally stood two metres high.

In the middle of 'The Avenue', 25 metres from the north east entrance and 77.4 metres (247 feet) from the Altar stone were two 'Heelstones'. Only one remains in place. The remaining 35-tonne monolith is an eroded pillar 5.9 metres (20 feet) high, of which 1.2 metres (4 feet) is buried underground.

Just inside the north east entrance were three 'Portal Stones'. Again, only one remains, the so-called Slaughter Stone. It's about the same size as the Heelstone. Just within the defining bank at points approximately north, south, north west and south east were four 'Station Stones', made of undressed sarsen stone, a form of sandstone dating from the Oligocene period (up to 34 million years old). The north and south Station Stones once stood in the centre of their own circular mounds, but the stones themselves are now missing. The other two stones are still in place.

Stonehenge Three Phase II

It's in the period of Stonehenge Three Phase II, dating from 2600 BCE to 2400 BCE, that we see the work that has made the site so famous.

It's in this approximate time frame, and we don't know how many people were involved or how long the work took, that workers made major additions. Firstly, an inner horseshoe arrangement of five 'trilithons'—two upright sarsen stones topped by a sarsen lintel. The open end of the 13.7 metres (45 feet) horseshoe faces north west, in alignment with 'The Avenue'. These sarsens are the largest stones in the site. The largest of all, 'stone 56' is nine metres tall (6.7 metres or 22 feet above ground) and weighs an estimated 50 tonnes. Two of the trilithons were still standing in modern times. One was re-erected and two remain fallen.

Surrounding the trilithons was a 33-metre (110 feet) ring of 30 sarsens, co-centric with the Altar Stone. Each stone stands 4.1 metres (13 feet) above ground, 2.1 metres (6.9 feet) wide and weighs around 25 tonnes. Atop this circle was a ring of lintel stones, each roughly 3.2 metres x 1 metre x 0.8 metres (10 x 3 x2.6 feet).

Although in recent years Stonehenge has become a sacred site of New Age Druid revivalists, the site predates the Celtic invasion of Britain and the original Druids had nothing to do with its construction.

Phases III–V

Current thinking posits that Phases III, IV and V somewhere between 2300 BCE and 1930 BCE, involved moving the bluestones from their former position outside the sarsen circle to their present position of two concentric rings within the circle. In Phase V at some point bluestones were removed from the inner circle to leave a horseshoe shape of 19 remaining standing stones that mimic the five trilithons—the Bluestone Horseshoe.

Speculation continues to abound as to why Neolithic people expended so much energy to build Stonehenge but we don't really know anything. Even the name is relatively modern, coming from the Old English 'stan hen(c)en'—stone gallows. The only obvious certainty is that the rising sun of the midsummer solstice aligns directly with the Heelstone and Altar Stones, but any other astronomical alignment or use is guesswork. Since its completion Stonehenge has gradually fallen into ruin and only between 1901 and 1964 did it undergo extensive restoration.

The site has remained the focus of considerable day dreaming, with all sorts of historically inaccurate assertions and legends building up around it. In the Middle Ages Geoffrey of Monmouth wrote that Stonehenge was built by Irish giants who carried the stones from Africa to create a place of healing. And much to the potential disappointment of Neo Pagans, the facts are that the Celts had nothing to do with its construction or use, since they didn't even arrive in the area until about a thousand years after the completion of Stonehenge. Nevertheless, the site is now a favourite among British NeoDruids to enact whatever rituals their imaginations, and the English Heritage organisation, let them.

The Army of Dreams

It's difficult to imagine how megalomaniacs think unless you happen to be one yourself. How does a man who spent a lot of money during his lifetime on quack 'immortality' cures nevertheless make elaborate preparations for his own tomb? The First Emperor of China, Qin Shi Huang Di, thought nothing of mobilising an entire nation around his own aggrandisement, both in this world and the next. Thus he wanted to make absolutely sure that his vision of life after death would be just like life before death, only more so.

After a lifetime spent on pillaging, raping and despoiling competing states, the man born as Ying Zheng, King of Qin finally succeeded in putting an end to the decadent Zhou Dynasty and united China, The Middle Kingdom, in 221 BCE. By all accounts Shi Huang Di was an unpleasant man, but he did do some good.

His achievements included starting the Great Wall, building an extensive road system and standardising weights and measures. But he also outlawed Confucianism, buried intellectuals alive and encouraged mass book burnings involving many irreplaceable historical documents. Naturally, this made him some enemies and he lived through so many assassination attempts that he took to sleeping in a different place every night.

After only 11 years on the throne, he died in 210 BCE at the age of 49. Apparently he accidentally poisoned himself after ingesting mercury pills, then thought to confer immortality. At the time, he was in Shaqiu, two months travel from the capital of Xianyang, which is today the city of Xian, much more centrally located than the modern capital of Beijing.

By the time the entourage arrived at the capital the emperor's body was in an advanced state of decomposition. The Big Man hadn't left a will, but everyone knew what to do; they'd been preparing for it for the past 36 years.

The Emperor's Final Resting Place

A combination of the records of the historian Sima Qian, who was writing over a hundred years after the events in question, and modern archaeology tells us the following.

The emperor had chosen a site halfway between Mount Li and Xianyang, a rectangular area with a long due north-south axis 2 165 metres and due east west axis of 940 metres (1.35 miles x 0.59 miles)—an area of about 2.5 square kilometres (618 acres), bordered by a wall 8 metres (26 feet) wide

Even from its earliest stages of history, everything about China is big. What other civilization would have come up with a terracotta army? And for all we know, what we see today is only a fraction of what Emperor Shi Huang Di caused to be made.

and originally as much as 12 metres (40 feet) high. Over time, this outer wall has eroded to a small stretch of just 2–3 metres (6.5–10 feet) high. In the centre of the area there is a smaller walled rectangle of 1 355 x 580 metres (0.85 x 0.36 miles). Nested within that is an area 460 x 392 metres (1 500 x 1 286 feet) bordered by an underground wall 2.7–4 metres (9–13 feet) deep below ground.

This is the actual tomb of the emperor. The whole area was covered with a tumulus, an artificial tree- and grass-covered hill that was originally 115 metres (337 feet) high and even after 2000 years is still 50 metres (165 feet) high.

Much of this area is still unexcavated, but so far diggers have unearthed over 400 separate deposits of grave goods, including a half-life-sized pair of canopied bronze chariots complete with drivers and four bronze horses a piece. Reconstructed from 3 500 pieces, one arrangement weighs 1.2 tonnes. In other places, kneeling statues are buried alongside the remains of real horses.

Sima Qian describes the inner tomb as being a three-dimensional model of the world, complete with 100 'rivers' flowing with liquid mercury, an artificial subterranean landscape upon which was built 'palaces, scenic towers...wonderful objects' and roofed with a ceiling depicting the heavens. Archaeologists have yet to venture there, so what has so far grabbed the most attention is the terracotta army.

There are four pits, about 1.5 kilometres (0.93 miles) to the east of the tumulus about 5 metres (16.5 feet) deep. Within the rammed-earth walls of the pits are rows of life-sized terracotta military figures, an army of about 7 000 to 8 000 soldiers, 130 chariots, 520 chariot horses and 150 cavalry horses. All the figures are unique, most arranged in rows facing east as if in readiness for an attack from the conquered states.

The largest pit, Pit 1, has eleven corridors, most over three metres (10 feet) wide, with infantry standing at attention. Pit 2, slightly to the north contains cavalry, infantry and war chariots. Pit 3 is a 'command post' with high-ranking officers. Pit 4 is empty and archaeologists think it was unfinished.

An Army of Workers

The figures show evidence of mass production for the bodies, with individuality and exquisite attention to detail left to the faces, uniforms and accessories. Scholars even believe that the faces are portraits of real people. Each figure, once complete, was glazed, then fired at 950°–1 000° Celsius (1 742°–1 832° Farenheit). This is a considerable investment of energy, but no less than for other elements, both structural, such as drainage pipes to keep the area dry throughout, and funerary, such as bronze swords and gold, silver and bronze harnesses for the horses.

Sima Qian tells us that over 700 000 people laboured from 246 BCE until 210 BCE to complete this memorial to one man's ego. But the lessons involved in creating the funerary complex were never forgotten, and the mass production techniques the workers devised went on to influence the development of the Chinese ceramics industry right up to the present day.

wives and many of the builders of the tomb to be buried alive within it. Who knows what we might find?

Preserving an Emperor's Ego

Preservation of the site is of some concern. Chinese officials claim that pollution from coal burning plants nearby is causing degradation of the statues.

Within a few years of his death, Shi Huandi's empire collapsed. Three years after the emperor's interment, the Chu nobleman and future king, General Xiang Yu had raided the tomb to provide some of the rebellion with instant weaponry so well made that even today the swords can still penetrate a shield. Having taken his plunder, Xiang then set fire to the necropolis. The blaze was so large that it is supposed to have lasted an unbelievable, and certainly exaggerated, three months. Of the thousands of statues, only one survived intact.

What we see today is a reconstruction of what must be the world's largest jigsaw puzzle, begun after the site was rediscovered by Chinese peasants in 1974.

But for all the damage and erosion, enough of the tomb remains to bear testament to one of the world's great examples of excellence in logistics, and the power and brutality of a single individual to realise his vision. And enough of the tomb remains buried to provide future generations with many more surprises. Tradition states that the second emperor ordered all of his father's childless

Metropolitan Cathedral
of Brasilia

The spectacular Metropolitan Cathedral of Brasilia in the capital of Brazil is the grand vision of architect Oscar Niemeyer. The 16 parabola-shaped concrete columns weigh 90 tonnes altogether and represent hands moving up towards heaven.The cornerstone was laid in 1958 and the building was dedicated in 1970.

Petra

The Roman Jewish historian, Josephus, had mentioned it by its ancient name of Rekem as the capital of the Aramaic-speaking Semetic tribe known as the Nabateans, although, to be honest, we're not sure what the Nabateans called it. Pliny the Elder also wrote about it and it's even mentioned in the Dead Sea scrolls, but no-one in the West had ever seen Petra (from a Latin word for 'rock') until Swiss explorer Johan Ludwig Burchhardt came upon it in 1812.

What he found was a city, carved into the slope of Mount Hor, in Arabah, Jordan, hidden in a niche that's part of a valley bordering Israel.

An excellent overhead view can be seen by searching for 'Petra' in in Google Maps on satellite view.

The first impression you get is how isolated and desolate it seems, but it wasn't always like this. At their height, the Nabateans controlled the nexus of a land trading route that carried incense on camel trains from Yemen, 1 600 kilometres (1 000 miles) to the south. The incense would then find its way to altars as far west to Egypt, north east to Persia and north-west to Greece, Rome and beyond.

Even today, the journey is hard. The limiting factor is water. But the Nabateans had mastered the art of channelling and storing what little rainfall there was. They created an artificial oasis, and they charged traders and travellers plenty for the one commodity most precious in the desert.

The Nabateans spent the wealth they took from excise taxes and water fees on luxuries and building themselves tombs using whatever architectural style seemed to be in vogue at the time. The result was an eclectic mix of visual elements unique in their juxtaposition.

Like anyone with lots of money and no taste, the Nabateans did what they thought was classy and they spent years carving masterpieces into rock, only to cover them over in plaster and gaudy paint. In time, the plaster wore away, revealing the true beauty of the rock beneath—an ever-changing pattern of colours and lighting effects that the builders themselves never intended.

We don't know when Petra's history began, but the best guess is around 500 BCE, and it was still going strong from 200 BCE to 50 CE. In 106, Petra lost its independence, but under Roman rule it became the capital of the province of Arabia Petrea and it reached the height of its glory during the reign of Alexander Severus (222–235 CE). But when Alexander's assassination sparked 50 years of Roman chaos and with the rise of Palmyra in Syria as a major trading centre, and the incense route moving south via the Red Sea, Petra fell into a decline.

An earthquake in 363 ruined the water supply and the few remaining inhabitants left. The tombs, long raided, are all that's left of the vision of their creators.

The Deir Monastery, or ad-Deir, in Petra. Thought to be built around 100 BCE, it was probably not a monastery at all but the grand vision of Obodas I, a king.

The Temple of Angkor Wat in the jungles of north-west Cambodia—imagine the surprise of the French rediscoverers when they stumbled upon these ancient ruins.

Angkor Wat

Another contender for the title of the 'greatest investment in post mortem ego' is Angkor Wat (In Khmer it means 'city temple').

Located in the jungles of central north-west Cambodia, 5.5 kilometres north of Siem Reap, Angkor Wat is enclosed within a roughly square moat, around 1.4 kilometres to a side. The moat is 190 metres (623 feet) wide and within it is a rectangular island, a walled 'outer courtyard' 4.5 metres (14.75 feet) high, 1 024 (3 360 feet) metres wide on an east west axis and 802 metres (2 631 feet) north south surrounded by a 30 metre (100 feet) wide apron before the terrace meets the moat. This outer wall encloses an area of 820 000 square metres (203 acres)—a shallow step pyramid that takes up a volume of 272 336 cubic metres (356 202 cubic yards) of earth and rock.

Successive concentric rectangular terraces form the inner arrangement. Terrace One: 215 x 115 metres—height 3.2 metres (705 x 377 and 10.5 feet). Terrace Two: 115 x 100 metres—height 6.4 metres (377 x 328 and 21 feet). Terrace Three: 73 x 75 metres—height 1.8 metres (239.5 x 246 and 5.9 feet).

The central terrace and its structures are what we normally see when look at photographs of Angkor Wat. Each corner of the terrace has a 32 metre (105 feet) high

tower, and at the centre of the complex is a tower 42 metres (138 feet) high crowned with a carved lotus pinnacle 65 metres (213 feet) above the moat level. The complex's orientation is due west. So to get to the centre you need to cross the moat on a causeway and walk about 600 metres (0.375 miles), through a cruciform terrace until you reach the wall of the first terrace.

As you reach the inner area there's a gallery wall carved with about 1000 square metres (10,764 square feet) of shallow relief carvings depicting scenes from the Mahabharata and the Ramayana. This level of detail is everywhere in Angkor Wat, and the intricate carvings represent an even bigger investment of time and energy than that required to move the earth to excavate the moat and to build the terraces.

Angkor Wat looks as if it's built entirely out of two types of sandstone, medium-grained for the main walls and fine-grained for the gallery walls. The stone came from Mount Kulen, 45 kilometres (28 miles) north east of the site but its use is principally for facing slabs around a core of local laterite. This is handy because unskilled labourers can carve laterite, which then hardens in air. Skilled stone carvers and masons then give the building its finished look but, nevertheless, the stones were placed without mortar, so the whole structure is held together by gravity.

We have no idea exactly how many people were involved in Angkor Wat's construction. It was built between 1113 and 1145 but, judging by other similar projects, we can guess that the workforce numbered easily into the hundreds of thousands.

A Tomb For a King

And what was it all for? King Suryavarman II intended it as his mausoleum. Angkor Wat's original name was Preah Pisnulok, in homage to Suryavarman's posthumous title of Paramavishnuloka ('he who has entered the heavenly world of Vishnu'). The original name of the central temple is unknown, although Vrah Vishnulok is a good guess. The king's religious dedication of the building to Vishnu and its intended use as a tomb explains why the temple is oriented to the west, towards the setting sun, although you can also access the site from an eastern causeway too.

For all the work done, the complex was still unfinished when the king died and some reliefs remain uncarved. This isn't entirely surprising as there is considerable evidence that the project bankrupted the country.

In 1177 the traditional enemies of the Khmer, the Chams, under the leadership of Jayavarnam VII, sacked the city of Angkor, and built a new capital and state temple at Angkor Thom, a more modest complex within a much larger area a few kilometres north of Angkor Wat. Jayavarnam wanted grandeur, but he didn't seem to be as keen on destroying the economy as was his predecessor.

Some 200 years later, Angkor Wat became a centre of Theravada Buddhism and it remains so to this day. The moat around it seems to have protected it from the encroaching jungle. It's in excellent condition in contrast to other projects built in tropical latitudes, like the Mesoamerican pyramids, but it still required extensive restoration during the 20th century. Close to three-quarters of a million people visit Angkor Wat every year, about half of all those who travel to Cambodia.

The Taj Mahal

The Mughal Emperors of India combined the very worst and the very best of human feeling, often in the same individuals. Does absolute power corrupt absolutely, or does such power just give free rein to the imagination for both the darkest and brightest visions?

Akbar, third of the Mughal Dynasty, once had 30 000 unarmed farmers hacked to pieces for rising up against him. In a later incident he built a pyramid out of the skulls of 2 000 other rebels as a warning to anyone else who had any ideas about challenging his rule. And yet, Akbar also enjoyed culture and philosophy and would pass down this love of finer things to his favourite grandson, Jahan. After Akbar died in 1605, the crown passed to Jahan's father, Jahangir, an altogether milder man.

A man smitten

In the early 1600s there was a custom that once a year the ladies of the nobility would hold a charity market. In 1607 Princess Arjumand Banu Begum, the 14-year-old cousin of Jahan, was selling trinkets at such a market stall when the young prince met her. It was in such unlikely circumstances that one of the great romances of history began. Jahan was instantly smitten. The two became engaged, but they would have to wait five years before Arjumand became Jahan's third wife.

It was obvious to everyone that Arjumand was THE GREAT LOVE of Jahan's life, and he bestowed upon her the title of Mumtaz Mahal—'beloved jewel of the palace'.

Duty required Jahan sire one child from each of his other wives, but enthusiasm kept Mumtaz Mahal in an almost continuous state of pregnancy or childrearing for the rest of her life. This didn't deter Jahan from bringing Mumtaz along with him on his expeditions to every corner of his vast empire.

After his father died from the long-term effects of alcoholism in 1627, Jahan became emperor in his own right and demonstrated his trust in Mumtaz by giving her the Imperial Seal, a sign that effectively said 'you and I are equals', an extraordinary gesture for a Muslim ruler to make to his wife.

The Taj Mahal. Imagine another one just like it right next to it but made of black marble and you'll see a vision grand enough, and expensive enough to bankrupt TWO empires.

Every account of their marriage documents the extraordinary closeness of the imperial couple, but their happiness couldn't go on forever. Love really doesn't conquer all, as much as we might like it to. In their years of marriage Mumtaz gave birth to 13 children, of whom only six had lived passed their early childhood.

Then on 17 June 1631 Mumtaz was in Burhanpur, having accompanied her husband on a campaign in the Deccan Plateau, when she went into labour with their fourteenth child. The birth was difficult and Mumtaz bled to death. She was only 38. The child, Princess Gauhara Begum, would live to be 75.

A Monument To Love

The legend goes that as she lay dying, Mumtaz asked Jahan to build a monument to their love and made him promise never to marry again. He promised. His adored Mumtaz was temporarily buried in Burhanpur, and the emperor hastily finished the Deccan campaign. Mumtaz was disinterred in December 1631 and brought to Agra in a golden casket.

Jahan had lapsed into deep, inconsolable grief and went into secluded mourning for a year, at the end of which, the chroniclers say, he emerged, stooped, worn-faced and white-haired. Meanwhile, the couple's eldest daughter Jahanara Begun, became her father's emotional support and the power behind the throne.

After his seclusion, Jahan dedicated the next 20 years to the building of his memorial to Mumtaz. The site, which belonged to Maharaja Jain Singh, is on the south bank of the Yamuna River, south of the city of Agra. Jahan gave Singh a palace in Agra in exchange for it. Workers excavated and then levelled a 1.2 hectare (3 acre) area to a height of 50 metres (164 feet) above the river bank.

They then constructed a 15-kilometre (9.3-mile) long rammed earth bank to carry the building materials. Teams of 30 oxen were needed to transport the main blocks. The scaffolding for the building was made of brick and was in itself a huge job that took years to build and dismantle.

The complex is set within a garden, 300 metres (984 feet) square. At the far north end on the east and west sides are two, mirror-image identical buildings.

The western one is a mosque, which features a floor inlay of 569 'prayer rugs' in black marble. The eastern building, a jawab, has no fixed function and exists purely for aesthetic balance. It may have been a guest house at some time. Framing the inner section are four minarets, 40 metres (131 feet) tall.

But it is the central building that inspires the most awe. Built on a plinth base, a square 55 metres (180 feet) to the side, the main central mausoleum is 35 metres (115 feet) high, on top of which is a cylindrical drum section, 7 metres (23 feet) tall. Sitting atop the drum is an onion dome, 28 metres (92 feet) tall, topped in turn with what was originally a gold spire, now of bronze.

Twenty thousand labourers worked to create this white marble architectural jewel, aligned precisely north to south. Stonecutters came from Baluchistan, sculptors from Bukhara, calligraphers from Persia and Syria, working under a core creative team of 37 master craftsmen.

The decorations, thousands of them, in line with Muslim prohibitions about representing the human form are geometric, calligraphic or botanical motifs. There is extensive use of lapidary, employing 28 varieties of both precious and semi-precious stones. The materials came from all over India and beyond—Rajasthan marble, Punjabi jasper, Afghani lapis lazuli, Sri Lankan sapphire, Arabian carnelian, Chinese crystal and jade— all but the marble blocks transported on the backs of over a thousand elephants.

Surahs from the Quran on the theme of judgment are written in jasper, inlaid into the marble on the exterior of the building. As you enter through the main gate of the mausoleum you pass under calligraphy that reads 'Oh Soul, thou art at rest. Return to the Lord at peace with Him, and He at peace with you'.

The plinth and main building took 12 years to complete, with a further 10 years to complete the minarets, mosque and jawab and the gateway that leads in to the front garden.

Jahan's End

In 1657 a false rumour of Jahan's death had spread, leading to a violent war of succession. The building of the Taj Mahal—the Crown Palace—had bankrupted the nation. The cost, estimated at 32 million rupees at the time, is virtually incalculable by modern standards. Hundreds of billions of dollars would be a fair estimate, considering the productive capacity of the empire at the time.

The body of Jahan now lies buried next to that of his beloved wife and the Taj Mahal remains one of the most famous and recognisable buildings in the world. Although the Taj Mahal is a tomb, it is unusual in that it wasn't built for self-aggrandisement, but as an act of love, an expression of grief.

Jahan had originally planned to create a mirror image of the Taj in black marble as his own mausoleum. Such a scheme would have bankrupted two empires, but what a grand vision that would have been.

Ceausescu's House of the People

In many ways the complete antithesis of the Taj Mahal is the central government administrative complex built by the regime of Romanian dictator Nicolae Ceausescu. Constructed between 1983 and to this day complete, but unfinished, the Palace of the Parliament as it's now called, might have rivalled the Ryugyong Hotel for the title of the 'world's worst building,' but for the fact that at least the palace is usable.

In true communist style, Ceausescu called it the 'House of the People', but it was nothing of the sort. The house was meant to be a lasting monument to the power of one man's ego—a complete overproduction in masonry. Ceausescu demolished half of downtown historic Bucharest, inconveniently dividing the centre of the city. Clearing the site involved the destruction of 3 Protestant and 19 Orthodox churches, 6 synagogues and 30 000 residences.

All this to build what is simultaneously the world's largest civilian administrative building, the most expensive administrative building and the world's heaviest building.

The 270 x 240 metre (886 x 787 feet) building rises from 9 metres (29.5 feet), two levels below ground to 12 storeys, 86 metres (282 feet) above ground. The structure and fitting of its 1100 rooms include:

- 1 million cubic metres (1.307 million cubic yards) of Transylvanian marble
- 700,000 tonnes of steel and bronze—for doors and windows
- 900,000 cubic metres (1.77 million cubic yards) of mostly Romanian elm, oak, sweet cherry, sycamore, maple and walnut—for parquetry and wainscotting
- 200,000 square metres (2.153 million square feet) of woollen carpets—some of which are so large they had to be woven inside the building to fit them in
- 3500 tonnes of crystal—for 480 chandeliers

Ceausescu didn't live long enough to really get the run of the place. When the people overthrew and assassinated him in 1989 the building was mostly structurally finished, but unfurnished. The building now houses the Romanian lower house—the Chamber of Deputies—but much of the palace of the Parliament is still under-utilised.

Only in
America

With its status as the world's richest country, and having the benefit of the most economically profitable portions of an entire continent, the United States of America has the resources and population base to materialise some of the grandest visions in the industrial world.

And yet for all the technology available to contemporary generations, when it comes to enduring monuments to memory, nothing says it, nor lasts, quite like solid rock. There's a simplicity and solidity to stone that ensures that any artefacts carved from it will outlast even the civilisation that created them.

Mount Rushmore

The Lakota Sioux called the mountain near Keystone, South Dakota 'The Six Grandfathers'. In 1930 the Americans named it after New York lawyer Charles E. Rushmore, 45 years after Rushmore visited the site as part of a mining survey.

The Mount Rushmore idea was the brainchild of South Dakota farmer historian Jonah LeRoy 'Doane' Robinson, who in 1923 conceived a monumental sculpture as a way of attracting tourists to the area. The next year Robinson seconded Confederate Memorial Carving sculptor Gutzon Borglum to look at the

area and it was Borglum who chose the Mount Rushmore site because of the strength of its granite and its well lit south-west elevation. With no consideration of whatever spiritual significance the Six Grandfathers might have had to the Lakota Sioux, Congress approved the plan to portray George Washington and three other presidents on the site—two Republicans and one Democrat—at President Calvin Coolidge's insistence. Might this have had something to do with Coolidge, himself, being a Republican?

Presidents elected

Congress authorised the Mount Rushmore National Memorial Commission on 3 March 1925 and Borglum selected the three other presidents—Thomas Jefferson, Abraham Lincoln and Theodore Roosevelt—because they had all contributed to expanding US territory. Washington with the foundation of the nation itself, Jefferson for the Louisiana Purchase, Lincoln for the consolidation of the northern and southern states, and Roosevelt for his role in Panama, although his opinions on the conquests of 'savages' by 'whites' couldn't have gone down too well with the Sioux, or any other native Americans for that matter.

Nevertheless, the work went ahead, and from 4 October 1927 Borglum and 400 other

workers blasted and chipped away at the mountain, 1 745 metres (5 725 feet) above sea level. Jefferson's face was originally intended to be at Washington's right, but Borglum found that the rock there was unstable and ordered it blasted away. Jefferson ended up at Washington's left, leading to Roosevelt's rather cramped position today.

Washington's face was finished by 4 July 1934, Jefferson's in 1936 and Lincoln's on 17 September 1937—the 150th anniversary of the signing of the Constitution.

The 450 000 tonnes of granite removed to produce the sculpture were left where they lay and now form an interesting feature of the site.

No-one died during its construction, and the project cost exactly $989 992.39 (or almost $50 million today). Charles E. Rushmore donated $5 000 ($300 000) to the project that bears his name—the largest single contribution— but he would never live to see it. He died in 1931. Coolidge never saw it either. He died in 1933. And neither did Borglum, who died of an embolism in March 1941, only six months before work on the site ended.

His son, Lincoln Borglum, saw the work to its completion, or at least its half completion. The sculptures were originally designed to be depicted down to waist level, and you can still see this in photographs of Borglum's original model. Borglum had also planned an additional, massive panel in the shape of the Louisiana Purchase commemorating the Declaration of Independence, The Constitution and the major territorial acquisitions of the US to his time but this grand vision was never realised.

The work was finished on 31 October 1941, when the project ran out of money, but just in time for the United States to experience yet another expansion of its territory in the wake of World War Two.

Crazy Horse's Head

In 1939, in response to the Mount Rushmore project, or perhaps in protest, Chief Henry Standing Bear wrote to sculptor Korchak Ziolowski, who was working on Mount Rushmore at the time. Bear wrote 'My fellow chiefs and I would like the white man to know that the red man has great heroes too.'

It wasn't until 1948 that Ziolowski took up Bear's suggestion of creating a giant sculpture of Oglala Lakota hero Crazy Horse in the face of Thunderhead Mountain in the Black Hills of South Dakota, 13 kilometres (8 miles) from Rushmore.

Privately funded by the Crazy Horse Memorial Foundation, Ziolowski turned down two offers of a federal grant of $10 million ($40 million) by the US government because he didn't want the project compromised.

Unfortunately, this idealism didn't help the progress of the sculpture. Ziolowski died

in 1982 and to date only Crazy Horse's face is finished. It was dedicated in 1998.

The project remains controversial, even in the Native American community, with the argument being that carving into a wild mountain is an act of desecration, contrary to the spirit of Crazy Horse's life. In fact, in his lifetime, Crazy Horse avoided being photographed, so it's interesting to speculate how he might have felt about the sculpture.

But if it is ever finished, Crazy Horse will be the world's largest sculpture—195 metres (645 feet) wide and 172 metres (563 feet) high. At full height Crazy Horse's head alone will be 27 metres (87 feet) high compared to the 18-metre (60 feet) high faces of the 'grandfathers' on Mount Rushmore.

The Mountain of Names

One mile up in Little Cottonwood Canyon in the Wasatch Range of Utah, about 20 miles (32 kilometres) south-east of Salt Lake City is the Granite Mountain Record Vault. The Vault is an excavated hollow 600 feet (200 metres) deep into Granite Mountain. Within The Vault, in a dry controlled environment are stored 2.4 million rolls of microfilm and 1 million sheets of microfiche—the equivalent of about 3 billion pages of family history records.

Every year, the Church of Latter Day Saints increases these records by up to 40 000 further rolls of microfilm, and since 1999 the faithful have been in the continuous process of digitising this huge amount of information which comprises the largest concentration of family records in the world.

Why are the Mormons doing this? Two billion names are stored there, behind 14-tonne steel doors. Why are they burying this huge record of the family tree of the whole human race in a place that even an atomic bomb wouldn't be able to reach?

They're doing it as a service to humanity.

A core tenet of the Mormon faith is that the dead can be posthumously baptised in the Church. Baptism is necessary for salvation, and families can continue to exist as Mormons in the afterlife forever if all their members are baptised.

Aside from the fact that some of us may not want to spend eternity with our relatives there are many people in the world who like their religion and aren't particularly interested in post-mortem conversion. Jewish rights advocates were among the first to object to the Mormon grand vision of eternity and others have since followed.

Nevertheless, in spite of the controversy, the Mountain of Names has been a great boon to family historians even if, in the words of Mormon Church historian Marlin Jensen, some of the afterlife baptisms are the work of 'well-intentioned, sometimes slightly over-zealous members'.

Grand Visions for the Future

If the past is anything to go by, the future looks good for even grander visions. If people in the past were able to produce things like the Panama Canal, the Empire State Building and the Sydney Opera House what might people be able to create in coming centuries, millennia or beyond?

Several things have to happen before a grand vision can turn into a grand reality.

The first is imagination, someone, somewhere has to dare to dream.

Second is the necessity. This can come about because there's a true economic need, or simply because there are enough people who want it to happen.

Thirdly there has to be the will. So many things have to happen before an idea in someone's head can end up as a construct in the physical world, there are so many obstacles that we have to overcome that we can bring them into being only if we have the will. There are already a lot of really important things that should be happening, like curing world hunger or ending stupid, pointless wars, or reclaiming the deserts that human beings have created over the past five thousand years. These things are technically, logistically and even economically possible, but they aren't happening simply because there isn't enough will yet to make them happen.

Fourth there are the practical issues. The real world works under the laws of physics and if you ignore those laws whatever you want to happen won't happen no matter how hard you dream, no matter how urgent the need and no matter how powerful your will. Some projects require the creation of technologies that simply don't exist yet, but that doesn't stop us from dreaming about them.

Here then is a brief look into the crystal ball.

A Really Big Bridge

Twelve thousand years ago, at the tail end of the ice age and with a lot of the world's water trapped in vast, continent-covering ice sheets, the level of the world's oceans was much lower than today. There was even a land bridge between Alaska and Eastern Siberia. People got from Asia to the Americas by walking. But when the big thaw came the oceans rose to their current levels, flooded the lowlands and the Bering land bridge became the Bering Strait.

The dream of being able to cross from the United States to Russia without getting your feet wet isn't new. In fact, Joseph Strauss, the dreamer behind the Golden Gate Bridge, submitted a design for an 89-kilometre (55-mile) long railroad bridge across the Bering Strait for his graduate thesis as far back as 1892.

Since then, engineers have come up with one possible solution for turning this dream into a reality.

The bridge would need 220 piers. Until global warming really kicks in, the Strait will be covered in ice for much of the year, so the piers would have to be cone-shaped in cross-sections to act like the bow of an ice-breaker ship. The only difference is that whereas a moving ice-breaker ploughs through the slow-moving ice, in this case the slow-moving ice would pass around the piers. The piers would have to weigh around 50 tonnes a piece

and be made of a special concrete that could withstand the extreme cold and the pressure of the ice on it—so special that the concrete in question hasn't been invented yet.

The climate also features icebergs, violent storms and winds at minus 40° celsius. The bridge itself would have to be about 200 feet above sea level, suspended from cables much like those which support the Golden Gate, although they'd also have to be sheathed in weather-resistant concrete.

At an estimated cost of $105 billion dollars, there wouldn't be enough traffic on the bridge to justify the expense. Who wants to pay a $10 000 toll? What would make the scheme economically viable would be pipelines on the lowest level of the bridge to bring oil and gas 4 000 miles from the Siberian fields for the ever-hungry American consumer. Above the oil pipeline would be an enclosed railway tunnel for two high-speed train lines. Above that would be an open highway for traffic, but again, until global warming kicks in, the highway could only be open for about four months per year.

If you want an even grander vision you could build a superhighway, making it possible to drive from Patagonia at the southern tip of South America to the Cape of Good Hope at the southern tip of Africa—a journey of about 50 000 kilometres (31 000 miles).

A Few Really Big
Tunnels

One major tunnel system is already under construction. By 2017 you'll be able to drive from Pollegio in Italy for 88.5 kilometres (55 miles) under the Swiss Alps using the Gotthard Base Tunnel. The whole journey from Zurich to Milan by train will take only two hours.

Currently, standard freight trains can't use the existing system because the gradient climbing up the Alps is too steep, but the Gotthard will be at near ground level, vastly increasing the route's freight capacity, making the $6.5 billion price tag for the tunnel worth its while.

But this is nothing compared to a proposal for a Transatlantic Tunnel (TAT). The TAT would be a huge concrete tube floating at a set depth in the ocean. It would be 4 987 kilometres (3 100 miles) long and would connect New York to London. The idea calls for building 54 000 prefabricated tube sections, each over 92 metres (300 feet) long, transported into position on the surface from specially designed immersion pontoons.

The sections would be steel-shelled, with an inner ring of buoyant foam. Engineers speculate that the tunnel sections would be anchored to the sea floor with over 100 000 tethers along the whole length of the tunnel.

The TAT would need to float around 45 metres (150 feet) below the ocean's surface to allow the safe passage of ships above it, and would have to be strong enough to deal with the sway of ocean currents.

The inner core of the tunnel would have three vertically arranged chambers. The lower chamber might service freight trains. The central chamber would have one track for eastbound trains, another for westbound, and a central track for emergencies. The upper chamber would serve tunnel-servicing trains.

The most extraordinary aspect of the TAT would be that its inner core would be devoid of air. The maglev trains would have to travel at 8 000 kilometres per hour (5 000 miles per hour). You could make the trip from New York to Paris in one hour, but not if you had to deal with air friction as well, so the system would require pumps to create a vacuum almost as hard as outer space. The cost of such a project could easily reach $500 billion dollars.

But if you wanted bigger, try a Transpacific Tunnel, linking Shanghai to Los Angeles. Such a tunnel would be 10 500 kilometres (6550 miles) long—more than double the Transatlantic.

These tunnels would make more of the earth accessible and unless population growth slows, we may may be looking elsewhere to live too.

Reaching for the Stars

Space beckons, but it's difficult and expensive to climb out of the earth's gravity. Because fuel has to carry its own weight, nearly all the mass of the fuel of the *Saturn V* rockets that took men to the Moon had to be spent to carry itself, leaving just a fraction to actually push the final stage of the rocket into orbit. After that, because there's hardly any friction in space at sub-light speeds, the rest of the way was relatively energy free.

One solution to this problem of expensive investments in fuel would be to build a space elevator. For that you'd need a rope to climb up in much the same way, almost, as Jack climbed his beanstalk.

The only trouble is that the beanstalk would have to be incredibly strong. There is as yet no substance that we know of that has the compressive strength to support its own weight in such a scenario.

A more feasible alternative would be to have a tether system. You'd then simply have a tether stretching from earth to a counterweight in geostationary orbit above. The rotation of the earth in synchrony with the tether would keep the tether taut. The tether wouldn't have to hold its own weight any more than a string with a ball attached to it has to hold its own weight as you swing it around your head. The problem is that the string would have to be incredibly strong. As yet, we know of no substance strong enough that has the tensile strength for such a task.

But scientists are working on such a problem, and carbon/diamond fibre nanotube composites may hold the key. To date, scientists have only created about 2 grams of carbon nanotube—not quite enough for a cable that would be about 100 000 kilometres (62 000 miles) long.

In the medium distant future we'd be looking to colonise planets. The only two in our immediate neighbourhood that would be suitable are Mars and Venus. Both would require a lot of work to convert to environments suitable for humans. Mars would need a lot of atmosphere and water, which you might be able to get from crashing enough ice asteroids onto its surface.

Venus would be an even bigger challenge. You'd have to bind up a lot of its atmosphere into rocks to get the pressure down to a level where it wouldn't crush you and to get the greenhouse effect down so that the surface wouldn't be hot enough to melt lead. Then you'd have to find a way of speeding up its rotation so that its day isn't as long as its year.

Going further out would be hard too. The distances between the stars are so great that at velocities below the speed of light the trip would be so long you'd have to build starships that could carry crews for generations, but such ships would require air and food recycling systems of unparalleled efficiency. Of course, you wouldn't have to do this if you could crack the light speed barrier.

But assuming you can't, you could expand your real estate by building a Dyson Sphere.

First proposed by Freeman Dyson in 1959 the Dyson Sphere involves building a sphere of artificial planets around a star, to make the most of its heat and light.

No longer is the sky the limit when it comes to grand visions.

In a world of ever-increasing population and ever-diminishing resources, space may hold the key to the future of the human race. At the very least, some grand visions of the future may require the harnessing of vast energies and the transformation of whole planets.

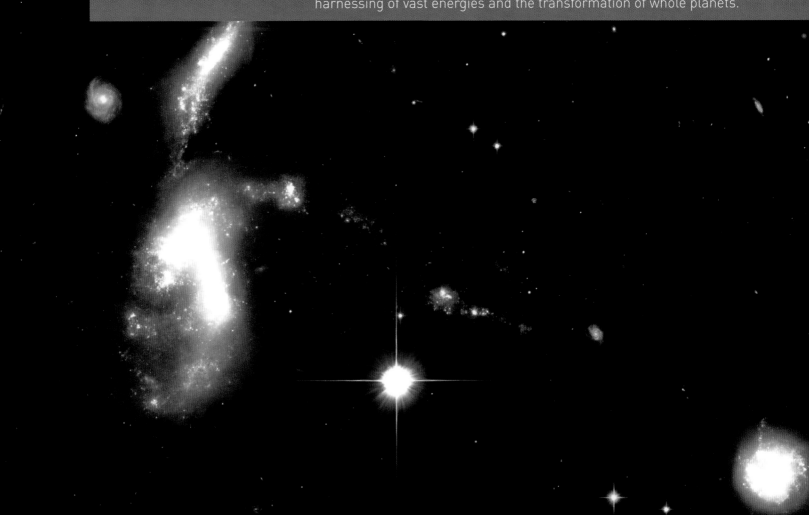

Internet References

Amazing Art 2008, Amazingart.com, viewed 17 December 2008, www.amazeingart.com/seven-wonders/ziggurat.html

Avery, RE, 1913, America's Triumph in Panama, The L.W. Walter Company, Chicago, IL via Serve.com 2008, viewed 17 December 2008, www.serve.com/CZBrats/Builders/FRCanal/failure.htm

Beijing 2008, Official Website of the Beijing 2008 Olympic Games, viewed 17 December 2008, http://en.beijing2008.cn/news/olympiccities/beijing/n214213908.shtml

Burj Dubai Official Website 2008, EMAAR Properties, Dubai, viewed 17 December 2008, www.burjdubai.com

Carroll, R 2007, Guardian.co.uk, viewed 17 December 2008, www.guardian.co.uk/uk/2007/sep/11/britishidentity.past

Creighton, S, The Giza Codex. 2008, viewed 17 December 2008, www.thegizaoracle.co.uk/Flash/GPW-I...gent-Design.swf

Cyberspace Orbit.com 2008, Cyberspace Orbit, viewed 17 December 2008, www.cyberspaceorbit.com/phikent/japan/japan.html

Discovery Communications 2008, Discovery Communications LLC, viewed 17 December 2008 http://dsc.discovery.com/convergence/engineering/archives/archives.html

Endersbee, L, 2008, The National Forum, Online Opinion, Australia, viewed 17 December 2008, www.onlineopinion.com.au/view.asp?article=992

Endex.com 2008, Endex.com, viewed 17 December 2008, www.endex.com/gf/buildings/bbridge/bbridgefacts.htm

Feuerstein, G 2008, Great Buildings.com, viewed 17 December 2008, www.greatbuildings.com/buildings/Brooklyn_Bridge.html

Housden, T 2002, BBC News Online, BBC.co.uk, viewed 17 December 2008 http://news.bbc.co.uk/2/hi/south_asia/1768109.stm

Incatrail-Peru.com 2008, Incatrail Peru.com, viewed 17 December 2008, www.incatrail-peru.com/inka-trail/en/history-of-the-qhapaq-nan.php

ITP Digital 2008, ITP Digital, 2008, viewed 17 December 2008, htpp://arabianbusiness.com

James, JL, Suzie Manley.com 2005, Egypt Pyramid History.com, viewed 17 December 2008, www.egyptpyramidhistory.com/pyramid_names.htm

Jones, T 1990, Tyler Jones June 29.com, viewed 17 December 2008, www.june29.com/Tyler/nonfiction/pan2.html

Kevin Matthews and Artifice, Inc., 1999–2007, Great Buildings.com, viewed 17 December 2008, www.greatbuildings.com/models/Sydney_Opera_mod.html

Linda Hall Library 2002, Linda Hall Kansas Missouri, viewed 17 December 2008, www.lindahall.org/events_exhib/exhibit/exhibits/civil/canal_zone.shtml

Maidencastle.com 2005, Dorchester Tourism Information, viewed 17 December 2008, www.maidencastle.com/

Mazalien 2008, OneStat.com, viewed 17 December 2008, www.mazalien.com/the-great-pyramid.html

McKinney, V, 2007, Sea Level Rise and the Future of the Netherlands, ICE Case Studies, viewed 17 December 2008, www.american.edu/ted/ice/dutch-sea.htm

NASA 2007, NASA, viewed 17 December 2008, www.nasa.gov/vision/space/workinginspace/great_wall.html

Nash, Andrew 2003, Jules Verne.ca, viewed 17 December 2008, www.julesverne.ca/greateastern.html

NewGraingeIreland.com 2008, Mythical Ireland.com, viewed 17 December 2008, www.mythicalireland.com/ancientsites/newgrange-facts/construction.php

Onkst, D. K. 2003, U.S. Centennial of Flight Commission, viewed 4 January 2009, www.centennialofflight.gov/essay/Explorers_Record_Setters_and_Daredevils/Hughes/EX28.htm

PBase.com 2008, PBase.com, viewed 17 December 2008, www.pbase.com/ericdeparis/versailles_gardens

Pettitt, P 2002, British Archaelogy Issue 66, viewed 17 December 2008, www.britarch.ac.uk/BA/ba66/feat1.shtml

Public Broadcasting Service 1995–2008, PBS.org, viewed 17 December 2008, www.pbs.org/mormons/etc/genealogy.html

Public Broadcasting Service 1995–2008, PBS.org, viewed 17 December 2008, www.pbs.org/wgbh/amex/hoover/peopleevents/pandeAMEX92.html

Public Broadcasting Service 1995–2008, PBS.org, viewed 17 December 2008, www.pbs.org/wgbh/amex/hoover/timeline/index.html

Public Broadcasting Service 1995–2008, PBS.org, viewed 17 December 2008, www.pbs.org/wgbh/amex/tcrr/peopleevents/p_cprr.html

Public Broadcasting Service 1995–2008, PBS.org, viewed 17 December 2008, www.pbs.org/wgbh/nova/pyramid/explore/builders.html

Royal Caribbean Cruises Ltd 2008, Royal Caribbean Cruises Ltd, viewed 17 December 2008, www.oasisoftheseas.com/

Skyrock Network 2008, Skyrock Network, viewed 17 December 2008, http://berdom.skyrock.com/

Snowy Hydro Ltd 2007, Snowy Hydro Ltd, viewed 17 December 2008, www.snowyhydro.com.au/

Taylor, D 2008, Bellrock.org.uk, viewed 17 December 2008, www.bellrock.org.uk/

Toast Net 2008, Moon and Back Graphics, viewed 17 December 2008 http://members.toast.net/rjspina/Japan%27s%20Underwater%20Ruins.htm

Tour Egypt 1996–2005, Tour Egypt, viewed 17 December 2008, www.touregypt.net/featurestories/pyramids.htm

Treat, J 1994, University of Pennsylvania, viewed 17 December 2008, http://ccat.sas.upenn.edu/arth/zoser/zoser.html

Wisconsin University 2008, Digital Collection Library, viewed 17 December 2008, http://digicoll.library.wisc.edu/cgi-bin/DLDecArts/DLDecArts-idx?type=header&id=DLDecArts.AdamRuins&isize=M

Books and other media

Abrams Harry N., 1983, The Great East River Bridge 1883–1983, The Brooklyn Museum Inc., New York.

Bauval, R and Gilbert, A, 1994, The Orion Mystery, Mandarin Books, London.

Bennett, I, 1915, History of the Panama Canal, Historical Publishing Co., Washington, DC.

Cameron, I, 1971, The Impossible Dream, William Morrow & Co Inc., New York.

Coates, R, 2006, Maiden Castle, Geoffrey of Monmouth and HÐrÐn al-RašÐd, published academic paper, University of West England, UK.

Chandler, T, 1987, Four Thousand Years of Urban Growth: An Historical Census, St. David's University Press, Lampeter, Wales

Chidsey, D, 1970, The Panama Canal, An Informal History of its Concept, Building, and Present Status, Crown Publishers Inc., New York.

Clayton, P A, 2006, Chronicle of the Pharaohs, Thames and Hudson, London.

Collins, A, 2007, The Cygnus Mystery, Watkins Publishing, London.

Dunn Jr., Jerry Camarillo, 2002, The World's Greatest Landmarks, Publications International, Lincolnwood.

Graf, Bernhard and Reichold, Klaus, 1999, Buildings that Changed the World, Prestel, London.

Harpur, James and Westwood, Jennifer, 2003, The Atlas of Legendary Places, Burlington, London.

Harris, Stephen L, 1985, Understanding the Bible, Mayfield Publishing Company, Palo Alto, California.

Lynch, D, 1992, Titanic—An Illustrated History, Madison Press Books, Toronto.

Marks, Robert B., China's Population Size During the Ming and Qing: A Comment on the Mote Revision, Remarks given at the 2002 annual meeting of the Association for Asian Studies, Washington DC.

McCarter, Robert, 1997, Frank Lloyd Wright, Phaidon, London.

McCullough, David, 1977, The Path Between the Seas: The Creation of the Panama Canal, Simon and Schuster, New York.

Scarre, Chris, Ed., 1999, The Seventy Wonders of the Ancient World, Thames and Hudson, London.

Shapiro, Mary J., 1983, A Picture History of the Brooklyn Bridge, Dover Publications, Mineola, New York.

Steinman, D.B., 1945, The Builders of the Bridge, Harcourt, Brace and Co., San Diego.

St. George, J., 1982, The Brooklyn Bridge: They Said It Couldn't Be Built, G.P. Putnam's and Sons, New York.

Trachtenberg, Alan, 1965, Brooklyn Bridge: Fact and Symbol, University of Chicago Press.

The Seven Wonders of the Industrial World, BBC Productions, 2003.

Wagner, Geraldine B., 2002, Thirteen Months to Go, New Burlington Books, London.

Zhang, Lin, 2005, The Qin Dynasty Terra-Cotta Army of Dreams, Xi'an Press, Xi'an, China.